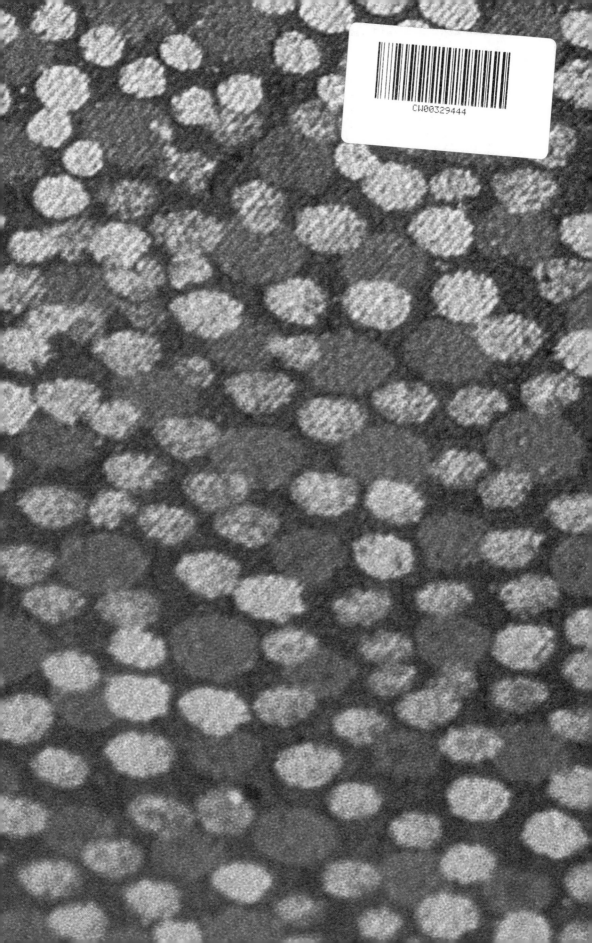

ABORIGINAL ARTISTS
OF THE WESTERN DESERT
A Biographical Dictionary

ABORIGINAL ARTISTS
OF THE WESTERN DESERT
A Biographical Dictionary

Vivien Johnson

CRAFTSMAN HOUSE

Also by Vivien Johnson
THE ART OF CLIFFORD POSSUM TJAPALTJARRI, 1994

Distributed in Australia by Craftsman House,
20 Barcoo Street, Roseville East, NSW 2069
in association with G+B Arts International:
Australia, Austria, Belgium, China, France, Germany,
Hong Kong, India, Japan, Malaysia, Netherlands,
Russia, Singapore, Switzerland, United Kingdom,
United States of America

ISBN 976 8097 81 7

Front cover photograph   *Grenville Turner*
Design   *Caroline de Fries*
Cover Design   *Caroline de Fries and Nevill Drury*
Printer   *Kyodo, Singapore*

Contents

Acknowledgments

I would like to thank everyone who has helped me with the dictionary project over the past five years: firstly the artists of the Western Desert whose paintings inspired this document, and many of whose lives are recorded in it — especially those who patiently bore my questioning. Thanks, too, to the art coordinators of the various painting companies, without whose assistance and support the task of collecting biographical data would have foundered: Daphne Williams, Janice Stanton and Fay Bell for Papunya Tula Artists; Christine Lennard, Glenn James and Geraldine Tyson for Warlukurlangu Artists, Yuendumu; Dorothea Zufall, who was running Yuelamu Artists at Mt Allan in early 1991; Janet Chisholm for the Napperby artists; Michael Rae for Warlayirti Artists for Balgo Hills biographies and special thanks for his generous support of the project; Janet Long Nakamarra for collecting the Willowra biographies and translating these artists' statements; Kerry Williams for Maruku Arts and Crafts, Mutitjulu community, Uluru; Kate Race and Jenni Dudley for Ernabella Arts Inc.; Marina Stocci for the Haasts Bluff biographies; Chris Hodges for CAAMA/Utopia Art, Sydney, for Utopia biographies and general support; Gabrielle Weichart for Nyrripi biographies; David Roennfeldt and Mary-Anne Malbunka for the lone Hermannsburg biography; Lee Cataldi and Peggy Napurrurla Rockman for researching the Lajamanu biographies and Christine Nicholls for an historical perspective on events at Lajamanu and general support; Roslyn Premond, Mark Lennard (now of Gondawana Gallery) and Veronica Johnson for the Centre for Aboriginal Artists, Alice Springs; Anne Gatti and others from Jukurrpa, IAD, Alice Springs; Glenice McBride from The Gap Neighbourhood Centre; Janet Holt from Delmore Gallery for Utopia biographies; Wally Caruana, National Gallery of Australia, and Luke Taylor, National Museum of Australia, for biographical data; Peter Los for Hidden Valley artists' biographies; Anne Mosey for Mt Allan contact; Tim, Tania and Ruby Johnson, for their love and forbearance; Macquarie University Research Grants for a starting grant to initiate the project in 1989 and to AITSIS for a grant to complete it in 1991/2. For photographs of the artists, I would like to thank Lee Cataldi, John Corker, Hank Ebes, Jon Falkenmire, Rodney Gouch, Chris Hodges, Jennifer Isaacs, Neil McLeod, Anne Mosey, Christine Nicholls, Grenville Turner, *The Sydney Morning Herald*, Dean Wilmot.

Introduction

Ten years ago, a complete biographical dictionary of Western Desert painters would have included no more than fifty entries. The original group of artists at Papunya who in 1971 began painting their traditional Dreaming designs in western materials numbered less than thirty. Others tried their hand at painting in those early years and then re-joined Papunya Tula Artists in the boom times of the late '80s, but it was these thirty pioneers of the art movement who persisted in their endeavours in the face of both market indifference and the hostility of their Aboriginal neighbours. Throughout the '70s, they laboured to invent the secularised painting language on which all contemporary forms of Western Desert art are based. By the end of the decade, they had been joined at Papunya by another twenty or so artists who were also painting regularly for Papunya Tula Artists. One or two others were working independently in Alice Springs, making what were then referred to as 'Papunya' or 'dot' paintings. But no-one else was yet prepared to take the step of committing their Dreamings to western art.

The burgeoning reputation and growing trade in the Papunya painters' work as the '80s progressed saw Papunya Tula Artists on a firm financial footing by the middle of the decade. The stage was set for the unprecedented artistic activity that occurred across the entire Western Desert during the late '80s, to which the more than five hundred biographical entries in this volume (and it is still far from complete) attest. Papunya Tula Artists at last had the resources to encourage the development of new artists, and the number of painters on its books swelled rapidly, reaching almost one hundred by the beginning of the '90s. At several neighbouring settlements, the production of canvases, which until that time had been occurring sporadically and individually, began to be organised into artists' cooperatives loosely modelled on the Papunya company. These organisations took responsibility for supplying the emerging painting groups with materials and marketing their work.

At Yuendumu, 100 km to the north of Papunya, Warlukurlangu Artists Association was formed in 1985. Napperby and Mt Allan (Yuelamu Artists) soon followed. By 1990 painting enterprises had sprung up as far north as Lajamanu, west to Kiwirrkura and Balgo, across the Western Australian border, in South Australia at Ernabella, Amata and Fregon, and east of Alice Springs in Alyawarre/Aranda country around Utopia. There was hardly a general store on any of the dozens of small communities dotted across the vast distances of the Western Desert that did not stock acrylic paints and canvas to sell to local artists, who ranged from teenagers to octogenarians. Almost every day new painters were taking up their brushes. The entire adult population of Aboriginal Central Australia, it seemed, was in the process of adopting the vocation of artist. What had begun as a small local art enterprise transformed itself in the space of about five years into a social and cultural movement embracing the entire Western Desert — and beyond.

The Dictionary Concept

This dictionary was originally conceived as a way of coming to grips with these amazing developments. In March 1989, when I began work on the project, the Western Desert acrylic painting movement already embraced hundreds of artists and about half a dozen communities who were mounting exhibitions of their artists' work in cities around Australia. The plan was to make contact with every group in Central Australia engaged in producing paintings in a style derived from the original Papunya painters and obtain brief accounts of the life histories and careers of as many as possible of the individual artists.

Only two of the hundreds of artists I interviewed for this dictionary really questioned me closely about this methodology. Everyone else readily agreed to answer a few questions about themselves in response to my initial explanation that I was writing a book about 'all the artists, not just the "big names" but every "dot painter"[1] in Central Australia' and wanted to include them. One of the exceptions was Benny Tjapaltjarri, who has been on the fringes of Papunya Tula Artists ever since its inception without ever becoming one of its 'big name' artists. Benny's resentment of the limited resources to paint which this status would often have entailed in the difficult first decade of the painting company's existence spilled over one day in 1980 when he sent his wife to knock on the door of the Papunya artists' house and ask for painting materials for him. 'My husband must have canvas; he is an artist!', she said. Nine years later, Benny Tjapaltjarri and his family had settled at Kintore, the Pintupi homeland community 20 km inside the Northern Territory/Western Australia border that was established at the start of the '80s. Despite the remoteness of the community, Papunya Tula Artists's improved fortunes ensured a more regular supply of painting materials for all the painters — though still not in sufficient quantities for Benny's liking. He had agreed after the usual short discussion to sit with me outside the art adviser's flat and be interviewed for the dictionary. However, when I started to explain the kinds of things I wanted to know, he stopped me and asked abruptly why he should give me this information. How would this book of mine benefit him?

I was ready for his question. One obvious merit of a biographical dictionary as a way of coming to grips with the extraordinary proliferation of Western Desert art since the mid '80s was that the artists' participation in the study could be based purely on self-interest. Benny Tjapaltjarri understood the relationship between an artist's recognisability and the saleability of their work in the art marketplace. From several books already produced on the work of the Western Desert artists, in which he had not been mentioned, he had observed the effect on dealers of being able to find an artist's name in a book. Over the preceding decade, he had experienced firsthand the star-making operations of the art world, which single out a handful of artists and exclude the remainder from the art historical process — and sometimes even from the supply of paint and canvas. This invidious system falls on Aboriginal and non-Aboriginal artists alike, but Western Desert artists are doubly disadvantaged. On top of the basic processes of elimination, there are colonialist assumptions about 'Fourth World' peoples which hinder recognition of the Western Desert painters' achievements as the work of individual artists.

In those intervening years, as debate raged in Australian art circles over the desirability of the Western Desert painters' emerging status as contemporary artists, I had often thought about the words of Benny Tjapaltjarri's wife. They directly contradict claims that there is no equivalent in any Western Desert language for the western concept of artist. Its introduction, through the success of the art movement, was said to threaten the fragile social structures of traditional Aboriginal societies with the bourgeois cancer of individualism. Such an argument could only be proposed by someone who had never met anyone in Benny Tjapaltjarri's position. To anyone who has had the privilege of spending time in the company of the people of the Western Desert, the idea that Aboriginal people are somehow devoid of personal identity, let alone a healthy portion of egoism, is laughable.

Tribalism as a social structure does not logically entail collectivism as a personality structure. The assumption that it does is a hangover from the days when practitioners of tribal art forms were presented to western audiences as not only anonymous, but located in an 'ethnographic present' which bore no relation to world historical time frames. The work of this dictionary in identifying the artists as individuals and tracing their personal histories in relation to the wider growth of Western Desert art will hopefully help to dispel these lingering misconceptions, which the extreme paucity of biographical information on even the highest profile artists in the art movement has hitherto reinforced.

The other person who challenged the concept of this dictionary was Michael Jagamara Nelson, whose experience of the art star system has been the very antithesis of Benny Tjapaltjarri's. When I spoke to him about the dictionary, Michael had not long returned to Papunya from New York, where he and Billy Stockman Tjapaltjarri had attended the 1988 opening of the prestigious 'Dreamings: Art of Aboriginal Australia' exhibition at the Asia Society Galleries in New York, whose catalogue features his 1985 'Five Stories' on the cover. It was the inclusiveness of the dictionary's proposed coverage of Western Desert art — which had attracted the participation of less well-known artists — that puzzled Michael Nelson. He seemed genuinely mystified as to what my interest could be in collecting information about hundreds of unknown artists.

I could have answered that I had learned never to underestimate the capacity of any painter to come up with something extraordinary, which would justify their inclusion in a comprehensive study of Western Desert art. It does not seem to matter how indifferent the artist's past performance nor how prolific or sparse their previous output, nor their age or years of experience painting in western mediums. The power of cultural practices within Aboriginal society dating back millenia, from which Western Desert artists draw their inspiration, seems the only possible explanation of their ability to confound the expectations of art audiences by continually turning up with astounding new paintings. That is, the kind of elitist thinking endemic in the white art world, applied to Western Desert art, has proven not only capricious and blind in its neglect of the very different sources of these artists' inspiration from their non-Aboriginal counterparts. It is also counter-productive, from the point of view of the student, collector or dealer in Aboriginal art, to proceed on such principles in the quest for the next great painting to come out of the Western Desert.

However, I doubt that Michael Nelson would have been much satisfied with this response. He was looking for an epistemological rather than an utilitarian answer. Why study Western Desert art — apart from its leading figures — at the level of individual biographies? Sociologists are supposed to proceed from the assumption that it is collectivities that make history — even art history. Such a history of the recent proliferation of painting enterprises in Central Australia is presented in the essay 'Domino Effects: The Spread of Western Desert Art in the '80s', which follows this Introduction. And yet, is it not self-evident that collectivities ultimately make history only through the actions of the individuals who constitute them? A biographical dictionary of Western Desert artists permits the mapping of individual artists onto the generalised history of the painting movement, providing a comprehensive account of how the influence of 'Papunya painting' actually spread out from its point of origin in Papunya. It also provides an understanding of the forces which are still shaping and re-shaping the contours of Western Desert art.

What is a Western Desert artist?

As new painting enterprises continued to blossom across Central Australia, the work of collecting biographies for the dictionary progressed into its second and then a third year. A principle of closure was partially enacted by the contraction of the marketplace in the early '90s, restricting the entry of new artists and cutting off some of the newer artists who had not established names for themselves before the recession closed in on Aboriginal art. But I had long since come to terms with the practical impossibility of including each and every Western Desert painter in the dictionary. In every Aboriginal community in the Western Desert where people had the resources to paint, artists can be found: the task of collecting all of their biographies is one of truly Herculean proportions.

In gathering the over five hundred entries included in this volume, the practical assistance of people coordinating the painting enterprises at the various communities has been absolutely invaluable. However, their participation in the task of data collection also required the early abandonment of the initial ideal of completeness. Art advisers, teachers, station owners, outstation managers, storekeepers and others involved in assisting the artists to produce and distribute their work have neither the time nor the incentive to dignify with the title of 'artist' (by their inclusion in an artists dictionary) the efforts of everyone who has ever tried to paint. They are under enough pressure from the people who already paint regularly. (Literacy workers, who collected the information for me at some communities, were under no such constraint, and at Lajamanu they prepared the biographies of over one hundred Lajamanu artists from a population of seven hundred people!) The need arises, then, for some account of what I mean by a 'Western Desert artist', so that those whom this research has for practical reasons not encompassed (this time around anyway) need not feel excluded from the company of

Western Desert artists as defined by this volume.

Perhaps no dictionary would be complete without some quibbling over the meaning of words, but a lot more than semantics is involved in setting the boundaries to what is meant here by the term 'Western Desert artist'. Thus far, I have been using the term as roughly co-extensive with painters working in the 'dot style' pioneered by the Papunya Tula artists during the '70s and early '80s. So it was, when talk of 'Western Desert' art first began filtering into art world circles. But this assumption is clearly no longer adequate. As the criterion of a Western Desert artist, style alone is at once both too exclusive — and not exclusive enough. In the hands of the group of artists I am trying to characterise here, the so-called 'dot style' has transformed itself in the intervening decade to the point where the trademark dots are no longer characteristic of the work of many leading Western Desert artists. On the other hand, in the '90s the geographical spread of Aboriginal (and other) artists painting in a style virtually indistinguishable from the classic 'dot style' of Western Desert art extends well beyond the geographical or cultural boundaries of the Western Desert. 'Dot painters' are everywhere, and whether they are crass imitators of, or draw genuine artistic inspiration from, Western Desert art in either case they are not themselves Western Desert artists. This is not the place to try to draw the lines between these two possibilities, but simply to note that both groups do in principle exist and lie outside the definition I need to construct here.

As an anthropological designation, the term 'Western Desert' refers to a cultural/ linguistic demarcation, rather than a strictly geographical one. The concept is based on particular religious or ritual manifestations which give an image of homogeneity across the very broad area encompassed by what Aboriginal linguists call the Wati group of languages (i.e. all those languages or dialects in which 'wati' is the word for 'man'). The Western Desert tribes enjoyed the distinction of minimal contact with missionaries and administrators and Europeans generally for longer than anyone, and are consequently prime movers in the struggle for the maintenance and renewal of traditional culture. This region, because of its isolation, has perhaps always been something of a heartland of Aboriginal law and custom. Anthropological documentation exists of the influence of Western Desert groups moving out to affect neighbouring groups even prior to the European occupation of the continent.[2] This process has become more, not less, significant in the post-contact period. Since the '60s, Western Desert influence has noticeably moved outwards in every direction, just as the painting movement has done: indeed the painting movement is one of the ways in which the impetus for renewing the Dreaming has been spread.

Through such intra-Aboriginal historical processes, tribal and pan-tribal groupings in Aboriginal social reality have always been more fluid than the anthropological efforts to solidify them into a set of neat conceptual compartments like 'Western Desert' can possibly accommodate. Applied to the acrylic art movement, the anthropological definition would mean excluding Arrente and Alyawerre artists like Norbett Lynch Kngwarreye and half the painters at Utopia, whose status as exponents of the Western Desert style has never been in question, even though these language groups are not

11

within the designated Western Desert 'enclave'. Some dealers have introduced the term 'Eastern Desert' artists to promote these painters, muddying the emergent art historical usage of the term 'Western Desert art'. In this usage, which I have adopted for the purposes of this dictionary, 'Western Desert art' describes a school of painters from Central Australia and adjacent regions who are socially, and in a broad sense culturally, part of Western Desert society. They paint their inherited Dreamings in acrylics on canvas or board using variants of the visual language based on the traditional iconography of the Western Desert peoples devised by the Papunya Tula artists during the '70s.

A few Western Desert artists whom I interviewed for this dictionary inclined to a more stringent definition, applying the criterion of one's ritual credentials to paint the Dreaming, which have always been central to the intra-Aboriginal debate about the painting movement in Central Australia.[3] They questioned the entitlement of artists to paint the Dreaming designs if they had not been through the full set of ceremonial procedures which define custodianship of the particular Dreamings depicted in their paintings — regardless of their social and cultural connections with Western Desert society. Their concerns seem to overlap with the preconceptions of the many who seek 'authenticity' in Western Desert paintings — and find it in proportion to the painter's seniority and ritual eminence. But the influence of such Primitivist thinking within the mainstream Australian art world is as weak as the elders' is strong in the homelands of Central Australia: no-one else would dream of questioning the applicability of the title 'Western Desert' artist to an Aboriginal acrylic painter working out of Alice Springs, regardless of their ritual knowledge. The resolution of such issues lies well outside the non-evaluative codes of dictionary compilation, which require a broader usage encompassing both the so-called 'town painters' — for whom such remarks are intended — and their critics, as exponents of Western Desert art. This designation still takes for granted that a Western Desert artist's work is grounded in some personal connection to Western Desert lands and the stories told in their paintings. The difficulty of sustaining any further subdivision of the definitional domain is by itself a rather compelling argument for the method of assemblage of individual artists' biographies adopted in this study as a way of representing an extremely complex artistic and social development.

Vivien Johnson, Sydney, 1991

Footnotes:

1. The terms 'dot painter' and 'dot painting' were used in these conversations with the artists, because these terms (despite their pejorative use in other contexts) were the most efficient way of communicating to them, the group of artists which is the subject of this study. Of course, there are many artists of the Western Desert who do not use dotting as a primary technique or acrylic paint on canvas as their medium: the Arrente watercolourists and the Mutitjulu woodcarvers, to name some obvious examples.

2. I am indebted to John Stanton of the University of Western Australia Museum of Anthropology (interviewed Perth, June 1986) for this understanding.

3. see *The Art of Clifford Possum Tjapaltjarri*, Vivien Johnson (Craftsman House, 1994), Chapter 3: 'Papunya Painting': The 'Secret/Sacred' Controversy, pp.35–40, for a more detailed discussion of this point.

Domino Effects
The Spread of Western Desert Art in the '80s

The origins of the acrylic painting movement in Central Australia lie back in the late '60s and early '70s, in events at Papunya which have already been described in numerous publications. While the Aboriginal side of that story is yet to be told — and the full history of Papunya Tula Artists still awaits comprehensive description and analysis — the focus of this book is on what happened in the Western Desert after the long night of the '70s. The following series of short essays delineate the growth of painting enterprises at the various communities associated with the artists entered in this dictionary. They are intended to complement the biographies of individual painters with an overview of their collective participation in this extraordinary art movement. The first two essays, on the last decade of Papunya Tula's development and the emergence of Warlukurlangu Artists at Yuendumu, cover some familiar territory, but in ways which seek to emphasise the processes at work in the explosion of painting right across Central Australia since the mid '80s.

1. Papunya Tula Artists of Papunya, Mt Leibig, Kintore, Kiwirrkura etc.

The 1980s marked a turning point in the recent history of the peoples of the Western Desert. A movement for the re-settlement of tribal homelands was gathering momentum. The European term for these homeland communities: 'outstations', conceptualises the movement as a strategic withdrawal from the ravages of settlement life. However, from the point of view of the tribesmen and women themselves, especially the older members of these communities, the focus was on restoration of ceremonial links to country after decades of dislocation. It was a calculated assertion of the fundamental importance of these connections to the cultural survival of Western Desert society. Nowhere was the homelands movement stronger than at Papunya.

Officially opened in 1961, Papunya was the last of the network of government settlements set up across Central Australia after World War II under the policy of centralisation of desert dwellers, and gathered together major groupings of about seven different tribes. These included about two hundred Pintupi people presumed to have been the last still pursuing their traditional lifestyle in the remote country across the Western Australian border, and who were brought in by the Northern Territory Welfare Branch patrols during the mid '60s. By the beginning of the '70s, there were close to fifteen hundred people at Papunya, in what proved to be a far more explosive social mix than at most of the older settlements, where one language group tended to dominate.

Just as the arrival of the Pintupi, with the strength of their immediate, practical continuity of connection with country, may have precipitated the emergence of the painting movement at Papunya (rather than at any of a dozen other communities from which painting enterprises have since emerged), so it was the Pintupi exodus back to their own country that spearheaded the homelands movement in the Western Desert. The last to leave their country, and the least versed or worst placed in the complex politics of resource allocation on settlements, they had perhaps the least reason to stay. In 1981 they established Kintore, a Pintupi township three hundred strong just inside the Western Australian border deep in the heart of Pintupi country. By 1985 they had pushed another 250 km further west across the Western Australian border to Kiwirrkura.

The paintings had served the Pintupi tribesmen during the decade of exile as a way of passing on their Dreamings to the next generation while educating the rest of the world in the ancient traditions of the Western Desert peoples. With the re-settlement of country and re-establishment of the ceremonial links which the paintings depicted, these functions gave precedence to a more 'professional' approach to art-making. Painting provides one of the few avenues to financial independence available to Aboriginal people living on these remote communities. A majority of current Papunya Tula painters nowadays live far to the west of the original settlement — at Kintore, Kiwirrkura and places beyond. In those two small Pintupi communities alone, there are over fifty artists. Income derived from the paintings remains vital to the viability of these and other homeland communities requiring cashflow to sustain their modified traditional lifestyles — a lesson not lost on their Western Desert countrymen and women. Many who had originally opposed the action of the Papunya painters had begun to re-think their position.

Back in Papunya, the exodus of the Pintupi precipitated many other departures. Some of the Warlpiri artists moved to the new township at Mt Leibig in the direction of Warlpiri country, where they continued to paint for Papunya Tula Artists, along with others who started painting at Mt Leibig after 1986 when the company began making regular buying trips there. Some of the artists moved into town and increasingly based themselves in Alice Springs, where the gradual acceptance of their urban lifestyles by the company began to transform perceptions of the 'town painter' (see this chapter, 5. *Alice Springs*). Others moved to small outstations in their heritage countries, and painted only intermittently when materials were available. About twenty artists, mostly from the Anmatyerre, Luritja and Warlpiri language groups, are still based in Papunya itself, amongst them a handful of the original 'painting men' and some of the Papunya Tula company's best known younger artists.

During the '70s Papunya Tula's fortunes had been too uncertain to allow the encouragement of new artists. As the '80s advanced, the company was able to extend its operations to include regular field trips to Kintore and the Pintupi communities further west and south. Its expanded resources had been focused in the meantime on Papunya and had become available to a new group of artists at the settlement working alongside the older group of senior men, many of them young — and some of them women. For a long time, the idea of 'painting women' seems to have occurred to no-one at Papunya. During the '70s everyone was preoccupied with the survival of the painting enterprise as a cultural initiative of the older ceremonially knowledgeable men. Women's increasing participation as assistants on the dotted backgrounds of their husbands' or fathers' canvases reflected the progressively more secular orientation of the original group of artists towards the painting enterprise as the decade progressed. However, until the '80s, the only artists actually on the company books were men. The first women at Papunya to begin painting in their own right were these wives and daughters, who were already highly proficient in the contemporary Western Desert style. They immediately received the recognition accorded by purchase by major public galleries, helping to ensure the women's emergence from their assistant roles, henceforth to be recognised as independent producers.

This 'second generation' of Papunya Tula artists from the outset painted highly sophisticated canvases for the western art market, producing stylistic variations within the mature Papunya style. In them, the transformation of the Western Desert painters from ethnologists of Aboriginality to contemporary artists was complete. Some have pursued and extended the trajectory to international acclaim as artists which had been blazed by the original 'painting men'. Since the 'Dreamings' exhibition, which show-cased the Papunya painters' achievement in the USA, word has spread rapidly in art circles around the world. The reputation of its artists, and the list of major overseas exhibitions involving Papunya Tula Artists, most in the last five of its twenty-five year existence, continues to grow.

Papunya Tula Artists Exhibitions

The following list is far from exhaustive, but gives an indication of the increasing prestige and internationalism of the company's showings over the past two decades.

1973–4   Walbiri and Pintubi Art Travelling Exhibition, Dept of Interior (finishing at the Residency, Alice Springs, NT, September1974)

1974   'Art of the First Australians', Australian Museum, Sydney
Anvil Art Gallery, Albury, New South Wales

1975–9   Peter Stuyvesant Cultural Foundation Travelling Exhibition, Ontario, Calgary, Montreal, Quebec, Toronto and touring worldwide

1977   Nigerian Festival Exhibition, Lagos, Nigeria
Realities Gallery, Melbourne
Christ College, Oakleigh, Victoria

1978   Collectors Gallery, Sydney

1979   Art of Man Gallery, Sydney

1980   Randells Mill, Adelaide Festival of Arts Exhibition, Adelaide

1980   'Aboriginal Art of the Western Desert', Macquarie University Library, Sydney

1980–1   'Contemporary Australian Aborigine Art', Pacific Asia Museum, Los Angeles

1981   'Contemporary Art of the Western Desert', Orange City Art Gallery, Orange, New South Wales
'Mr Sandman Bring Me a Dream', USA, UK

1982	Art of the Western Desert, Georges Gallery, Melbourne
	Brisbane Festival, Brisbane
	Aboriginal Arts Australia, Sydney
1983	Mori Gallery, Sydney
	Roar Studios, Melbourne
	XVIIth Sao Paulo Bienal, Sao Paulo, Brazil
1984	'Painters of the Western Desert', Kintore Gallery, Adelaide
	'Papunya and Beyond', Araluen Arts Centre, Alice Springs, Northern Territory
1985	'Dot and Circle': A Retrospective Survey of the Aboriginal Acrylic Paintings of Central Australia, Royal Melbourne Institute of Technology, Melbourne
	'The Face of the Centre: Papunya Tula Paintings 1971–84', National Gallery of Victoria, Melbourne
1986	Roar Studios, Melbourne
	Galerie Dusseldorf, Perth
1987	Gallery Gabrielle Pizzi, Melbourne
	Undercroft Gallery, University of Western Australia, Perth
1988	Wagga Wagga City Art Gallery, Wagga Wagga, New South Wales
	'The Inspired Dream: Life as Art in Aboriginal Australia', Queensland Art Gallery, Brisbane
	Expo '88, Brisbane
1988–9	'Dreamings: Art of Aboriginal Australia', Asia Society Galleries, touring New York, Chicago, Los Angeles, Melbourne, Adelaide 1988–9
1988	John Weber Gallery, New York
1989	Gallery Gabrielle Pizzi, Melbourne
	'Mythscapes: Aboriginal Art of the Desert', National Gallery of Victoria, Melbourne
	Centro Cultural Arte Contemporaneo, Mexico City, Mexico
	'Anatjari Tjakamarra', John Weber Gallery, New York
1990	'East to West: Land in Papunya Tula Painting', Tandanya Aboriginal Cultural Institute, Adelaide
	'Friendly Country Friendly People', Araluen Arts Centre, Alice Springs, Northern Territory, touring other states in 1991–2
	Papunya Women's Ground Painting, Tandanya Aboriginal Cultural Institute, Adelaide
1990	'Songlines', Rebecca Hossack Gallery, London
	'Contemporary Aboriginal Art from the Robert Holmes à Court Collection', Harvard University, Harvard, USA
	Isaacs Gallery, Toronto
	Gallery Gabrielle Pizzi at the Palazzo Bianchi Michiel, Venice
1991	'The Painted Dream', Auckland City Art Gallery and National Gallery of New Zealand, Wellington

See also listings of individual artists for solo exhibitions at Gallery Gabrielle Pizzi, Melbourne, Australia of Papunya Tula artists Joseph Jurra Tjapaltjarri, Warlimpirringa Tjapaltjarri, Michael Jagamara Nelson, Maxie Tjampitjinpa, Ronnie Tjampitjinpa, Pansy Napangati, Anatjari Tjakamarra, William Sandy, and Mick Namarari Tjapaltjarri

2. Warlukurlangu Artists of Yuendumu

'At Yuendumu, there used to be only kangaroos, there were no people. People would go right through to a good country. They would go to Wakurlpa and other places to live. Afterwards, white men came here. They built a bore and houses here. They never asked the people, they went ahead building ... The name of this place is 'Yurntumulyn', which was the name of a dreamtime woman. Today, everybody calls it Yuendumu. However, Yuendumu is over there, east, where we go on the road to Alice Springs, beside the hills. Yakurrukaji is the name of the place where the houses stand, where the soakage is. This is the land of the honey and dreaming'. [Honey Ant Dreaming ed.]

This statement, from a press release issued to accompany Warlukurlangu Artists' 1986 exhibitions in Perth and Adelaide, gives one reason why Yuendumu was the first place to which the painting movement spread from Papunya. The communities of Napperby and Mt Allan, where painting enterprises started a few years later, are even closer to Papunya than Yuendumu, but they are both cattle stations, which exist to fulfill an economic function. So long as there was no market for 'dot paintings', there was little incentive for anyone to provide the Aboriginal people living on stations with art materials. By contrast, Papunya and Yuendumu were settlements, which had no economic purpose — in fact, there was absolutely nothing of an economic nature for most people to do there. Even the traditional hunting and gathering was not available: the concentration of population at the settlements meant that the area around them had been foraged out years ago. In the early '70s the superintendent of Yuendumu who boasted of employing one hundred and eighty people at his 'model settlement' may well have been the source of the expression 'painting rocks white' for useless work, for that was what many of his Aboriginal workers reportedly did.

By the '80s such 'solutions' to Aboriginal unemployment were no longer available.

Community advisers, particularly in the field of education, searching for something that would involve the people to whom they were now supposed to be administering self-determination, were bound to hit upon the idea of emulating Papunya's success. This is more or less how the painting enterprise got started at Yuendumu — and subsequently at Lajamanu, Balgo, and many other smaller centres. The Aboriginal response to these initiatives was electrifying to those who observed it. It was a scenario repeated at many Western Desert communities: as soon as art materials were made available there was a wild outburst of painting in the community, accompanied by an enormous sense of cultural pride in the activity. A succession of intermediaries, who came after the idealistic but sometimes impractical initiators of painting, struggled with varying success to channel this activity into viable art enterprises.

So it was at Yuendumu. Individuals were painting long before the whole community got involved[1], but it took an assortment of researchers, teachers and free-floating art enthusiasts to create the environment in which these isolated efforts could be channelled into the establishment of the now flourishing enterprise of Warlukurlangu Artists. The new headmaster of Yuendumu School, Kim Bridgewater, and adult educator, Peter Toyne first initiated painting in the Yuendumu community. Some of the senior men were commissioned to paint the main Dreamings for the Yuendumu community on the thirty doors of the school. The project drew on the initiators' knowledge of the mural painted in 1971 on the Papunya school wall which originally set the art movement in motion. Researchers Francoise Dussart and Meredith Morris, who had a specific interest in culture, also came to Yuendumu in the mid '80s. Dussart's particular interest was in recording the women's body painting designs. They distributed art materials and encouraging a group of women in the successful project of earning enough money from their paintings to buy themselves a Toyota. These events were a factor in the radically different and major role which women have played in the painting movement at Yuendumu.

Dramatic changes in the non-Aboriginal community's appreciation of the importance of women as social and ceremonial agents in Aboriginal society had translated into pressure of demand in the art world for Papunya women's paintings. But it was the senior women at Yuendumu whose large collectively produced canvases, flamboyantly coloured and painted and glowing with pride in their own cultural heritage, so quickly drew the art world's attention in 1986 to the new work coming out of Yuendumu. Women still constitute a majority of the Warlukurlangu artists, a pattern which has been repeated in most of the Western Desert painting enterprises established since.

Yuendumu painting's first significant exposure to the Australian art world was in Sydney just before Christmas 1985. The media release prepared for the exhibition, containing 'some 50 works of traditional art ... on sale at prices ranging from $100 to $3000', told a now-familiar story:

'Aboriginal painters from a remote Northern Territory settlement are hoping to set the international art world alight and follow in the footsteps of the nearby Papunya tribe whose original sand paintings have achieved universal acclaim.'

The press release's concluding comment, calling the Warlpiri works from Yuendumu 'less contrived, freer and less stylised than other desert paintings ... the effect ... more contemporary, even post-modernist, in the striking application of colour', announced the sophistication of this pathfinding assault by a rival group on the niche which Papunya painting was beginning to carve out for itself in the art marketplace. The paintings were indeed different from what the art audience was coming to recognise as Western Desert art — though in fact not so different from Papunya paintings of a decade earlier, when those artists were likewise making the transition to canvas and the acrylic palette. The effect was strongest in the massive painting of the Milky Way Dreaming in red, yellow, black and white which dominated the show, and was sold to the Australian National Gallery for the exhibition's top price of $3000. From this and a few other sales, enough went back to support the establishment of the proposed Yuendumu crafts centre and the Warlukurlangu Artists company was born. In June the following year, Warlukulangu Artists enjoyed their first critical and marketing triumph with a sell-out show at the Editions Gallery in Fremantle, Western Australia.

Warlukurlangu Artists has since gone from strength to strength, building on the lessons of Papunya Tula Artists's experience of running a painting company. For example, under the favourable conditions in which they entered the market, they were able to introduce a commission system to mitigate the ongoing problem for all Western Desert painting companies of maintaining a cash flow to pay the painters and buy new materials. Under the Yuendumu system, the artist would receive a small amount on receipt of the painting, and the balance of their 60% share of the purchase price when the painting sold. Warlukurlangu's location in Yuendumu itself was also a departure from the way Papunya Tula Artists operated. The Papunya company had been based in Alice Springs for the preceding decade, opening its own gallery there in the mid '80s to gain access for its artists to the lucrative local market. Being based on the community does limit Warlukurlangu's access to this market, which in turn limits the number of artists it can afford to keep on its books, particularly in the difficult economic times of the early '90s. However, it has also engendered higher levels of both community involvement with the art enterprise, and art adviser accountability to the artists. While this situation is not without its problems, in Yuendumu it has produced an organisation characterised, like the Warlpiri people themselves, with a very strong sense of collective purpose and cultural pride. The 'Dreamings: Art of Aboriginal Australia' exhibition which toured hte USA in 1988–9 helped to establish Warlukurlangu's international reputation — Papunya and Yuendumu being the only Central Australian communities represented. It was further bolstered the following year in Europe by their widely acclaimed participation in 'Magiciens de la Terre' in Paris and most recently reinforced by 'Aratjara: Art of the First Australians', touring Germany, the UK and Denmark in 1993–4.

Warlukurlangu Artists Exhibitions 1985–91

October 1985	Araluen Arts Centre, Alice Springs
December 1985	Hogarth Galleries, Sydney
June 1986	Editions Gallery, Perth
July 1986	Araluen Arts Centre, Alice Springs
October 1986	Victorian Artists Society, Gabrielle Pizzi, Melbourne
	RSASA Gallery, Adelaide
January 1987	Achille Lauro, Perth
May 1987	Portsmouth Festival, England
June 1987	Roar, Gabrielle Pizzi, Melbourne
August 1987	Reconnaissance Gallery, Melbourne
September 1987	Chapman Gallery, Canberra
December 1987	Opera House Gallery, Sydney
February 1988	Lewis-Wara Gallery, Seattle, USA
March 1988	Anima Gallery, Adelaide
	'Yuendumu: Paintings Out of the Desert', South Australian Museum, Adelaide
May 1988	FOE Community Arts Space, Melbourne
July 1988	Bellas Gallery, Brisbane
August 1988	Linden Gallery, Melbourne
September 1988	NT Tourist Commission, Auckland, New Zealand
	Dreamtime Gallery, Perth
October 1988	'Dreamings: Art of Aboriginal Australia', Asia Society, New York
December 1988	FOE Community Arts Space, Melbourne
February 1989	Painters Gallery, Sydney
May 1989	FOE Community Arts Space, Melbourne
	'Magiciens de la Terre', Centre Georges Pompidou, Paris
June–August 1989	'Mythscapes', National Gallery of Victoria, Melbourne
August 1989	Chesser Gallery, Adelaide
October 1989	FOE Community Arts Space, Melbourne
November 1989	Hogarth Gallery of Dreams, Sydney
	Chapman Gallery, Canberra
February 1990	'A Sense of Dreaming': Paintings from the Christensen Fund, Perth
March 1990	South Australian Museum Shop, Adelaide Festival
June 1990	'L'été Australien', Musée Fabre, Montpellier, France
July 1990	Darwin Performing Arts Centre, Darwin
August 1990	'Tigari Lai: Contemporary Aboriginal Art from Australia', Third Eye Centre, Glasgow, UK
October, 1990	FOE Community Arts Space, Melbourne
	Bond University Campus Gallery, Queensland
November 1990	Hogarth Gallery of Dreams, Sydney

3. Yuelamu Artists of Mt Allan

Mt Allan station, home of Yuelamu Artists, is situated some 250 km west of Alice Springs, astride the Tanami Road. Nearby is Yuelamu, one of the main Honey Ant Dreaming sites for this whole area of Central Australia, from which Dreaming tracks of the ancestral Honey Ants radiate in several directions across the country. The area remained in Aboriginal hands later than neighbouring parts of the region; cattle stations had been established at adjacent Napperby and Coniston in the early years of the century. These pastoral operations attracted many Mt Allan families, wanting to gain access to rations and become part of the station workforce as stockmen and domestic servants. The Coniston massacre of 1928 and the reprisals that went on for years afterwards drove more people away from the area, many of whom congregated after World War II in the newly established government settlement at Yuendumu. As a result of these processes, when Didi Smith took out the Mt Allan lease in 1946 it was decreed to be over land on which there was no local population.

The new station owner went to Yuendumu to ask for volunteers to re-settle the land and help build up the cattle operation. Many people with customary responsibilities in the Mt Allan area returned. Didi Smith ran Mt Allan station for the next thirty years until it was purchased in 1976 on behalf of the Mt Allan Aboriginal community by the Aboriginal Land Fund Commission. Then his son D.D. Smith stayed on as manager. With Mt Allan coming under Aboriginal control, traditional owners of the Honey Ant sites on the western side of Mt Allan (Yuelamu) returned from Mt Denison. Others concerned with the site of Ngarlu on the southern part of the lease have also returned. Still others from Napperby more recently resumed responsibility for Emu and Dingo sites on the east side. The result of this gravitation was population pressure at Mt Allan, which the community dealt with by dispersal of these groups to outstations near their heritage sites: Yulyipinyu in the west and Pulardi on the east side. These developments could only strengthen the Anmatyerre land claim which had been lodged once the land was out of private hands. The claim was finally granted in October 1988.

The origins of the painting enterprise at Mt Allan follow directly from these events. After Mt Allan was restored to Aboriginal ownership, the people built a community store and the store manager started buying art works. From the mid '80s, Mt Allan artists began supplying some of the galleries in town. These events were part of a wave of painting enterprises — at Yuendumu, Napperby and Mt Allan — which emerged as the painting movement began to fan out in the wake of Papunya Tula's sudden rise to

21

popularity and marketability in the mid '80s. Mt Allan is distinctive within this group in that — at least in these initial stages — it exemplified another organisational model for the production side of the art movement, which has continued to stamp the way Yuelamu Artists operates. It is a model which is repeated at many other communities which I have not had the resources to include in this study — and at some which were included in the dictionary. In the latter instances, it may function in a more clandestine manner, alongside and in competition with the model of government sponsored artists' co-operatives exemplified by the Papunya and Yuendumu organisations.

The 'Mt Allan model' centres on the activities of the community general store, which goes into the business of art on a supply and demand basis. It sells paint and canvas to the artists (usually of a quality reflecting the restricted level of capital investment which the store can afford to put behind this arm of its operations), and buys back their paintings to re-sell on the open market. In the case of Mt Allan, the store manager's activities did later develop in the direction of raising the artists' profile in the art world. Subsequently, art advisers appointed by Yuelamu Artists took this process further. However, in the early years of Mt Allan as a painting community, the storekeeper was more of a middleman than an agent for the painters. Though based in and part of the Mt Allan community like the Yuendumu art adviser, the storekeeper's role in the situation was somewhat more akin to the dealers in Aboriginal art who now operate freelance out of Alice Springs. He dealt with no particular group of artists: Mt Allan store would sell materials to, and buy paintings from, all comers.

The store manager also sold paintings to all comers. He supplied passing tourists and galleries in Alice Springs, but he had an eye, too, to the ongoing development of the enterprise. He kept a card file of all artists whose paintings went through his books. These records were kept to assist in preparing annotations for the paintings, which he perceived were vital to the market's perception of them as 'authentic' Aboriginal art. For the purposes of this research, the artists' cards also provide a useful documentation of the form which the art movement took in the Mt Allan community in the late '80s. At different times, almost every adult member of the Mt Allan community seems to have tried their hand at painting. There appeared to be a very fast turnover of artists outside of the core group of local people painting regularly. Apparently, many people in Mt Allan had responded to the unrestricted availablility of art materials in the community by trying their hand at painting — and quite a few subsequently gave it away. There is also evidence of significant passing traffic, not usually found on the other communities so far mentioned. Sometimes they were people who had no access at home to paint and canvas because they were not on the books of their local painting company, but there were also people who usually worked for a painting company elsewhere but who might sell a painting to the storekeeper for funds when they were in Mt Allan, perhaps visiting relatives. A few people from more distant communities like Willowra, where no art materials were available as yet, took the opportunity of doing a painting and selling it to the storekeeper while in Mt Allan.

The painting enterprise at Mt Allan entered a new phase in April 1988 with the opening of Yuelamu Art Gallery and Museum, funded by a Bicentennial grant. What had started as a sideline for the storekeeper — or a service to the community — had become something the community identified with as its own project. Like the land itself on which the station stood, the enterprise was in the process of passing into Aboriginal hands. An art adviser was appointed to run the painting company, working out of the Museum and Art Gallery, which attempted — not entirely successfully — to separate its functions from the activities of the store. Exhibitions were organised, including 'Two Faces of the Desert' at the NT Museum of Arts and Sciences in April 1989. In the same year, a substantial body of work was purchased for the opening of the Caz Gallery, the first in the United States to deal during its brief existence exclusively in Aboriginal Art.

The art business has not run altogether smoothly for the Mt Allan artists and their representatives. A succession of difficulties beset them, involving the abrupt departure of the first art adviser, then a long gap, followed by his successor's struggle to pick up the pieces and keep the enterprise afloat. The organisation appears to be devolving into the earlier, more 'down-market' model. No successor was appointed to run Yuelamu Artists when the second art adviser resigned. In the interim, Don Morton Japangardi, one of the most senior men at Mt Allan, who told me proudly that the museum had been his brainchild, kept it going himself. Since the grand opening ceremony, which made the national media and focused attention on the artistic aspirations of the Mt Allan community, regular showings in established art galleries, which are required to establish the community's reputation in art circles, have not been sustainable through the various disruptions Yuelamu Artists has experienced in recent years. The significant percentage of transients selling through Mt Allan, and the high turnover of artists, have made it difficult to establish the kind of 'signature style' which identifies other painting groups in the marketplace. With the stunning exceptions one learns to expect in Western Desert art from even the most unpromising of painting conditions, Mt Allan paintings do at times reflect the 'uncoordinated' character of the painting enterprise there. They can generally be found at the lower end of the market — in tourist and museum-shop outlets which were once the usual destination of Aboriginal art, rather than 'up-market' commercial art galleries. Yuelamu Artists' basic operating structure, with its lower capital flow requirements, is well suited to leaner economic times. There are significant advantages in Mt Allan's situation compared with other painting communities which lack the infrastructure that has been built up in the Museum and Art Gallery. By linking the community into the tourist trade, they provide a useful source of income for the painters. These factors, and the strength of the artists' resolve, improve Yuelamu Artists' chances of survival, despite the current difficulties.

4. Napperby Artists

A third painting enterprise was established at the same time as Yuendumu and Mt Allan, on Napperby station, a six million hectare cattle holding on the edge of the Western Desert, 250 km north-west of Alice Springs. Napperby is one of the original pastoral properties in the region and has been owned and run by the Chisholm family for generations. The local Anmatyerre people, on whose tribal lands the station is located, have also worked for the station owners for several generations. They had no access to the community advisers, adult educators, welfare officers, art and craft advisers or government officials who were instrumental at many government and mission settlements in obtaining the materials and markets that enabled people in Papunya, Yuendumu and many other places to start painting. Yet Napperby's links with the painting movement which began in nearby Papunya in the early '70s were close. Kaapa Tjampitjinpa, Tim Leura Tjapaltjarri, Clifford Possum Tjapaltjarri, and Billy Stockman Tjapaltjarri, four of the founding group of Papunya Tula Artists, were born and raised on the station. Throughout the '70s and early '80s Clifford Possum regularly spent time painting at Napperby, away from the pressures of Papunya.

But the local market for Western Desert paintings was still so negligible by the mid '80s that few people ventured to paint without the support of Papunya Tula Artists (or the emerging painting company at Yuendumu) to supply them with art materials. The current owners of Napperby had kept touch with the development of the Papunya painting group since the start of the '80s and were impressed enough by the metropolitan art market's growing interest in Western Desert art to make canvas and paint available to the local Aboriginal community. In May 1986 the Napperby painting enterprise got underway. Cassidy Tjapaltjarri, an older brother of Clifford Possum, expressed the community's high hopes for it in an interview with a journalist who came to Napperby to cover the story :

'We will make our people the number one painters. We will make plenty of money. We have plenty of good painters here. It is something my people always do well. Even the young fellas are getting interested in this. We can do work for ourselves for a change and not just take your government money.'[2]

The local artists soon graduated from the small canvas boards initially provided to larger canvases. The station store set a room aside to display and store the paintings, which are purchased from the artists on completion. Napperby paintings are typically very neat and regular, skills which the women have also applied to decorating boxes and other curios with miniature dot work. This attempt to diversify their production was prompted by the serious glut of 'dot paintings' on the Alice Springs market. The plans of the Australian Aboriginal Design Company, which has been established to handle this side of the enterprise, include large ceramic pots and a range of other bathroom/kitchen designs to be launched in the US. To date, their productions have included a set of placemats decorated with Aboriginal designs.

Distribution from such an isolated community presents real difficulties for the Napperby artists. Their first exhibition at Hogarth Galleries in Sydney in July 1987 sold out, and another smaller exhibition organised by Coo-ee in Sydney in 1989 also sold well. In 1990 their work was shown at the Arts and Crafts Gallery in Canberra, followed by a mixed show in Sydney, and there were plans for an exhibition of Napperby artists in New York. Artists also sell their paintings independently to outlets in Alice Springs and nearby settlements. In 1991 there was another Napperby show at Hogarth Galleries in Sydney, which included several much larger canvases by younger artists like Peter Leo, Michael Tommy and Brenda Lynch. There were one or two new artists from Napperby, and one or two others migrating between settlements and painting communities in a pattern which is familiar for many Western Desert artists. The most noticeable difference from previous exhibitions was the relative youth of the painters, with only Kitty Pultara represented from amongst the senior men and women who have in the past painted at Napperby.

Though it is years since Clifford Possum lived or painted at Napperby, the influence of his style is still evident in some Napperby artists' works — along with the elements of symmetry and setting of symbols against the plane of the rest of the picture which characterise the Anmatyerre style in general. These features are also evident in the work of many of the Yuelamu artists — also Anmatyerre people — at neighbouring Mt Allan station. The variety of other discernible influences, including the Warlukurlangu painters at the predominantly Warlpiri settlement of Yuendumu, places generalisation about regional differences on shaky ground: there may be equally significant individual variations within each painting group. Unlike Papunya and Yuendumu — and even Mt Allan, which attracted early notice — the Napperby artists have had little media attention. However, with the move to larger canvases by a core group of young artists dedicated to establishing individual reputations through a high standard of work, the Napperby painting enterprise appears set to retain its proposed trajectory into the art world, while diversifying into smaller decorative items to maintain cashflow.

5. Alice Springs: Centre for Aboriginal Artists, Jukurrpa, Pertame, CAAMA

In Western Desert art, the term 'town painting' was originally applied to the work of established Papunya Tula artists, with the implication that they had done a hurried painting for some extra cash while visiting Alice Springs. The Papunya company discouraged its artists from painting in town on the grounds that the haste, and the distracting conditions of the fringe camps in which these paintings were generally produced, showed in their rougher workmanship compared to paintings produced by the same artists on the remote settlements in the desert. The company often refused to buy these 'town paintings', which were sometimes sold to passing tourists, but usually to either the Centre for Aboriginal Artists (known amongst the artists as the 'government gallery') or a variety of local shops and galleries in Alice Springs catering to the cultural tourist market.

Not all 'town paintings' were deserving of the label's derogatory connotations.

Notwithstanding Papunya Tula's caution, there must have been at least some exceptional works to spawn the insistent myth amongst many non-Aboriginal residents of Alice Springs that masterpieces could once be bought along Todd Street for the price of a flagon. There were also artists who were long-term residents of Alice Springs painting in the Western Desert style more or less independently of Papunya Tula Artists. Dick Lechleitner, for instance, had painted boomerangs with Clifford Possum before dot paintings were even thought of. He had been living at a town camp in Alice Springs known as Morris Soak for nine years, selling his Western Desert style paintings privately to the Centre for Aboriginal Artists and other outlets. His independence from the Papunya painters was recognised by the success of his application for an individual grant to the Aboriginal Arts Board in 1980. Wenton Rubuntja, a prominent figure in local Aboriginal affairs, who turned his talents sometimes to Namatjira style watercolours and sometimes to his distinctive paintings of traditional Aranda designs, also operated independently of Papunya Tula Artists. Willie Reilly Japanangka, who did some paintings for Papunya Tula Artists in the early '70s and now lives at Willowra, was selling his paintings to shops and galleries in Alice Springs in the late '70s and early '80s. Another interesting aspect of early 'town painting' is the role which the wives of some of the Papunya artists played in it. For example, there was a radical difference between the paintings produced by Kaapa Tjampitjinpa when in Alice Springs and his work from Papunya, thought by some local dealers to be due to his town-based wife Eunice Napangati having lent a hand in his town canvases. This supposition was confirmed when Eunice began painting in her own right in the mid '80s.

Papunya Tula Artists's rise to the upper reaches of the national and international art market in the latter half of the '80s had a dramatic impact on the Aboriginal art and craft trade which has flourished in Alice Springs since the tourist boom began fifty years ago. Local producers turned their talents to what is still widely designated in Alice Springs circles as 'dot dot' painting: at first rocks, then small canvas boards — in response to the dealers' assessment of the most marketable lines in the contemporary climate. Experience with other mediums of Centralian Aboriginal art making, including batik and watercolour landscape painting, is evident in the work of many of the Alice Springs based artists. However, for many other town-based painters in this dictionary, acrylic on canvas is the first medium in which they have produced art to sell. The popularity of the Western Desert style has encouraged greater participation in art making from all levels of the Aboriginal community. It is often the desire to become an artist which provides the motivation for individuals to seek out their affiliations with country from older relatives — so as to learn the Dreamings which they may paint.

The Centre for Aboriginal Artists was established in 1971 by Mary White, later the first chairwoman of the Crafts Council of the Australia Council. The Centre purchased art and artefacts direct from local producers, marketing them both in Alice Springs and in capital cities around Australia through other government supported galleries for twenty years before being sold into its present private ownership. The Centre was buying Papunya paintings in the early '70s before the painting company formally existed, and was for many years the official outlet for Papunya Tula's stock in Alice Springs. Then in the early '80s their access to the company's paintings was cut off over a dispute between Andrew Crocker, the previous art coordinator of Papunya Tula Artists, and Aboriginal Arts Australia, the government funded company managing the Centre and similar outlets for Aboriginal art and craftwork in all Australian capital cities. The case went to court and was eventually decided in favour of Aboriginal Arts Australia. During this long-running feud, the Centre began taking a more active interest in 'town paintings' to meet the growing local demand. When Papunya Tula Artists opened its own gallery a few doors down the street and began to market the company's paintings in Alice Springs itself, the Centre moved to establish its own source of supply and stable of artists.

Local artists and out-of-town painters began to work for the Centre on the premises in a bough shelter workshop constructed out the back to provide more favourable conditions for the production of quality canvases. The workshop filled a gap which had been created by the building in of the open space alongside the old office of Papunya Tula Artists at the back of the Centre. During the previous decade, Papunya artists used to sit and paint under the trees in this area whenever they were in town. The Centre's dynamic management in the late '80s oversaw the consolidation of a stable of painters and mounted a series of successful exhibitions of the artists' work, including 'Desert Paintings of Central Australia' at the Gauguin Museum, Tahiti, February '88; Expo 88, Brisbane Library, July '88; Linden Gallery, Victoria, August '88 (with Warlukurlungu Artists); Blaxland Gallery, Sydney, September '88; and Tin Sheds Auction (for Tranby Co-operative College for Aborigines), Sydney, October '88. They then left the Centre to establish their own gallery, Gondawana (which also stocks Warlukurlangu Artists' work), amidst the crowd of new outlets responding to the boom in Aboriginal art at the opposite end of Todd Street.

In early 1990 a new director took over the Centre, and despite the more difficult economic times in Alice Springs, it remained a viable and expanding enterprise, earning the Brolga Award of 1991 for Tourism Excellence in the Northern Territory. for its retail trading. Its leading artists have attracted major commissions: Eunice Napangati for the new Alice Springs airport and a travelling exhibition in the USA, and Polly Watson for an exhibition at the Australian Embassy in Paris. The studio at the back of the Centre was receiving less use, except for artists executing large commissioned works or working for an exhibition. Exhibitions of individual artists were a new development in the Centre's activities, beginning with Eunice Napangati and Maxie Tjampitjinpa's show at the Aboriginal Arts Australia Gallery in Sydney in February 1991. Then in 1992 Aboriginal Arts Australia went into liquidation, and the Centre was taken over by the former owners of Corkwood Gallery, operating as a commercial gallery under its old name.

The artists' organisation Jukurrpa, based at the Institute of Aboriginal Development in Alice Springs, is one of a handful of Aboriginal owned and controlled painting enterprises operating out of Alice Springs. 'Jukurrpa' is the Warlpiri term for the

Dreaming. The group was started in July 1986 by a group of Warlpiri women who were all students taking the General Literacy course at the Institute for Aboriginal Development in Alice Springs. The women were encouraged by their teacher to do some 'traditional style' paintings in the afternoons after formal classes. Starting on cardboard and commercial art board, they quickly gained confidence and began painting on canvas. Later in 1986 the Aboriginal Arts Board gave further support to the group in the form of a grant for materials. By this time they had ten members. In its seven years of operation, Jukurrpa has represented up to twenty artists from areas all over Central Australia, including Kintore, Ernabella and Papunya.

The group runs as a cooperative, with a portion of the income from each painting sold going into a group bank account to cover the cost of new materials. In June 1987 the Department of Aboriginal Affairs provided funds for the construction of an open shade structure for the women to use as a studio. In October 1987 the group had its first exhibition at the workshop. Four Jukurrpa artists entered the Alice Springs Art Prize that year, and then in 1988 two Jukurrpa artists were included in the ANCAA (Association for Northern and Central Australian Aboriginal Artists) exhibition 'Karnta' touring South East Asia, the South Pacific and Canada. In September 1988 the then chairwoman of Jukurrpa, Pauline Nakamarra Woods, won the National Aboriginal Art Award, the first woman to do so. In November 1988 the group had its first solo exhibition at the Anima Gallery in Adelaide and sold more than half the paintings. Sales for the period July 1987 to June 1988 averaged $700 per month; for the period July 1988 to September 1988 they averaged $4000 a month. About twenty artists from the Pitjantjatjara, Anmatyerre, Pintupi and Warlpiri tribal groups were now painting on a regular basis for Jukurrpa, and a few others, including Clifford Possum, Barney Daniels, Colin and Mary Dixon and Wenton Rubuntja, were using Jukurrpa as one of the outlets for their work. Pansy Napangati was a member of the original group, and is still a member of the General Literacy course at the IAD. For a time, she worked mostly with the Jukurrpa group in the outdoor shade area in the IAD grounds, taking out the 1989 National Aboriginal Art Award. One of the features of town painting in the late '80s is the predominance of women amongst the group of practising artists. The importance of senior women artists in the success of Warlukurlangu Artists was a significant factor in this development. Some of these painters, for example Peggy Poulson and Rosie Fleming, have since moved into Alice Springs and begun painting for outlets in town.

Jukurrpa artists have since shown in many more exhibitions (see below). Their paintings have been purchased by the National Gallery of Australia and sold to collections in England, America and Japan. The women have also used their art to teach others about Aboriginal culture, visiting many schools locally and interstate to show the paintings and explain the stories, songs and dances that go with them. Times have been hard for the organisation, due to the recession and a temporary decline in the local tourist industry. Both grant monies and income from sales have contracted dramatically. The artists are paid for their paintings on a consignment basis, which requires a high turnover of cash to keep up the supply of paintings. Money delays have hindered Jukurrpa's capacity to operate effectively as an agent for Aboriginal artists. In October 1991 the IAD arts development officer and coordinator of Jukurrpa resigned due to lack of funds to pay her salary. The sudden death in 1993 of the literacy teacher, who had been carrying on the job of coordinator, was another serious blow to Jukurrpa's fortunes. However, the original group of artists, with all the wealth of talent it contains, is still together and the organisation continues to mount exhibitions and remain a presence in a highly competitive marketplace.

Jukurrpa Exhibitions 1987–91

1987	18th Alice Springs Art Prize. Four Jukurrpa entrants: Sally Butler, Rachel Jurra (sold), Rene Robinson (recommended acquisition) and Pauline Woods (sold)
1988	Karnta Exhibition touring SE Asia, South Pacific and Canada — two Jukurrpa painters included: Pauline Woods and Rachel Jurra
1988	National Aboriginal Art Award — Jukurrpa entrant Pauline Woods first woman to win the award
October 1988	'Continuity of Perception: Two Aspects of Warlpiri Art' — seven paintings exhibited by Jukurrpa artists Rene Robinson, Mary Dixon, Pauline Woods and Rachel Jurra
December 1988	Anima Gallery Adelaide — Jukurrpa's first solo exhibition
March 1989	'Women's Business Exhibition' at Stonelea, Victoria, went on to tour Victoria and New South Wales
April 1989	'Two Faces of the Desert', Northern Territory Museum of Arts and Sciences (with Yuelamu Artists and Pmere) — included 18 Jukurrpa entries
June 1989	'One Country Two Views' Exhibition, Araluen Arts Centre, Alice Springs. Aboriginal and non-Aboriginal art. Two Jukurrpa entries: Linda Syddick and Bessie Liddle
July 1989	'Songlines' exhibition, Rebecca Hossack Gallery in London includes a painting by Bessie Liddle 'Desert Impression' Australian Conservation Foundation, Melbourne — Jukurrpa, Pmere and Utopia art
August 1989	Northern Territory Art Award, Araluen Arts Centre — three Jukurrpa entries: Joylene Abbott, Patsy Morton, Betty Egan (her *Murchison River* was highly commended)
September 1989	Jukurrpa exhibition, North Point College TAFE, Brisbane Jukurrpa entrants in 'The Timeless Dreaming' exhibition, New York
October 1989	'Minymaku' exhibition, Araluen Arts Centre — exhibition of Pitjantjatjara women's art, including Jukurrpa entries by Eileen Boko, Kitty Miller, Bessie Liddle, Betty Egan and Linda Syddick

November 1989	Jukurrpa 'Central Dreaming' exhibition Redcliffe, Queensland — 80 paintings exhibited
December 1989	'Nganampa Jukurrpa', Araluen Arts Centre — 80 Jukurrpa paintings exhibited. Australan National Gallery purchased five paintings
February 1990	Exhibition of Jukurrpa Art at Blackbooks, Sydney
March 1990	Australian Conservation Foundation, Melbourne — second exhibition of Jukurrpa art
April 1990	Jukurrpa exhibition, CSIRO, Melbourne
May 1990	Jukurrpa exhibition, Kamarga Aboriginal Arts, Brisbane
	Centralian Advocate Art Award — five Jukurrpa entries including Linda Syddick and Kitty Miller
	'From the Australian Desert', Lew Allen/Butler Fine Art, Santa Fe, New Mexico — featuring Linda Syddick's work
July 1990	'Nganampa Jukurrpa' exhibition, Friends of the Earth Gallery, Melbourne
December 1990	Jukurrpa exhibition, Albert Hall, Canberra
January 1991	Jukurrpa exhibition, Brisbane
March 1991	'Crossroads' — Jukurrpa exhibition, Araluen Arts Centre

Pertame artists are based at the Gap Neighbourhood Centre in Gap Road, Alice Springs. Funded as a welfare and childcare centre, at the end of 1985 the Centre began using art and craft as a focus for women's participation in its other activities. A group of ten Aboriginal women soon emerged as artists and took over a flat attached to the Centre for their work. Batik making, screenprinting and linocut printing were the main activities initially, and the influence of batik was evident in the paintings which the group went on to produce. Dots were used in their batik designs as early as 1986, but it was not until early in 1988 that the women began doing paintings in the Western Desert style, largely in response to the preference of local dealers in Aboriginal art and crafts for canvases. The women were also painting dotted designs on earrings for Walkabout Clay Crafts and have in the past painted dots on rocks after an idea started by people from Mt Allan. All of the painters working out of the Gap were brought up in Alice Springs, though their traditional country is further to the west in Luritja territory. Eight women from the Gap travelled to the Pacific Arts Festival and a design by the Pertame women is a feature of the centre court of the Yperrenye Shopping Centre in Alice Springs. The current coordinator of the Centre remains committed to the painting activity as a focus around which the Centre's other functions can be carried on informally. In December 1991 the group opened a shop on Gap Road to sell their work directly to the public.

The involvement of CAAMA (Central Australian Aboriginal Media Association) in marketing the work of Western Desert artists temporarily or permanently based in Alice Springs grew out of the establishment of another shop on Gap Road — to market the records and cassettes of contemporary Aboriginal music which CAAMA was beginning to produce (six albums on cassette at the time the retail outlet opened in 1983). Word soon spread amongst local artists that a shop controlled by an Aboriginal organisation had opened up. Their paintings and artefacts rapidly moved from a sideline to the major focus of the enterprise. In recent years CAAMA has diversified into clothing design, commissioning artists to prepare the designs for a range of T-shirts and fashion garments, and has transferred its business to a shop in the main shopping mall of Alice Springs. In 1988 CAAMA took over the management of the Utopia Women's Batik Group, from which some of the strongest new artists in the Western Desert style have emerged in the last few years. The Utopia community (see this chapter, 11. *Utopia*) is now the focus of CAAMA's art marketing activities, leaving the town-based artists to try their luck with commercial galleries, which now line both sides of the top end of Todd Street Mall. If these avenues fail, the artists can still resort to the small army of freelance art dealers who frequent Alice Springs hoping to find bargains or masterpieces of Western Desert art to market in the capital cities and overseas.

6. Warlayirti Artists of Balgo Hills, Western Australia

Warlayirti Artists company supports a vital painting enterprise centred around the communities of Balgo, Mulan and Billiluna in north-east Western Australia, some 300 km south of the nearest town of Halls Creek. Here, on the north-western perimeter of what anthropologists loosely define as the Western Desert 'bloc', is a thriving community of seven hundred people, of whom more than one hundred and fifty are artists, and about fifty paint regularly. Although located nearly 1000 km north-west across the Western Desert region from Papunya where acrylic painting began in the early '70s, the Balgo community was not unaware of this development. The Papunya artists were, it seems, the talk of almost every community in these parts for most of that decade. Their action of painting ceremonial designs in a European medium was highly controversial in every other community in the Western Desert. Thus in 1981, when the Pintupi moved from Papunya to establish Kintore 20 km from the West Australian border, the Papunya Tula artists took a decision that there should be no painting on outstations of the new settlement which lay across the border, in deference to the sensibilities of their countrymen at settlements like Balgo.

While feelings everywhere ran high about the supposedly destabilising effects of what was happening at Papunya on an already dislocated situation, the Aboriginal debate about whether people should be painting at all was offset by the sporadic presence of painting activity on many of these same settlements. Thus, at Balgo in the late '70s, the old men of the community did occasionally use bits of paper, board or canvas that were lying around to paint their traditional designs. A number of the artists whose biographies are included in this dictionary have links with other painting communities where they may have painted before starting up with the Balgo group, including Brandy, Kenny Gibson, Donkeyman and Patrick Oldoodi with Kiwirrkura and Alan Winderoo with Yuendumu. The old men at Balgo may also have been influenced to try

31

their hand at painting by the visits of members of the founding group of Papunya painters, some of whom had close relatives in Balgo. Anatjari Tjampitjinpa, for example, was a one-time resident of Balgo and recalled instructing people (including his younger brother, Dini Campbell Tjampitjinpa) in the use of paint and canvas. Like many of the original Papunya 'painting men', the older members of the Balgo community were born and grew to adulthood in the bush before their first contact with white society. People of this generation comprise about one third of all the artists working out of Balgo, and over the years they have exerted a profound influence on the course of the painting movement through the strength of their adherence to the Dreamings, which connect the painters to the places depicted in their paintings, as the foundation of their art.

Against this background, the opening of the St John's Adult Education Centre in 1981 under the caring and charismatic supervision of Sister Alice Dempsey was a turning point in the development of a painting enterprise at the settlement. The '70s had brought dramatic changes for the people of the Balgo Hills after a peaceful half century under the Catholic missionaries, who established Balgo mission in the 1930s. A nearby cattle station was bought and handed back to Aboriginal control, and the new communities of Mulan and Billiluna were established. Balgo itself became an Aboriginal controlled community, with the remaining Catholic missionaries concentrating their energies in education. The Centre offered a range of programs including art and craft activities, and at last provided the Balgo community with a regular supply of painting materials. At first the artists involved with the Centre were mostly young men in their early twenties. Their use of figurative and decorative elements reflected the lessons of the mission schoolroom to which their generation had been exposed.[3] However, the artists' approach to the depiction of Christian traditions in these paintings also applies Aboriginal ideas of journey paths and sites marked out along them where significant events occurred: Aboriginal ways of telling the stories of Christianity.

The initial move from basic ochres to acrylics stimulated a wave of experimentation with the new medium. The older men also became involved with the church paintings and some large paintings two and three metres long were completed for specific Christian celebrations like the Golden Jubilee of Balgo's establishment. From these banners for church festivals, the painters soon moved on to individual works. The Centre was struggling to keep up the supply of materials as the artists moved from small canvas boards to larger stretched canvases. People caught up in helping with the paintings at this time recall a frenzy of painting activity and working into the night to prepare calico canvases with whatever they could find for undercoat. People were painting on roller blinds, any materials they could get hold of.

At this point, the women also became involved in the painting enterprise, following the pattern of other communities where painting has recently started (rather than the model of Kintore or Kiwirrkura, where very few women paint regularly). As with women's painting in Yuendumu, it was very much a communal activity, with the older women standing around singing and dancing while others painted. A similarly collective approach was shown in the Luurnpa project, initiated by the artist Gracie Green Nangala, one of the original 'painting women' at Balgo, and later taken over by the old men. The huge canvas depicted the ancestral Kingfisher who came to rest on Uluru and then carried water in his neck to aid the Balgo people on their long trek across the desert to Balgo. During the 1985 ceremony when Uluru was formally handed back to its Aboriginal owners, the old men of Balgo carried the canvas right up the Rock to the point where Luurnpa drank, in a communal affirmation of the Balgo people's ties through this Dreaming to Uluru.

The establishment in 1985 of Kiwirrkura across the WA border, west of Kintore and south of Balgo, brought closer links between the Papunya Tula artists living there and the Balgo painters. There is strong evidence of artistic interchange between the two painting communities in the adoption of the technique of linked dotting that is characteristic of the work of many of the older Balgo artists by several artists at Kiwirrkura and Kintore in the late '80s — including Dini Campbell, who moved to Kintore in the early '80s and started to paint for Papunya Tula Artists.

In December 1986 the first solo exhibition of Balgo art was shown at the Art Gallery of Western Australia to wide critical acclaim. Considerable debate amongst the artists attended the selection of paintings for the show, especially a Lightning Brothers Dreaming, the inclusion of which was permitted only after lengthy discussion of claims that it breached Aboriginal laws of disclosure. After the success of the exhibition, an approach was made to the Aboriginal Arts Board for funding of an arts coordinator position and the founding of the artists' cooperative Warlayirti Artists followed. There have since been many exhibitions of Warlayirti Artists, and Balgo artists are represented in major private and public collections, including the state galleries of Victoria, New South Wales, Queensland and Western Australia, and the Australian National Gallery.

In a crowded field, Balgo paintings retain a distinctive vitality. Six main tribal groups make up the artist population of the Balgo area, with Kukatja-speaking desert people making up about half of all the artists and Walmatjari, Warlpiri and the Tjaru group from the Kimberley making up most of the remainder. Such diversity is unusual in remote communities, which are usually heavily dominated by one language group. The situation is reminiscent of Papunya in the early '70s when at least seven different tribal groups were thrown together in significant numbers at the settlement. There were conflicts arising from this situation, but there was also an unparalleled opportunity, particularly for the elders of these groups, to exchange religious knowledge and enlarge their ritual practice. Michael Rae, art coordinator of Warlayirti Artists from 1989 to 1992, noted 'the very sociable character of painting at Balgo, particularly amongst the older men and women, who are constantly sharing ideas and insights with each other as they work'.

Women now comprise a slight majority of Balgo artists. Many of them paint only intermittently, but some of the strongest Balgo painters are older women like Susie Bootja Bootja, Bye Bye Napangati, Eubena Nampitjinpa, Rita Kunintji, Lucy Loomoo, Bridget Mudjidell, Muntja Nungurrayai and Njamme Napangati. The younger women, like the younger men, show keener attention to design and execution than the older people. The traditional palette of black, white, red ochre and yellow ochre which dominated the earlier works is now supplemented with green and blue and brighter reds and yellows as artists seek to highlight their work. Recent exhibitions show the artists continuing to explore new ideas and experiment with techniques developed by other Aboriginal communities. But beyond the various inputs from school, church and, lately, television discernible in the rapidly evolving forms of Balgo art is its firm grounding in the artists' profound knowledge both of their Law and of the country to which it binds them.

Warlayirti Artists Exhibitions 1987–91

November 1987	'Art from the Great Sandy Desert', Art Gallery of WA, Perth
April 1988	'Australian Aboriginal Art', Coo-ee Emporium, Sydney
September 1988	'Art from Balgo Hills', Birnkmarri Gallery, Fremantle
October 1988	'Balgo Art', Gallery Gabrielle Pizzi, Melbourne
March 1989	'Balgo Art', Blaxland Gallery, Sydney
July 1989	'Balgo Paintings', Dreamtime Gallery, Perth
June–August 1989	'Mythscapes: Aboriginal Art of the Desert', National Gallery of Victoria, Melbourne
August 1989	'Recent Paintings from Balgo', Gallery Gabrielle Pizzi, Melbourne
October 1989	'A Myriad of Dreaming', Lauraine Diggins Fine Art, Melbourne
November 1989	'Warlayirti Artists', Coo-ee Aboriginal Art, Sydney
December 1989	'Balgo Paintings', Robert Steele Gallery, Adelaide
January 1990	'Australian Aboriginal Art', Wildlife of the World Gallery, Aspen, Colorado
February 1990	'Contemporary Aboriginal Art', Robert Holmes à Court Collection, touring the USA
March 1990	'Balance 1990, Views, Visions, Influences', Queensland Art Gallery, Brisbane
April 1990	'Songlines — Paintings from the Balgo Hills', Rebecca Hossack Gallery, London
	'Warlayirti Art', Birnkmarri Gallery, Fremantle
May 1990	'Innovations in Aboriginal Art', Hogarth Galleries, Sydney
	'Wimmitji Tjapangati and Eubena Nampitjin', Gallery Gabrielle Pizzi, Melbourne
July 1990	'L'été Australien à Montpellier', Musée Fabre, Galerie St Ravy, Montpellier, France
	'Paintings from Kukatja Country', Deutscher Brunswick St Gallery, Melbourne
	'Aboriginal Art Exhibition', Dreamtime Gallery, Broadbeach, Queensland

August 1990	'Balgo and Beyond', Dreamtime Gallery, Broadbeach, Queensland
	'Paintings from Balgo, WA', Hogarth Gallery, Sydney
	'Contemporary Aboriginal Art 1990', Third Eye Centre, Glasgow, UK
October 1990	'Recent Balgo Paintings', Dreamtime Gallery, Perth
November 1990	'The Singing Earth', Chapman Gallery, Canberra
	'Innovation and Tradition — Paintings from Warlayirti Artists', Gallery Gabrielle Pizzi, Melbourne
December 1990	'Balgo Paintings', Robert Steele Gallery, Adelaide
February 1991	'Il Sud del Mondo', Marsala, Sicily
	'World Council of Churches Assembly', High Court, Canberra
	'Circles and Cycles', Dreamtime Gallery, Perth
March 1991	'Mulan — The Art of the Great Sandy Desert', Coo-ee Aboriginal Art, Sydney
	'Paintings from Kukatja Country', Rebecca Hossack Gallery, London
	'Aboriginal Art Exhibition', Kookaburra Gallery, Hobart, Tasmania
	'Aboriginal Arts Festival', Guildford Grammar School, Perth
April 1991	'Balgo — Kimberley Art from the Desert', Creations Gallery, Broome, WA
	'Aboriginal Art', Grenoble, France
May 1991	'New Artists from Balgo Hills', The Prince and the Frog Gallery, Melbourne
June 1991	'Lions Haven Aboriginal Art Exhibition', Broadbeach, Queensland
	'Aboriginal Art from the Balgo Hills', Gallery Gabrielle Pizzi, Melbourne
July 1991	'Balgo Art', Birukmarri Gallery, Fremantle, WA
August 1991	'Warlayirti Artists', Hogarth Gallery, Sydney
	'Songlines — Aboriginal Art', Barbican Centre, London
September 1991	'Art from Balgo Hills', Shades of Ochre Gallery, Darwin
	'Women's Paintings from the Western Desert', Vivien Anderson Gallery, Melbourne
	'Aboriginal Women's Exhibition', Art Gallery of NSW, Sydney, then touring state galleries
October 1991	'Aboriginal Art', Union of Soviet Artists Gallery, Moscow

7. Lajamanu

Lajamanu's history as an Aboriginal settlement goes back to 1949, when several hundred Warlpiri people were trucked there from Yuendumu. Fears held by the authorities that there would be an outbreak of serious disease at Yuendumu unless the numbers there could be drastically reduced, prompted the establishment of a new depot at Catfish Waterhole, a safe 600 km north across the inhospitable Tanami Desert — just in case anyone felt like walking back to visit the relatives from whom they had been arbitrarily separated. The site of the new settlement was not even on Warlpiri lands, but located in the 'buffer zone' between the traditional territories of the Warlpiri and the Gurindji. Several times the people walked back to Yuendumu, but in the end they stayed and established a strong community, which was for many years one of the staunchest in its opposition to the painting movement.

> 'We did not do this ... to seek out praise, or honour. We only want the world to accept and respect our culture. We only want recognition that we have a culture, and that we remain strong, as Warlpiri people in Australia. We do not want to be venerated as "special". We just want to be recognised as part of the human race, with our own traditions which we maintain, as we always have. We will NEVER put this kind of painting on to canvas, or on to artboard, or on to any "permanent" medium. The permanence of these designs is in our minds. We do not need museums or books to remind us of our traditions. We are forever renewing and recreating those traditions in our ceremonies.'[4]

One of the most articulate of its opponents was Maurice Luther Jupurrurla, who vigorously and successfully opposed the development of a painting enterprise at Lajamanu from his influential position as Chairman of the local Community Council. On this occasion, he was explaining why he and eleven of his Warlpiri countrymen had travelled to Paris to construct a traditional ground painting for 'D'un autre continent: l'Australie — le rêve et le réel'. These elaborate sculptured mosaics of dyed plant, down and feathers which mark out the ceremonial area are the source of the symbolism of U-shapes, concentric circles and connecting lines which forms the distinctive iconography of contemporary Western Desert canvases. However, for Maurice Luther, it was one thing to create and destroy a ground painting as part of a public ritual that happened to be sited in an art gallery — but quite another to make a permanent image of one on a canvas and sell it on the white art market. Luther was adamant: 'We are not, and do not, ever, want to become professional painters ...'

The irony of Maurice Luther's untimely death in 1985 and the wave of painting activity that so soon afterwards broke over Lajamanu is that the pioneer painters of Papunya Tula Artists who started the art movement back in the early '70s had been just as intent on preserving the distinction between the sacred and the profane as he was. It was the widespread Aboriginal opposition, even the threat of censure under traditional law, that provided the spur to the artists' imaginations and drove the Papunya artists into the search for a de-sacralised painting language to encode a secularised vision of Western Desert culture. Whether or not one's ideological sympathies are with Maurice Luther's position that producing images of one's culture rather than the culture itself is alien and alienating with respect to its traditions, it is vital to an appreciation of the sophistication of the Aboriginal position on these issues to recognise that the artists themselves have long since had these debates with the ideologues of their own culture — and moved beyond them. The arguments that raged a few years ago in art critical circles about whether aesthetics, ethnography or the rhetoric of social justice is the more appropriate interpretive framework for these paintings really miss the point that the paintings are themselves translations of Western Desert culture for western audiences. The artists themselves address us from the space which these analytical discourses seek to occupy. Like all good translations, the paintings take us far enough into another world to let us know what we are missing.

It was John Quinn, the adult educator at Lajamanu who in 1986 precipitated the painting enterprise in the settlement by running a course in 'Traditional Painting', for which the Department of Employment Education and Training supplied $8000 worth of paint and canvas. At first only the men painted, but after about six months the women started painting in the jilimi (single women's camp). Such was the enthusiasm that in the end over one hundred people enrolled for the course — most of whom, to judge by the over one hundred entries for Lajamanu artists in this dictionary, are (or would, if they could be) still painting. It has not always been as easy for them to do so as for their countrymen on other settlements. There was no pre-sale of goods to an inter-mediary at the settlement, as in Papunya. Mimi Arts and Crafts, based in Katherine, was already coming to Lajamanu on buying trips for seed necklaces, coolamons etc. and began buying the paintings too. In 1986 Andrew Crocker, previously an art supervisor for Papunya Tula Artists (1980–1), came to Lajamanu and taught the artists stretching. He encouraged an Aboriginal adult educator at Lajamanu school to take on the job of coordinating the painting enterprise for six months. The money received from DEET had been placed in two cheque accounts, one for the men — Kurawari — and Yawulyu for the women, who had been encouraged by the involvement of a woman in the role of art coordinator to begin painting in earnest. These arrangements broke down in the financial misunderstandings that have almost invariably accompanied the beginning of painting companies at other settlements.

Towards the end of 1987 an exhibition of twenty to thirty paintings was arranged for the Gallery Gabrielle Pizzi in Melbourne. The show was highly successful: it virtually sold out — helped, no doubt, by the charismatic presence of Jimmy Robertson at the opening. Some of the artists were disappointed when their cheques from the sale of paintings came and were often not as large as the substantial deposits they had been paid when the paintings were consigned to the Gallery. Nevertheless, the painting enterprise was firmly established in the community after the work's favourable recep-tion in Melbourne, and a second successful show in London at the Rebecca Hossack Gallery the following year. The artists' requests to the Department of Aboriginal

Affairs for a funded art coordinator for years met with denial, apparently on the grounds that Yuendumu, the closest Warlpiri community (650 km across the Tanami) already had one for Warlukurlungu Artists. In 1988 the artists — fifteen men led by Tim Kennedy Jupurrurla — tired of waiting, occupied the staff room of the school to demand incorporation as an artists' company. Incorporation papers were drawn up in a series of meetings. An executive was appointed and a set of aims and objectives of the company composed, but as the years went by and there was no word, artists who wanted to paint in Lajamanu were obliged to fall back on the inferior — usually student quality — materials that were intermittently available from the community general store. Unlike Mt Allan, the storekeeper at Lajamanu was not in the business of buying paintings. The paintings made their way out of Lajamanu sporadically, either via exhibitions organised through the school principal as an extension of her involvement in the original Adult Education initiatives, or through private entrepreneurs amongst the non-Aboriginal residents of the community and passing travellers. In the peak years of the Aboriginal art boom, there was no shortage of triers.

Over the years, several Lajamanu artists have built up impressive individual reputations despite the lack of an organised attempt to promote or distribute their work. Many others struggled on, though the lessons about stretching and professional presentation for the marketplace often went by the board. Collectively they have forged for Lajamanu painting a distinctive identity, more distinctive perhaps than at some communities where the centralising effect of an art adviser position tends to flatten out the individualities of style.

8. Wirliyajarrayi Artists of Willowra

Willowra differs from the other two predominantly Warlpiri-speaking communities of Yuendumu and Lajamanu so far discussed in several key respects which have a bearing on the character of the painting enterprise in the Willowra community. Most members of the Willowra Aboriginal community are Lander River Warlpiri who have always lived in the area, whereas many of the residents of Yuendumu and Lajamanu came originally from distant places or other language groups. Willowra is also a pastoral property, rather than a government or mission settlement established to promote assimilationist policies of population consolidation. Before it passed into Aboriginal hands in 1973, and then into Aboriginal freehold title in 1983, Willowra station was run by a pastoralist whose attitude to the resident Aboriginal community acknowledged the importance of extended family ties and attachment to land. The relative isolation of Willowra on often impassable side roads has also contributed to the strength of traditional forms of social authority in the community, as reflected in the continuance until very recently of customary marriage practices, the stability of the population (few people leave, despite lack of employment) — and perhaps also the fragmented and tentative character of the local painting enterprise.

'Wirliyajarrayi' is not the name of a painting company. None exists, or seems likely to in the near future, at Willowra. It is a Warlpiri word meaning 'footprint', which is the Aboriginal name for the site of Willowra, and was suggested by Malcolm Jagamara as a suitable name for the painting group, if such a collective enterprise were to be formed in the community. As yet, painting is still organised on a very ad hoc basis in Willowra, with a few artists taking their work into town to sell, and occasionally selling it in Willowra to private dealers. Though for a period in 1989 the Community Development Employment Program coordinator made canvas and paint available, giving many Willowra residents their first experience of painting, there was not the same frenzy of painting activity which this factor produced in other more 'displaced' communities. Perhaps hostility towards the painting movement is still a factor: the community's formidable reputation as one of the strongest in the Law in the region guarantees that the debates in Willowra about the art movement during the '70s would have been memorably intense.

'You know what it really boils down to is when these paintings are actually being done, there's a division all of a sudden happening. There is a correct procedure for all of this to happen. There is a song and a dance and all of this. The real law is kurdus are owners, but without kurdungurlu the cycle is incomplete. For any ceremony, for anything to happen, there has to be kurdu/kurdungurlu relationship. Nobody talks about it for ceremonial purposes, because it's visual, it's so visual, the kurdu/kurdungulu relationships in that scenario. You can see people doing it, fulfilling that role. So there's this whole sharing aspect. All of a sudden, the other ones were excluded for the sake of one area. So there was more or less a broken chain of a continuity cycle that people couldn't come to grips with. Nobody actually said this to me, but the thing was, I could pick up in areas, "Oh yeah, you paint so-and-so, where's the kurdu sitting round singing songs for it? Where's the kurdungurlu sitting round serving a cup of tea and putting wood on the fire? Where's the karnta [women] on the sidelines dancing?" I mean, that whole chain of events was broken, really — in the form of transportable art. Now it becomes a bit confused through greed, a whole lot of different things, when it starts getting transferred onto canvas.'[5]

The speaker is Malcolm Jagamara, who returned to Central Australia in the mid '70s and observed the situation in Willowra closely during the '80s. According to him, the paintings remain contentious for some in the Willowra community even today. However, the original questions about the artists' right to paint at all have largely been replaced by more 'legalistic' debates about who has the right to paint what, which accept that the painting movement is a reality and seek to regulate certain aspects of it. According to Malcolm, Mervyn Rubuntja, the son of the eminent Wenton Rubuntja, was the first person to have the temerity to begin painting in Willowra in the late '80s.

9. Ernabella Arts Inc.

Along with Oenpelli bark painting in the North, Ernabella Arts Inc. was one of the first major attempts in Australia to manufacture and sell Aboriginal art. Ernabella Arts was the brainchild of Winifred Hilliard, who was Deaconess and later craft supervisor at Ernabella for almost thirty years. The settlement was established by the Presbyterian Church in the late '40s to minister to the Pitjantjatjara tribespeople of the far north-western corner of South Australia. Hilliard's original idea was to establish a rug-making industry using the wool from the mission's sheep property. The older women performed the semi-traditional task of spinning the wool into yarn, and the younger women dyed the wool and then hand wove it into rugs. The distinctive Ernabella designs, so evocative of the patterns of vegetation and shade in the desert, were first used on those rugs, having been devised in the Ernabella schoolroom by the same young women who were now working in the mission 'craftroom'.

The artistic careers of several of the Ernabella women who are included in this dictionary as 'dot painters' span nearly three decades with Ernabella Arts, in which their recent diversification into acrylics on canvas is but the latest episode. Nyukana Baker and the late Yipati Kuyata began designing, weaving and painting in the early '60s and started their training in batik with a workshop conducted at Ernabella in 1971. In 1975 they attended the Batik Institute in Jogjakarta, Indonesia, studying batik technique. Years of exhibitions and demonstrations of their batik-making followed, including two showings at the Museum of Ethnology in Osaka, Japan and 'Textiles of the Commonwealth', a travelling exhibition which toured the UK. Both women have travelled the world with their batiks. Their extensive curricula vitae, supplied by Ernabella Arts Inc., provide a fascinating historical documentation of the limited opportunities generally available to Aboriginal artists, and especially to Aboriginal women artists, until very recent times. Neither has had a solo exhibition of her work.

Hilliard's marketing strategy located the origin of the Ernabella designs in the schoolroom and the Pitjantjatjara's intimate knowledge of the environment and its patterns, rather than the ancient Pitjantjatjara forms of graphic expression which they also resemble. Ernabella Arts probably suffered from the stigma of non-traditionalism in times when such a status meant being neither 'Art' nor truly 'Aboriginal'. The move into batik and textile production provided a context less afflicted with these prejudices than the world of high art, thus ensuring the survival of Ernabella Arts Inc. But it also increased the art world's prejudice against them for working in a female-dominated (and thus 'uncreative', 'craft-orientated') medium. As the '80s progressed, however, there was a perceptible change in these attitudes.

Winifred Hilliard's retirement and the emergence of Utopia as a rival batik-making enterprise with the prestigious patronage of Holmes à Court meant that the '80s were years of some difficulty for Ernabella Arts Inc., even if they were also positively affected by the boom years in Aboriginal art generally towards the end of the decade. For many years, Ernabella Arts resisted the trend to 'dot painting' sweeping across the entire Western Desert region. A few artists originally from Ernabella moved to other communities and joined painting groups there, but in Ernabella itself, the influence of Winifred Hilliard's attitude that 'dot painting' was bandwaggoning continued to be felt right up to the end of the '80s.

Another factor in Ernabella's holding back in this area may be the historical residue of the controversies during the first half of the '70s about the secret-sacred content of some early Papunya paintings. The strongest protests seem to have come from the Pitjantjatjara peoples, who over the past two decades have remained constantly vigilant about unauthorised disclosures, to the extent of taking C.P. Mountford to court in 1976 for 'breach of confidence' in *Nomads of the Australian Desert* — and winning too. The fear of incurring the wrath of tribal authorities may also have underpinned the general reluctance of people in Ernabella to paint.

This may also be why the impetus for the commencement of painting in the dot style in the community came from outside. In 1988 Ernabella Arts were approached by HALT (Healthy Aboriginal Life Team) about a book presenting Pitjantjatjara perceptions of health through the medium of paintings. The 'Health Project' stimulated a lot of people to start painting in 1988/9. Eleven Ernabella artists are included in *Anangu Way*, published by the IAD and Nganapu Health Council in 1991. However, none of these eleven were amongst the biographies provided by Kate Race, the art supervisor of Ernabella Arts, who observed that after the initial burst of activity when a lot of people started painting, only a small core of artists had kept painting regularly. Questioned whether it was still controversial for them to do so, she said that the artists who paint were very aware of the sensitivity of their work in the community. About five or six Dreaming lines are currently being painted on canvas, and are being painted by people who are very closely tied to those lines.

An incident which occurred in November 1990 in connection with the 'Two Homes' exhibition of Ernabella paintings and batiks at Tandanya Aboriginal Cultural Institute in Adelaide strengthens the argument for the overriding significance of such issues for the people of this community. A video was made to accompany the exhibition, in which artists talked about their paintings in the show. After long debate, part of the Pitjantjatjara sound track explaining the significance of a particular section of one of the paintings was taped over with the soundtrack of some footage from a ceremony. The English sub-titles to the spoken Pitjantjatjara were not erased, and while it is perhaps doubtful that they bore a very close relationship to the Pitjantjatjara version, it is significant that the vital concern of the artists was that other Pitjantjatjara speakers should not be privy to this information, not whether outsiders to Western Desert society read the written translations. Nor was there any objection raised to the painting itself being included in the exhibition.

10. Amata, Fregon, Indulkana

Acrylic painting began at Amata, Fregon and Indulkana, all Pitjantjatjara communities in northern South Australia, about the same time it began in Ernabella, also in connection with the HALT *Anangu Way* project of 1988/9. As at Ernabella, painting activity has since died down to a core group of a few people after the initial burst of enthusiasm produced by the 'Health Project'. Tjurma Homelands Inc. at Amata returned only two biographies in response to my inquiries about Amata 'dot painters' for inclusion in the dictionary, Indulkana and Fregon none, though there are, no doubt, quite a few people in these communities who still paint occasionally.

11. Utopia

Utopia lies 240 km north-east of Alice Springs, on the eastern perimeter of the Western Desert 'bloc', astride the traditional lands of the Eastern Anmatyerre and Alyawarre peoples. The territory of the Eastern Arrente comes up from the south to meet it. Utopia was the name of the first pastoral lease taken out on the area in 1927, with the usual effect of depopulating traditional areas of occupancy as local tribesmen and women were drawn to homestead encampments to work as stockmen (and sometimes women) and domestics. In 1977, the Aboriginal Land Fund Commission acquired the lease for the Utopia community and precipitated a move back to heritage country similar to what was happening on nearby Mt Allan station. People began to establish themselves at isolated encampments on their traditional lands, ignoring attempts by the Northern Territory government to establish a centralised settlement along the lines of Papunya and Yuendumu. The successful land claim in 1979 returning the lands to the Utopia community under inalienable freehold title accelerated this process, which has proven an effective way of accommodating the region's cultural diversity.

The batik program was started in 1977 by school teacher Toly Sawkeno and adult educator Jenny Green as a source of income for the women which could be adapted to the widely dispersed demographic structure of Utopia. In the preparations for the land claim hearings, and the presentations of traditional culture which that process involved, it acquired new significance. During the hearings the women displayed their batiks to demonstrate the economic viability of the outstations, and also as an expression of their Dreaming rights and responsibilities to the country. The Utopia work was immediately distinctive for its rawness and energy, arising partly from the camp conditions in which it was produced, and partly from the women's attitude to the activity. A succession of art advisers appointed to Utopia encouraged them in these bold, exploratory attitudes to the work and within a few years they were beginning to carve out a niche for themselves alongside such long-established enterprises as Ernabella Arts Inc. After a show at the Araluen Arts Centre in Alice Springs in 1980, Utopia batiks were shown in the 1981 Adelaide Arts Festival in a major exhibition 'Floating Forests of Silk: Utopia Batik from the Desert'. Twelve of the artists attended the opening and attracted considerable media attention. Exhibitions of Utopia batiks at cultural festivals around the country followed. However, recognition of the batiks as art rather than beautifully crafted dress material remained elusive, despite purchases by some major public galleries.

CAAMA took over the marketing and finances of the Utopia artists in 1987. During the first months of 1988, each artist in the group was commissioned to do a batik. The resulting collection of eighty-eight batiks, one by each of the artists, was the opening exhibition at the new Tandanya Aboriginal Cultural Institute in Adelaide in October 1988, and later toured to Ireland, accompanied by artist Gloria Petyarre. The batiks were purchased by the Robert Holmes à Court Collection, whose patronage of the Utopia artists over the next few years played an important role in their emergence as painters. Later in 1988 CAAMA mounted its first overseas exhibition in St Louis Missouri. The show featured Utopia batiks and the work of Western Desert artists who sold their work through the CAAMA shop. These included at the time Clifford Possum Tjapaltjarri, who travelled to America with the CAAMA representative for the opening. The attitude of museums in the United States, who were even more resistant than their Australian counterparts to the idea of regarding the batiks as art rather than craft, made the move to acrylic painting almost inevitable as the Aboriginal fine art market continued to boom.

That move came with the 'Summer Project' of 1988–9. One hundred small canvases identical in their dimensions, and the four basic colours of the Aboriginal palette — black, white, yellow ochre and red ochre — were distributed. In the end eighty-one artists participated in the project. The works were initially placed on the market at $100 each, but later purchased as a group by the Holmes à Court collection. Later that year they were exhibited as 'A Summer Project: Utopia Women's Paintings (The First Works on Canvas)' at the S.H. Ervin Gallery in Sydney. The exhibition produced a dramatic and almost instantaneous alteration in the perception of the Utopia artists within the local art world.

In many of the Western Desert communities so far considered, people have learnt to paint for ceremony, but apart from perhaps a settlement schoolroom as children, have no previous experience of working as artists or in European mediums. The Utopia women, by contrast, were already experienced artists when they made the move to canvas and acrylic paints. The influence of the batik-making is evident in their work, not only in the designs they use, but also in considerations of scale and form pertaining to fabric and being worn. The technical skill and assurance of the artists quickly brought them to the attention of the art world. Emily Kngwarreye's immediate and phenomenal success — universal acclaim, acquisition by major public and private collections, solo exhibitions, inclusion in the 'Abstraction' show at the Art Gallery of NSW, and artist-in-residence at Perth ICA — helped pave the way for other Utopia artists like Ada and Lyndsay Bird, Loiue Pwerle and Gloria Petyarre, who have also established individual careers.

Perhaps because of the pre-history of the Utopia painting enterprise in batik-making, which is conventionally perceived as 'women's work', the Utopia artists are overwhelmingly female, more so than any other group of Western Desert artists. Men take a role in the enterprise in some ways analogous to women's participation in the Papunya company. As with the Papunya model, they are mostly the husbands of women who paint. Most became involved only when painting began, but a few men have also crossed the line and made batiks. Both men and women have a long history as wood carvers of traditional implements as well as lizards and snakes decorated with poker-work for the tourist trade. In the past few years, this skill has been turned to the production of carved and painted sculptures in a wide variety of new forms. Wombats, echidnas, kangaroos, camp and devil dogs and human figures are sold by Utopia Arts in Sydney, which also markets the acrylic paintings collected in the field by CAAMA. The Utopia artists' work is the subject of Michael Boulter's recently published *The Art of Utopia: A New Direction in Aboriginal Art* (Craftsman House, Australia, 1991).

Selected Utopia Art Exhibitions 1981–92

1981   'Floating Forests of Silk: Utopia Batik from the Desert', Adelaide Festival Centre, Adelaide

1988   'Time Before Time', Austral Gallery, St Louis, USA
        'Painting and Batik from the Desert', Utopia Art, Sydney
        'The Inspired Dream', Queensland Art Gallery, Brisbane
        'Peintures Aborigines', Arte Productions, Paris

1989   'Utopia', Utopia Art Sydney
        'Utopia Women', Coventry Gallery, Sydney
        'Paintings from Utopia', Austral Gallery, St Louis, USA
        'Twelve Men and an Echidna', Utopia Art, Sydney
        'Aboriginal Art Now', New England Regional Art Museum, Armidale, New South Wales
        'Utopia Batik', Araluen Art Centre, Alice Springs
        'Utopia Batik', Darwin Museum and Gallery, Darwin
        'A Summer Project: Utopia Women's Paintings (the First Works on Canvas)', S.H. Ervin Gallery, Sydney; Orange Regional Art Gallery, Orange, New South Wales
        'Aboriginal Art from Utopia', Gallery Gabrielle Pizzi, Melbourne
        'A Continuing Tradition', Australian National Gallery, Canberra
        Lyndsay Bird Mpetyane, Syme-Dodson Gallery, Sydney

1990   'A Picture Story', Tandanya Aboriginal Cultural Institute, Adelaide; Royal Hibernian Academy, Dublin
        'Utopia Men and Dogs', Austral Gallery, St Louis, USA
        CAAMA/Utopia Artists-in-Residence Project: Louis Pwerle and Emily Kame Kngwarreye, Perth Institute of Modern Art, Perth
        'Art from Utopia', Orange Regional Gallery, Orange, New South Wales
        'The Figure', Utopia Art Sydney
        'Utopia Artists', Flinders Lane Gallery, Melbourne
        'Art, Cars and the Landscape', William Mora Galleries, Melbourne

'New Year — New Art', Utopia Art, Sydney

'The New Images of Utopia', Gallery Gundulmirri, Warrandyte, Victoria

'Contemporary Aboriginal Art', Carpenter Center, Harvard University, Harvard, USA

'Tangari Lia: My Family', Third Eye Centre, Glasgow

'ACAF2: The Second Australian Contemporary Art Fair', Exhibition Centre, Melbourne

Emily Kame Kngwarreye, Utopia Art, Sydney

Ada Bird Petyarre, Utopia Art, Sydney

Louis Pwerle, Utopia Art, Sydney

1991   'Utopia Batik', Utopia Art, Sydney

'Long Hot Summer', Utopia Art, Sydney

'A Picture Story', Meat Market Gallery, Melbourne

'Camp Scenes', The Gallery at the Prince and Frog, Melbourne

'Aboriginal Art and Spirituality', High Court of Australia, Canberra

'Contemporary Aboriginal Art', Art Gallery of New South Wales, Sydney

'Australian Perspecta 1991', Art Gallery of New South Wales, Sydney

Gloria Petyarre, Utopia Art, Sydney

Lyndsay Bird Mpetyane, Utopia Art, Sydney

Emily Kame Kngwarreye, Utopia Art, Sydney

Lily Sandover Kngwarreye, Utopia Art, Sydney

1992   Utopia Batik from the Robert Holmes à Court Collection, Shangri-La Hotel, Bangkok

'Flash Pictures', Australian National Gallery, Canberra

Australian Prints, St Louis Print Fair, St Louis, USA

◆ ◆ ◆ ◆

As a spin off from CAAMA's 'Summer Project', a second artists' group was established in 1989 by the owners of Delmore Downs station, which adjoins Utopia Aboriginal land on its southern boundary. Many of the Utopia artists have a long association with the station, Emily Kngwarreye having worked stock there for the Holt family as a young woman. The station owner's wife Janet Holt (née Wilson) assisted Dick Kimber, running Papunya Tula Artists in the mid '70s, and when some of the women living near the station approached her with a request for materials so they could continue painting, she responded enthusiastically. The Delmore Gallery has since been established to market the work, and several major exhibitions have been mounted in capital cities around Australia. A few of the CAAMA Utopians also paint with this group, most notably Emily Kngwarreye, who has family associations going back several generations to the Holt family. This situation created some intense rivalry between the two organisations in the late '80s; however, nowadays this commerce is more in the spirit of the way Papunya or Yuendumu artists will occasionally sell their work through Yuelamu

Artists at Mt Allan. The Utopia painters working exclusively for Delmore Downs have developed a distinct regional variant of the Utopia style, which is influenced, like the CAAMA artists, by the women's prior experience of batik-making — though differently. The work is often characterised by large, sometimes very loose design elements surrounded by row upon row of immaculate painstakingly minute dotting. Unlike the CAAMA group, a significant proportion of the Delmore Downs artists are men, including Louie Pwerle and David Pwerle Ross, who are very senior lawmen for this whole area.

12. Nyirrpi

The painting movement started up at Nyirrpi in 1985 through the initiative of local school teacher Wendy Baarda. Its development at Nyirrpi shows strong parallels with both Papunya Tula Artists and Warlukurlangu Artists at Yuendumu, including the idea of painting a series of murals on the school buildings. Nyirrpi is a very 'young' community, to which Aboriginal people have moved mainly from Yuendumu. It began as an outstation of Yuendumu, and gradually developed its own independent resources, including a community store, which in the early '90s became the focus of painting in the community. For some years before this, Warlukurlangu Artists had made regular trips to the community, but discontinued the practice as part of its cost-cutting strategies for the '90s. All the Nyirrpi artists have very strong connections with neighbouring communities and outstations, especially Yuendumu. Most are also related to one another in some way. Since there have until recently been no records of Nyirrpi paintings except of those sold through Warlukurlangu Artists, and the artists themselves usually did not know exactly how long they had been painting, the 'late '80s' in their biographies for when they started painting is only a rough estimate. Their work was shown in Sydney at Artspace in 1990, and a group of Nyirrpi artists has travelled to Japan to accompany an exhibition of their paintings.

13. Mutitjulu Community, Uluru, Maruku Arts and Crafts

People began doing carvings to sell to the tourists when the road to the Rock was first opened up in the Great Depression. The activity has continued ever since, despite attempts by white authorities in the early years to discourage it. The Mutitjulu community is renowned for decorated wooden artefacts and weapons. The majority of producers are women, but the skills needed to produce the artefacts are widely distributed throughout the adult members of the community, as indicated by the surge in the number of producers in 1985/6 when there was an upsurge in local (tourist) demand for carvings due to publicity surrounding the formal handing back of the Rock to Aboriginal ownership.

Uluru's subsequent status as a National Park led to some difficulties for the craftsmen and women of the Mutitjulu community. Shortages in the supply of wood for carving were the main reason for the diversification into painting. Maruku Arts and Crafts's strong reputation for wood carving made them understandably reluctant to attempt breaking into a new and already crowded field by initiating acrylic painting in the community. Good quality canvas and paint only became available to the painters in 1990, replacing the cotton duck and student paints of the initial attempts. Some of the Mutitjulu artists whose biographies are included in this dictionary are exclusively painters, some are primarily carvers who paint occasionally. In these biographies the artists refer to the difference between decorative work for tourist consumption, teaching paintings that instruct the young in the Dreaming stories and 'history paintings' which portray contemporary events and social problems in the Western Desert style.

Maruku Arts and Crafts comes under the organisational umbrella of the Mutitjulu Community Incorporated at Uluru National Park. In addition to the fifty artists at the Rock itself, the Centre services over seven hundred producers living outside Uluru National Park at a number of communities on Pitjantjatjara lands.

1994 Postscript

Even as the research for this dictionary was being conducted between 1989 and 1991, Aboriginal art was radiating out from all its established centres of production, just as Western Desert art had been disseminated from Papunya across most of Central Australia during the '80s. Arnhem Land bark painting was in resurgence, and previously minor centres were expanding into major new producers in the Kimberley, Bathurst Island, North Queensland and the Torres Strait. The waves of art spread out like the roundels on a Western Desert painting — until they joined up. This extraordinary outpouring of creative energy is finally sweeping away the antiquated 'traditional vs contemporary' classification of Aboriginal art, which denied both the historical contemporaneity of tribally oriented artists, and the cultural authority of 'non-traditional' artists. However, it has also created difficulties in de-limiting the geographical scope of Western Desert art which were not even thought of when this dictionary was commenced.

Determinations about which new enterprises lie within the boundaries of Western Desert art and which lie outside them seem increasingly to obscure continuities rather than make useful distinctions. The influence of Western Desert art is strongly evident in the distinctive regional styles of many new painting communities, especially those whose land-bases abut the central desert. Of these, I regret not having the resources to incorporate in this dictionary several communities along the borders of the region who are both working within the Western Desert style and culturally linked to its existing practitioners (most recently the Ngaanyatjarra people of Warburton in Western Australia). However, the research for the dictionary was substantially concluded and written up over three years ago. My limited efforts to update the manuscript for its belated publication have been focused on the heartlands of the original art movement.

The study's coverage of town-based artists was improved in late 1992 by the addition of twenty or thirty biographies collected by a research assistant working out of Alice Springs. It has not been possible to undertake the extensive field research required to bring the project to its original ideal of completeness, nor to iron out other unevenness (due to the diverse avenues through which biographical data was collected) in its coverage of the communities discussed in 'Domino Effects'. One noteworthy exception is a small group of painters who recently began working out of the Ikuntji Women's Centre at Haasts Bluff, on whom biographical details were obtained at the eleventh hour.[6] During the '70s and early '80s, Haasts Bluff was home to a group of artists, several of whom were members of Geoffrey Bardon's original painting group at Papunya. Over the years, they developed a distinctive 'Haasts Bluff' style of alternating bands of brown and yellow background dotting which influenced many other artists in the movement. The resurgence of painting in the Haasts Bluff community after almost a decade in decline is being led by a group of painters with close family ties to the original group of Papunya Tula artists. Hopefully this is a pattern which will in time be repeated at many other communities in this study, with each new generation of painters inspired to continue the work of the last.

Mindful of the sensitivity of the issue in traditional Aboriginal communities, I did make a point of trying to check whether any of the artists already included in the dictionary had died since their biographies were collected. Given the advanced age of many of the leading practitioners of Western Desert art, and the high casualty rates in Central Australian Aboriginal society generally, I was surprised at the small number of painters from each community who were recently deceased. The relative affluence of the artists within these communities, due to the extra income they receive from their paintings, may well be a factor in their comparatively low death rates.

To finish, here is a story from the 'Dreamtime Strip' (that astonishing assortment of galleries and shops lining either side of the Todd Street Mall in Alice Springs selling Aboriginal culture to the tourist trade) which says a lot about the changes in Western Desert art since this project was commenced. On my last visit in late October 1993, something caught my eye in a garbage bin set back in a park midway along the Mall. It was a small oval-shaped painting in a Western Desert style. The design-work was shaky but strong and executed in charcoal grey edged with white dots, with a yellow ochre and 'punk' pink dotted background. I showed it to an artist at Papunya who could not identify the design but judged it to be the work of someone from town — perhaps their first attempt at painting. Presumably they threw it away after failing to sell it.

How different this is from the experience of the majority of artists in this dictionary — except, of course, the first fifty pioneers of the painting movement, many of whose early works were thrown out in the '70s and early '80s when there was no demand at all for Western Desert art. In the late '80s, when most people began painting, new artists could be confident of selling even their first attempts to shopkeepers and art dealers in Alice Springs eager to stock up for a market insatiable for 'dot paintings'. But these are different times. With no reputation to help market their work, the would-be artist stood little chance of ever seeing their work added to the piles of small canvases and boards already lining the walls of the tourist shops.

Ironically, that same week an Austrian art dealer in Australia on a quest for rare and fine pieces for the booming European market in Aboriginal art had paid $7000 to a Sydney dealer for what was reputedly Emily Kngwarreye's second painting, the next one she did after the 1988–9 'Summer Project'. That figure represents a 700% increase in four years on the asking price of $100 on the painting in CAAMA's exhibition of 'The First Canvases'. However, the dealer estimated that the painting might fetch ten times that amount on an overseas market now as hungry as the Dreamtime Strip used to be for Western Desert art — and prepared to pay fine art prices for its leading exponents. But there too, as on their homeground in Alice Springs, Western Desert artists still face a capricious and often uncomprehending audience, in serious need of the kind of information contained in this dictionary about individual painters and their work.

There remains only to acknowledge once again the radical incompleteness of the task as originally undertaken, and to express the hope that some day a revised edition of this dictionary will come closer to a complete listing of artists. In the meantime, a beginning has been made in assembling the detailed and comprehensive documentation which this remarkable art movement so richly deserves of its scholars.

Footnotes:

1. Like George Jampijinpa Robertson, whose painting *Lightning and Thunder Dreaming* from the mid '70s is reproduced in the *Dreamings* catalogue

2. *Sydney Morning Herald*, 11 July 1987

3. see R. Crumlin (ed.), *Aboriginal Art and Spirituality*, Collins Dove, Victoria 1991

4. Maurice Luther Jupurrurla in *D'un autre continent: l'Australie, le rêve et la réel*, ARC/Musée d'Art Moderne de la Ville de Paris, 1983

5. Malcolm Jagamara interview, Vivien Johnson, Alice Springs, 1991

6. Biographical data on JACK, Eunice Napanangka, JUGADAI, Narputta Nangala, JUGADAI, Daisy and JUNABEE Napaltjarri was supplied by Ikuntji Women's Centre, Haasts Bluff

Map of Painting Communities

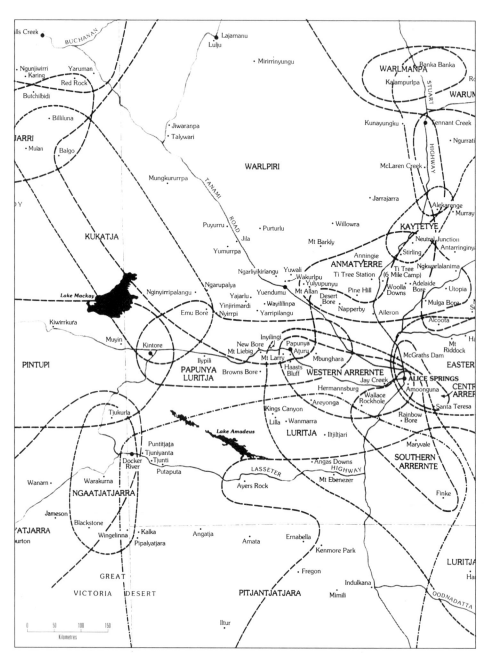

Map (detail) of Current Distribution of Central Australian Languages reproduced with the permission of the Institute for Aboriginal Development.

Notes on the Biographies

'Andy Warhol didn't have a CV either. I mean — they're not artists on the make. They're not part of the whole career structure.'[1]

Compiling these biographies has been an education in the social fabric of Western Desert society in general and of Western Desert art in particular. It has also taught me the impossibility of condensing into the rigid simplifications of the conventional 'artist's resume' who any of these five hundred and something men and women really are. That might perhaps be said of anyone (with the possible exception of Andy Warhol himself). But for the men and women whose artistic identities are the subject of this book, the ordinary limitations of the brief biographical form are compounded by cultural differences which render even the most basic categories of information problematical. At the outset, I should like to point out some of the many ways in which these artists' lives escape the categories of either conventional artistic biography or the modified version which has accompanied the arrival of Aboriginal artists in the domain of contemporary art.

Dates of Birth

Take the most prosaic of items in a biographical entry: the artist's date of birth. The fact is that most people I interviewed for the dictionary had no idea how old they were — at least, not in calendar years. In the case of the older artists, this is because they were born and grew to adulthood in the desert, beyond the reach both of regimes of official registration and the cult of the birthday. Those who were born at missions and government settlements where records were kept of births may have a vague idea of the year in which they were born, but the information has no practical significance in their lives, and is usually recalled with difficulty. Even for those who do utilise such accoutrements of western culture as driver's licences (and, in a few cases, passports), the dates of birth which appear on these documents have little connection with their personal biographies. The Aboriginal Population Register in which their births are recorded seems to have routinely updated its information on the first of January and the first of July every year — at least that is the most plausible explanation I can think of for so many people's birthdays (when they have one) falling on those dates. Of course, there are also people who can tell you an exact birth date which is neither of these dates, though as yet they are a minority amongst the artists of the Western Desert.

Such greyness might complicate the biographer's task, but however uncertain people may be about answering the question: when were you born? — at least there is no disagreement about what it means. More profound cultural differences appear when we approach the even more basic category of names. For a western artist, nothing could be more fundamental to one's individuality. Or more clearcut — except in the unusual cir-

51

cumstance that someone paints under another name than the one they are usually known by. For Western Desert artists, however, such cases may be the rule rather than the exception ...

Names

Pupiya Napaljarri sits in the driveway of her home in Lajamanu surrounded by members of her family, enjoying the sweetness of the twilight together as the blazing sun finally sets over the Tanami Desert. An esteemed senior woman and leading figure in the ceremonial life of this Warlpiri community, she smiles a welcome, for my European companion is an old friend of hers. They greet each other using the common form of address within most Western Desert communities — skin names: 'Hello Napaljarri.' 'Hello Napurrurla'. (In the course of her long association with the Lajamanu community, my friend has acquired the skin 'Napurrurla' as a signifier of her connection to it.) Pupiya gets to her feet and invites us into the house. Motioning us to come closer, she points to the back of some shelves beneath a dripping sink where her painting materials are stored away. She pulls out a crumpled bundle of water-stained cotton duck and unrolls it to reveal her latest work. The large blood red flowers of the Medicine Vine Dreaming bloom across a roughly painted black background covered in undulating white dots. To an enthusiast of Western Desert painting it says, unmistakably: 'Louisa Lawson', the European-given name Pupiya uses in her dealings with the art world. She is one of the most highly regarded artists to have emerged from Lajamanu in the six short years since painting started up in the community. But in Lajamanu, amongst her fellow Warlpiri countrywomen and men, the name Louisa Lawson could fail to evoke recognition even amongst her closest relatives, so completely external is it to her life there. Her Warlpiri name 'Pupiya Napaljarri' is the key to her social and Dreaming identity, 'Louisa Lawson' a mere handle to facilitate transactions with another part of the world, which bestowed it on her in its own obdurate monolingualism. To my friend, however, she is clearly both: their friendship encompasses the duality which is an intrinsic part of Western Desert art as a cultural and artistic enterprise. Pupiya offers to sell the painting to my friend, and the offer is accepted with alacrity befitting the work's radiance. The Louisa Lawson and the cheque exchange hands; photos are taken of the artist holding up her painting; questions about its meaning are asked and answered. The transaction completed, talk returns to conversation — perhaps about a planned trip to the country depicted in the painting.

The biographer of Western Desert artists must take on board the knowledge that the names under which people appear in this dictionary are not necessarily how they are known to their neighbours and kinsmen and women, but may only be the labels used to identify their work for the western art audience. The extreme forms of bi-culturalism exemplified by Pupiya Louisa Napaljarri Lawson's case are produced by Lajamanu's relative isolation from western culture. However, there are plenty of examples of painters using their 'bush' names to identify themselves to the art world, and plenty of examples of artists whose European names are as familiar as their skins within their communities of residence. 'Bush' names may also designate sites with which the bearer is closely associated; if the places are secret, so may their names be. Others know them, but they may not be spoken. European names, in some cases, provide an alternative form of address.

Yet another complication needs to be addressed in the naming of artists. Everywhere in the Western Desert, people observe customary mourning rites which proscribe for an interval the use of both European and/or 'bush' names if they resemble those of the dead. In such circumstances, Pupiya might adopt the title 'Kumunjayi' (Warlpiri spelling, meaning 'taboo'), or her European name, or perhaps another name altogether, within the local Warlpiri community. Underneath this variety of relationships between artists and their appellations, which is to be found right across the Western Desert, runs the common thread of the relatively tenuous and contingent status of 'first names' in this society. For the purposes of this dictionary, Pupiya goes under the name of Louisa Napaljarri Lawson — but how little this says about the complex dualisms of her existence.

In these circumstances, skin names function effectively as a mode of address because one's skin group (or 'subsection', to use anthropological terminology) is one thing that does remain constant through the many transformations of individual labelling.[2] One's skin group also determines one's relationship to the complex system of Aboriginal copyright which regulates the distribution of rights and obligations in the Dreaming, the real core of individual identity in Western Desert society. And here we enter the special territory of 'Aboriginal biography': the conventions that have arisen for the presentation of Western Desert and other Aboriginal artists to the art world.

Tribe

The most obvious signifier of the special biographical treatment accorded Aboriginal artists by contemporary art institutions is the notion of the tribe. The orthodoxy in the presentation of Western Desert canvases in art galleries and museums is to give the title of the painting (usually invented by an art adviser or gallery owner rather than the artist), followed by the artist's name, a date of birth whose probability of accuracy has just been commented upon, and a tribal identification. The *Dreamings: Art of Aboriginal Australia* catalogue and exhibition, which established some important precedents in this as in other areas of the presentation of Aboriginal art and artists, introduced the substitute terminology of artist's language: 'The term does not mean simply "language spoken" but "language of formal affiliation" or "language-group identity" ... (frequently "tribe")'[3]. Not surprisingly, this usage has not yet found much favour with increasingly populist-oriented cultural institutions who fail to see in this any ground for replacing a straightforward term by a confusing one.

For similar reasons of clarity, I have not taken issue with the concept in the biographical entries themselves, but in this context let it be noted that Western Desert tribal identifications participate in the fluidity of post-contact forms of Aboriginal community. Old tribal boundaries have been dissolved by inter-marriage and there is much greater personal mobility than was possible when 'foot-walking' was the only form of transportation. Tribal identity might depend on the dominant language of the settlement where an artist lives. Under the conditions of settlement life, the tribe has taken on new significance as a political and cultural grouping vis-à-vis settler society, with practical implications in the distribution of communal resources. Rather than always belonging to the 'out-group' of a minority cultural enclave, individuals may move through marriage and other associations into the sphere of the majority 'tribe'.

Individual artists may have changed their tribal identifications with their communities of residence at least once and sometimes several times in their lives, significantly complicating the task of presenting their biographies both accurately and succinctly. Louisa Lawson's husband, Ronnie Jakamarra Lawson (also one of Lajamanu's best known artists), is a case in point. Though his sacred sites lie well within Pintupi territory, he identified himself to me as Warlpiri. In his case 'language spoken' is an important guide to his language-group or tribal identity, over which contingencies such as residence in the Warlpiri-dominated settlements first of Yuendumu and then of Lajamanu, and marriage to a woman of Warlpiri descent, apparently exercise a determining influence.

Unravelling the tangled web of tribal affiliation in the case of Old Mick Tjakamarra, one of the most venerable artists of the painting movement, will illustrate how complex the answer to the simple question of tribal identification can be. Old Mick was one of the two senior custodians of the Papunya Honey Ant Dreaming (Old Tom Onion Tjapangati was the other) who gave permission for the painting of the school mural which started off the still-expanding process whose historical agents are recorded in the pages of this dictionary. When I first talked to Old Mick about his biography in 1986, he gave his tribal affiliation as Arrente/Luritja. Yet, in annotations of his paintings prepared by Papunya Tula Artists from the mid to late '70s, his tribe is given as Ngalia. Geoffrey Bardon says in *Papunya Tula — Art of the Western Desert* that he is 'Anmatyerre/ Aranda' (Arrente).[4] The Australian National Gallery's on-file biography for Old Mick says his 'Language' is Luritja/Warlpiri.

Rather than jumping to the 'obvious' conclusion that all but one of these attributions must be mistaken, and trying to decide which one is the correct one, a more satisfactory explanation of Old Mick's multiple tribal affiliations involves the initial assumption that they might all be partially right: capturing, as non-exclusive alternatives, a more complex set of social arrangements than the one-dimensional notion of the 'tribe' encompasses.[5] According to the National Gallery's notes, Old Mick's first wife had Luritja, Anmatyerre and Arrente connections. At different times over the last twenty years, these or other family associations may have dominated the artist's living arrangements to the point of tribal affiliation. Old Mick also raised his sister's son, Don Tjungarrayi, after his Warlpiri father died, adding Warlpiri connections to the list of languages spoken. This makes sense of the National Gallery's classification, but the Ngalia reference is more problematical. A mistake on the part of whoever wrote these annotations for Papunya Tula Artists is unlikely, since they would all have been done at this time in the company's history by or in association with Dick Kimber, whose meticulousness in such matters is justly renowned. Ngalia lands, as they appear on

Tindale's map, did lie in the vicinity of Papunya, which Old Mick once told me was his birthplace. The Australian National Gallery's biography also notes that the artist's great authority derives from his association with Papunya — as well as his great age. The extensiveness of the associations which the artist has formed over a life of more than ninety years with other groups is reflected in the variety of his tribal attributions over the past two decades. But what on earth is the assiduous biographer or art curator to write in her entry for the artist?

Spelling

The sub-heading 'Also cited as' is employed in many of the biographies in this dictionary to indicate alternative spellings of the artist's name, as well as alternative names by which they might be referred to. There is no implication in this that these are 'misspelled names or other names not considered by the authors to be valid or established alternatives'[6], which the *Dreamings* catalogue designated them. The problem here with these kinds of authorial rulings, made by the editors of *Dreamings* to avoid confusing novitiates of Western Desert art, is that they can have the unintended consequence of dismissing as an 'invalid alternative' the artist's own spelling of his or her name.

For example, when Michael Nelson was asked to sign his BMW Art Car he wrote along the driver's running board in large rough letters big enough to be seen in all the publicity photographs: 'Michael Jagamara Nelson'. He writes his name this way because that was how he was taught to write it in the mission schoolroom at Yuendumu, where a now obsolete Warlpiri orthography was imposed by his teachers. However, the *Dreamings* book does not even list this as an alternative to its 'Michael Nelson Jakamarra'. This spelling of the artist's skin adopts the current Warlpiri orthographical orthodoxy, which is used uniformly throughout the *Dreamings* biographies for all Western Desert artists rather than the regional variant of 'Tjakamarra' which is employed by the dominant school of Pintupi/Luritja linguists based in Papunya. The Papunya Tula company has adopted the 'Tjakamarra' spelling, which consequently appears on the annotations and catalogues of most exhibitions in which the artist's work is displayed.

In this dictionary, priority has been given to the factor of actual usage over the creation of a tidy uniformity which may ultimately confuse the reader attempting to use it as a reference book connecting the authorship ascribed to specific paintings with the biographies of their creators. In general, however: Tjakamarra/Tjungarrayi/ Tjampitjinpa / Tjapanangka / Tjangala / Tjapangati / Tjapaltjarri / Tjupurrula spellings specified by contemporary Pintupi/Luritja linguists are used for the Papunya Tula artists. Warlayirti Artists at Balgo has followed Papunya Tula's practice (except for Tjungurrayai/ Nungurrayai and Tjampitjin/Nampitjin). Artists from the Napperby community also conform to Papunya Tula's usage except for Nungurrayi/Tjungurrayi and Jupurrula. Jakamarra / Jungarrayi / Jampijinpa / Japanangka / Jangala / Japangardi / Japaljarri/Jupurrurla, the current linguistic orthodoxy for Warlpiri, is used for artists from the predominantly Warlpiri communities of Yuendumu, Mt Allan, Willowra and Lajamanu[7].

Country and Dreamings

Two categories of biographical information did emerge from the rigorous testing ground of data collection as capturing Western Desert social realities with some degree of accuracy: Country and Dreamings (or 'Totems' as the *Dreamings* catalogue expressed it by way of meeting its American readership halfway). Country and Dreamings initially became part of the standard information sought about artists when collecting their biographies for this dictionary because they were what everyone was interested in talking about. No-one was interested in what year they were born, tribal identifications could be vague and even shifting, but people were always very definite about what country and Dreamings were theirs to paint. A comprehensive cross-referencing of all this information is beyond my current resources, but would make up a fascinating register of Aboriginal copyright.

Warlukurlangu Artists's listing of all the current painters in the Yuendumu community and their Dreamings and country in Appendix B takes this a step further, providing a glimpse of another level of complexity: the relationship between skin and Aboriginal copyright. Each Dreaming is the shared responsibility of individuals from different skin groups in the complementary roles of kurdu (owner) and kurdungurlu (manager). While artists mostly paint the Dreamings over which they or close family members personally have ownership, they may also on occasion paint other Dreamings and sites to which they stand in manager relationships. The records of painting companies like Warlukurlangu Artists constitute a far more detailed and accurate record of these matters — let alone what the authorities within the Aboriginal community could provide if they wanted to. This is a partial but public record, and hopefully one which will help to shed light on the complex patterns of ownership of Dreaming stories in Western Desert society. These are in turn inextricably linked to rights in land, which continue to be the focal point of the artists' interest in the painting enterprise.

Vivien Johnson

Footnotes:
1. Chris Anderson interviewed in *Market of Dreams*, Kennedy/White Productions, (Adelaide, 1990).
2. Though there are still exceptions. As a system for determining potential marriage partners, skin names exhibit flexibility within the basic requirement that incestuous relationships be avoided. A few people in this dictionary also have double skin names, where children have taken skin names from each parent in a second-choice marriage.
    A succinct account of Western Desert skin systems is provided in *Current Distribution of Central Australian Aboriginal Languages* (Institute for Aboriginal Development, Alice Springs, 1990, prepared by John Hobson for IAD). See also *Pintupi/Luritja Kinship* (IAD, Alice Springs, revised edition 1979).
3. *Dreamings: the Art of Aboriginal Australia*, ed P. Sutton (Viking, New York, 1988) p 235.
4. Bardon, G., *Papunya Tula: Art of the Western Desert* (McPhee Gribble, Australia, 1991) p 69.
5. Just to complicate matters further, 'Luritja' may well be an emergent tribal grouping, initially a term for others applied by Arrente people living on their own lands at Haasts Bluff Aboriginal Reserve in the '40s and '50s to all non-Arrente tribesmen in residence at the settlement. Nor is it the only tribal designation said to be of recent origin: 'Pintupi' is likewise said to be a term invented by non-Pintupi to describe the 'wild ones' who were being trucked in from the west in the '60s.
6. *Dreamings*, p 235.
7. There is another twist to this tale. Spellings of artists' skin names at Mt Allan have recently reverted to the forms used by the Department of Social Security for decades: Jabanardi, Jabanunga, Jambatjinba etc — similar to the original Papunya Tula Artists' spelling of artists' skin names. The contemporary Warlpiri orthography which was previously in use at Mt Allan has been retained in the dictionary to avoid further confusion.

The Biographies

A

ABBOTT, MARY

An Arrente/Luritja speaker in her late forties, Mary Abbott was born c.1943 at Hermannsburg, where she received European schooling. From there she moved to Alice Springs, where she now lives. She has relatives whom she visits in Papunya. Began painting in 1988 with the Jukurrpa group. Her work is very precise with intricate designs. She paints Honey Ant and Wild Onion Dreamings.

ABIE JANGALA
Also cited as: Abe Jangala

Born in 1919 at Kurlpurlurnu, Abie Jangala's language/tribe is Warlpiri and his country Kurlpurlurnu/ Parrulyu/ Puyuuru [Mikanjijangka — Kurlpurlurnukurra — from Mikanji through to Kurlpurlurnu] — a wide-ranging set of country. Main Dreamings are Ngapa (Water) and Watiyawarnu. He and Jimmy KELLY share Dreamings. Abie started painting in 1986 in the Traditional Painting course at Lajamanu. He was one of the first active painters at Lajamanu — the 'grand old man' of Lajamanu painting. Important ceremonial leader and a most charming and personable old man. In 1989 he visited the Dreamtime Gallery in Perth for several months and painted in the gallery. His late wife used to paint too. In 1993 he had his first solo exhibition at Coo-ee Gallery in Sydney. Collections: National Gallery of Victoria

ADA NAPALJARRI, see ANDY, Ada Napaljarri

ADRIAN TJUPURRULA

Lives at Kintore. In his early thirties, he has three wives, and is a youth worker for HALT (Healthy Aboriginal Lifestyle Team). He paints for Papunya Tula Artists. Collections: Holmes à Court

ALLAN, MARY NANGALA

Born c.1950, Mary Allan is of the Anmatyerre tribe. Her heritage country is Mt Allan and she paints Honey Ant, Emu, Turkey and Bush Plum Dreamings. She is married to Teddy Jungarrayi and resides in Mt Allan.

ANATJARI TJAKAMARRA d. 1992
Also cited as: Anitjari Jagamara, Anatjari No. 3

Born in the early 1930s deep in Pintupi country at the site of Ngaanyatjarra (Ngumatja) in the area of Kulkuta, a large rockhole near the Pollock Hills in the Baron Ranges across the Northern Territory border in Western Australia, and some of the most isolated country in Central Australia. In 1964 Anatjari, his two wives and two daughters were the last people to be brought out of the desert into Papunya by the NT Welfare Branch patrols. This particular patrol is the subject of Douglas Lockwood's book, *The Lizard Eaters*. The group had encountered the patrols the year before in 1963. Anatjari and his family subsequently demonstrated elements of their traditional lifestyle for the cameras of Ian Dunlop's documentary film *Desert People*. Anatjari Tjakamarra was part of the original group of 'painting men' at Papunya in the early '70s. He and UTA UTA Tjangala were working as the school gardeners when the mural which set the painting movement in motion was painted on the Papunya school wall. Anatjari's early work shows the particular influence of KAAPA Tjampitjinpa in its masterly line-work. In the early '80s he established Tjukula outstation, between Kintore and Docker River, and was based there for most of the '80s, selling his work independently of Papunya Tula Artists. In the late '80s he then moved to the new settlement of Kiwirrkura, 250 km west of Kintore over the Western Australian border and began painting again for Papunya Tula Artists. Between painting spells, Anatjari pursued other employment, such as maintenance work. His paintings depict Tingari stories including a Snake Dreaming from Kulkuta which travels west through Kiwirrkura, Water, and a Dingo Puppy Dreaming sited around Kintore. In 1989 and 1991 he had solo exhibitions at the Gallery Gabrielle Pizzi in Melbourne. He also showed at John Weber's New York Gallery in 1989. Anatjari's *Tingari Cycle Dreaming*, purchased by the Metropolitan Museum of Modern Art, became the first work by a Western Desert artist to enter one of the world's major international art collections. Other collections in which his work is represented include: Burke Museum, University of Washington, Seattle, Museums & Art Galleries of NT, Flinders University Art Museum, Art Gallery of WA, National Museum of Australia, Canberra, Art Gallery of SA, National Gallery of Victoria, Queensland Art Gallery, Australian Museum, Sydney, Holmes à Court etc.

ANATJARI TJAMPITJINPA
Also cited as: Anitjari Jampijinpa, Anatjari No. 1

One of the group of tribesmen and women who walked in to Papunya from the Pintupi homelands in the west in the early '60s, Anatjari joined the founding group of Papunya Tula Artists in the early '70s, and though now in his sixties (born c.1927) is still one the company's most consistent and dedicated painters. His country, where he grew up and spent the first forty years of his life, lies across the NT border in WA, south of Jupiter Well. The artist now resides in Kiwirrkura, after spells in Yai Yai, Lampara, Inyaling, Mt Leibig, Kintore and Balgo since those early days in West Camp Papunya when the painting movement was just beginning. While in Balgo visiting relatives, he instructed people about painting with canvas and acrylics, including his younger brother, Dini CAMPBELL, who later moved to Kintore and began painting for Papunya Tula Artists. Anatjari's sons, George YAPA YAPA and Ray James, now also paint. His work was shown in 'Face of the Centre', National Gallery of Victoria 1985, the Asia Society's 'Dreamings: Art of Aboriginal Australia' exhibition and many other group exhibitions of Papunya Tula Artists. In 1989 he travelled to Brisbane with Paddy CARROLL for an exhibition of Papunya Tula Artists at the Queensland Art Gallery. Collections: University of WA Anthropology Museum, Museums & Art Galleries of NT, SA Museum, Queensland Museum, Holmes à Court, Kelton Foundation etc.

ANDERSON, ALISON NAMPITJINPA

Born in 1958, Alison Anderson is a Luritja speaker, and paints Honey Ant Dreaming for her home country Papunya, Women Dancing Stories and her Warlpiri father's Bushfire Dreaming, which starts at the site of Warlukurlangu just south-west of Yuendumu and comes across to Mt Leibig, to the north of Papunya. When in her late twenties Alison Anderson was appointed Administrator of Papunya, a position she has now held for many years. Her responsibilities in the community mean that she paints only intermittently, but she has been doing so consistently since the mid '80s. Collections: Holmes à Court

ANDY, ADA NAPALJARRI
Also cited as: Ada Napaljarri, Ada Napaltjarri Andy

Born in 1954 at Narwietooma station, Ada Napaljarri and her family soon afterwards moved to Haasts Bluff, where she grew up. She is a member of the Luritja/Warlpiri language group that emerged from the mix of dialects at that settlement. Later the family moved again, to the newly established settlement of Papunya. In the early '80s Ada started painting, at the same time as the first women to be on Papunya Tula Artists' books as artists in their own right: Daisy LEURA, Natalie CORBY, GLADYS Napanangka, and Ada's mother, ENTALURA Nangala. Like them, Ada may have learnt to paint from watching or assisting male relatives. Entalura's husband, DON Tjungarrayi, and her father's younger brother, TWO BOB Tjungarrayi, were both part of the new generation of painters who emerged at Papunya at the start of the '80s. However, it was perhaps Ada's husband Alistair, a school teacher with a keen interest in the art movement and a conviction that women were being excluded from painting, who influenced her to paint independently of Papunya Tula Artists — one of the very first women in Papunya to do so. That was in about 1982, and since then the artist has spent time living in a number of the communities included in this study while her husband was headteacher there — at Mt Allan, Lajamanu and Willowra. It is quite possible that Ada's interest in painting has been a factor in helping to interest people in painting at those communities also. Her heritage country is Mt Wedge (Kerrinyarra) and Ilpilli, which links her to the Warumpi Mother and Daughter Dreaming, also the Water and Women's Dancing Dreamings from Ilpilli. She also paints Yalka (Bush Onion) Dreaming. Her sisters, Nora ANDY Napaljarri, now living in Alice Springs, and Emily ANDY Napaljarri, who still lives at Mt Allan, also paint.

ANDY, EMILY NAPALJARRI

Born in 1953 at Narwietooma Station. Emily Andy, Ada ANDY and Nora ANDY are all the daughters of ENTALURA Nangala. Like her sister Ada, Emily's traditional country is Mt Wedge (Kerrinyarra) and her language group is Luritja/Warlpiri. She paints Bush Onion, Yala (Bush Potato), Wallaby and Honey Ant Dreamings and has probably been acquainted with the medium for some time, through the other members of her family, most of whom paint themselves. She lives at Mt Allan.

ANDY, NORA NAPALJARRI
Also cited as: Nora Napaltjarri/Napaljarri

Born in the late '50s at Haasts Bluff just before the establishment of Papunya settlement, where the family then settled. Now in her thirties, Nora Andy is the daughter of ENTALURA Nangala, who has painted for Papunya Tula Artists since the early '80s, and a Warlpiri speaker. She began painting in the late '80s while living in Alice Springs and still paints occasionally, usually selling her work through the Centre for Aboriginal Artists. She has also lived in Mt Allan and Mt Leibig and currently resides in Papunya. She usually paints the Bush Onion Dreaming around Haasts Bluff, which was her father's story. She exhibited at Gauguin Museum, Tahiti in February 1988. Her younger sister, Charlene Andy Napaljarri, has also recently begun painting, and her older sisters Emily and Ada ANDY Napaljarri have been producing for over a decade.

ANGELINA NA(NGA)LA PWERLE

Born at Utopia in the early '50s, Angelina is an Anmatyerre speaker, who has been painting stories relating to women's ceremonies and bush foods that grow in her country since 1988. She sells her work through galleries in Alice Springs, including the Centre for Aboriginal Artists in Alice Springs.

ANNE NAPANGARDI

Born at Ali-Curung (Warrabri) and belongs to the Warlpiri tribe. Her country is Mt Theo (Purturlu) and she lives in Willowra.

ATIRA-ATIRA, MICHAEL

Michael Atira-Atira was born 'in the bush' at Ernabella in about 1942. Both his parents were Pitjantjatjara speakers — his mother's country is on the Western Australian border at Pipalyatjara, and his father's country is closer to Ernabella, near Kanypi, a place called Mulayanyu. Michael grew up at the Ernabella mission, attending Ernabella school. After leaving school, Michael's work options were tending and shearing sheep on the mission and building many of the still existing buildings at Ernabella. During 1988 Michael spent some time in Alice Springs with his wife, Tjulkiwa ATIRA-ATIRA, and they both learnt to use acrylic paints there. Michael is currently living at Ernabella with his wife and six children, and is still enjoying using acrylics principally to depict scenes of his father's country.

ATIRA-ATIRA, TJULKIWA

Tjulkiwa was born on 8 January 1951 at Wataru (Mt Lindsay). She is Pitjantjatjara. Her father's country is Kuntjanu (SA) and her mother is from Walytjitjarta (NT). Her parents are now living at Kalka. Tjulkiwa is married to Michael ATIRA-ATIRA, and they have two sons, Tjiyangu and Wariri, and four daughters, Kawiny, Yilpi, Lexie and Laurabell. From 1968, as a school-leaver at Ernabella, Tjulkiwa started learning the various techniques practised in the craftroom of the settlement. She spent much of the next decade away from Ernabella; however, her artistic pursuits continued, and she spent a large amount of this time working at Fregon, producing batik works. In 1988 she returned to Ernabella and began exploring with acrylics on canvas. By the following year, she was working full-time with Ernabella Arts and was a featured artist in the 'Wirutjuta' Exhibition, Araluen Arts Centre, Alice Springs. In 1990, following the birth of her sixth child, she worked outside Ernabella Arts, further developing her skills with brushes and paint on canvas, and in November was a featured artist in the 'Two Homes' Exhibition at Tandanya Aboriginal Cultural Institute in Adelaide. In 1991 she moved out with her family to a homeland settlement about 80 km from Ernabella, where she continues to paint. In April the SA Dept of Arts leased one of her paintings, *Aralya Tjukurpa*. The Art Gallery of SA holds one of Tjulkiwa's acrylic paintings from 1988. Her subjects for paintings are often scenes from Aralya Tjurkpa and traditional bushfoods from Pitjantjatjara lands.

ATIRA-ATIRA, YILPI
Also cited as: Yilpi Michael

Born 7 November 1969, of the Pitjantjatjara language group. Yilpi was born at the mission hospital at Ernabella. Her mother, Tjulkiwa ATIRA-ATIRA, is from Wataru (Mt Lindsay). Her father, Michael ATIRA-ATIRA, was born near Ernabella. Both are Pitjantjatjara speakers now living on a homeland settlement at Pukatja. Yilpi attended Ernabella school. She is now married, and has one daughter, Nyukana. Yilpi began working in the batik workshop at Ernabella Arts in 1988. In July 1989 she sold her painting in 'Desert Impressions', the Australian Conservation Foundation's exhibition at the Friends of the Earth Gallery in Melbourne. In November 1989 she was a featured artist in Ernabella Arts' exhibition 'Wirutjuta' at the Araluen Arts Centre in Alice Springs. Yilpi's acrylic paintings show the same rapid refinement of the technical aspects as is evident in her work in other media such as batik scarves, where she also experiments with varied combinations of lines, shapes and colours.

B

BAGGOT, KATHY NAPANGARDI

Born in 1960, of the Anmatyerre tribe, Kathy's country Mt Allan. Dreamings she paints are Witchetty, Snake and the Bush Potato. She is married to David STAFFORD and resides at Mt Allan.

BAKER, BELINDA NAKAMARRA

Born at Lajamanu in 1965, her language group is Warlpiri and her country is Yawarrka and Pawurinji. Her Dreamings are Ngurlu and Purlukuku. A person of great drive, when Belinda began working at Lajamanu school she was non-literate, but taught herself and became an assistant teacher at the school. She also helps on husband 'Mad Bobby' Paton Japaljarri's canvases and has been painting since 1987. She resides at Lajamanu.

BAKER, Nyukana

Born at Ernabella on 13 November 1943. A Pitjantjatjara speaker, her mother's family are from Wingellina and her father's family from Kanypi. She grew up at Ernabella and attended Ernabella school, starting designing and weaving in the craftroom in 1963, as well as painting, and already showing exceptional design ability. Nyukana's chosen subjects for paintings are principally Dreaming stories associated with country around Kanypi — west of Ernabella.
1971: Studied under Leo Brereton at Ernabella; Dec. Designs were included in an exhibition of painted designs at Argyle Arts Centre, Sydney. 1972: Attended an exhibition of painted designs (by invitation), Age Gallery, Melbourne. 1973: Designs in an exhibition at Civic Gallery, Canberra. 1974: Jan. Darwin workshop to learn new skills; Attended first exhibition of Ernabella batik at St John's, Wahroonga, featuring craftwork from all Presbyterian missions. 1975: Jan./Feb. Attended Batik Institute, Jogjakarta, Indonesia to study batik technique. Later in the year extended skills when Vivianne McClintock conducted a workshop at Ernabella. 1976: Sept. Attended and exhibited at Grace Bros, Chatswood, Sydney. 1977: Sept. Attended and exhibited at Grace Bros, Chatswood, Sydney. 1981: Exhibited in Craft Expo '81. 1982: Exhibited and participated in workshop, Darwin; Exhibited at Grace Bros, Chatswood, Sydney. 1983: Sept. Two exhibitions and demonstrations at the Museum of Ethnology, Osaka, Japan; Oct. Travelling exhibition and demonstration at Albury/Wodonga, Wagga Wagga and Orange. 1984: June. By invitation, exhibition and Arts conference in Canberra. 1986–7: Participant, 'Textiles of the Commonwealth', travelling exhibition, UK. 1987: Nov. Demonstrated at the Gap Neighbourhood Centre, Alice Springs. 1988: April. Exhibitor, Texas International Festival; May/June. Exhibitor, 'Classics at

the Craft Centre', Crafts Council of NSW; Aug. Exhibitor, Fifth National Aboriginal Art Award; Nov./Dec. Exhibitor, ANCAA and Boomalli Exhibition, Sydney. 1989: May. Exhibition and demonstration, Plaza Dreamtime Gallery, Alice Springs; July. Exhibitor, 'Desert Impressions', conducted by Australian Conservation Foundation, Melbourne; Sept. Demonstration at 'Shades of Ochre' Gallery, Darwin; Cultural exchange at Tiwi Designs, Bathurst Island; Oct. Exhibitor, Bloomfield's Gallery, Sydney; Exhibitor, 'A Myriad of Dreamings', Lauraine Diggins Fine Art, Melbourne and Sydney; Nov. Featured artist, 'Wirutjuta', Ernabella works. 1989: Araluen Arts Centre, Alice Springs. 1990: May. Exhibitor, 'From the Australian Desert', curated by Silver Harris, Santa Fe, New Mexico; June. Art Award, Barunga Festival, acrylic on canvas; Sept. Exhibitor, Edinburgh Festival, curated by Tandanya, SA; Exhibitor and demonstrator, Plaza Dreamtime Gallery, Alice Springs; Nov. Featured artist, 'Two Homes' exhibition at Tandanya, Adelaide, acrylic on canvas and batik. 1991: April. Acrylic painting *Kanypi Tjukurpa* leased by SA Dept of Arts. Collections: Art Gallery of SA (acrylic on canvas, 1989), Crafts Council of NSW (batik), Holmes à Court (batik), Kelton Collection (acrylic and batik)

BANDY JUPURRURLA
Also cited as: Bandy Jupurrula
Born at Coniston, Bandy Jupurrurla is a Warlpiri speaker and custodian of Bandicoot Dreaming in this region. He lives in Willowra and has no particular connections with artists in his own or in other Western Desert painting communities. Just before canvas and paint arrived in the Willowra community in 1989 through the CDEP adviser, Bandy had been painting weapons like boomerangs and shields for the artefact market and quickly moved on to art boards when the opportunity became available. The artist takes an active interest in the ceremonial life of the Willowra community, remarking that 'sometimes I am interested in other ceremonies/purlapa/initiations etc.'.

BARNES, BERYL (PUYURRPA) NAKAMARRA
Born at Yumurrpa, c.1940. Beryl Barnes's language/tribe is Warlpiri and her Dreamings Yarla (Wild Yam) and Wapurti. She started painting in 1986 and lives at Lajamanu. Collections: National Gallery of Victoria

BARNES, LADY NAKAMARRA
Lady Barnes's country is Yumurrpa, where she was born c.1940–2. Her language/tribe is Warlpiri and her principal Dreaming is Yarla (Wild Yam). She lives at Lajamanu and started painting in 1986. She is the mother of Marjorie Nungarrayi WATSON. Collections: National Gallery of Victoria

BENNETT, JOHN JOHN TJAPANGATI
A Pintupi speaker, his country is Mukulurru, north of Docker River, the southernmost place visited by Tingari people; also Kulkuta, west of Lake McDonald, Western

Johnny Warangkula Tjupurrula (Photo: Grenville Turner)

Tim Payungka Tjapangati (Photo: Grenville Turner)

Mick Namarari Tjapaltjarri (Photo: Grenville Turner)

Turkey Tolson Tjupurrula (Photo: Grenville Turner)

Dini Campbell Tjampitjinpa (Photo: Chris Hodges)

Yumpululu Tjungarrayi (Photo: Jim Sheldon)

George Tjungarrayi (Photo: John Corker)

Pinta Pinta Tjapanangka (Photo: Grenville Turner)

Michael Jagamara Nelson (Photo: Grenville Turner)

Anatjari Tjampitjinpa and Freddy West Tjakamarra (Photo: Chris Hodges)

Australia, another important site on the Tingari route. He began painting for Papunya Tula Artists in the early '80s after the Pintupi move back to Kintore. Residence formerly Kintore, now south at Tjukula. Collections: Holmes à Court

BENNY JANGALA
Also cited as: Benny Tjangala

Born in the 1920s around Kintore, where most of his family now lives, Benny Jangala is a Pintupi speaker. He paints Emu and Bush Tucker Dreamings for the country around Kintore and lives at Nyirrpi. He has been painting since the late '80s.

BENNY TJAPALTJARRI

Born west of Kintore in the early 1930s at a rockhole known as Tuwiru, Benny grew up travelling around the Kintore area living in the old way. Eventually the group journeyed east to Hermannsburg to collect rations and bring them back to the bush around Kalimpinpa and later further east at Ilpilli. The family group continued the same lifestyle after Haasts Bluff was established and also began to distribute rations. Eventually one of the senior men of the group passed away and the remaining members walked in to Haasts Bluff. Benny worked on the construction programs at Haasts Bluff and later Papunya, building houses, working with his uncle, GEORGE Tjangala. He recalled the routine: Weetbix for breakfast, working all week and on Friday going back with the money he had earned to Haasts Bluff, where he spent the weekends hunting for kangaroo with rifles before returning to work on Monday. Then he 'shifted his swag' to Papunya with George Tjangala and his father, Charlie TARAWA. During Peter Fannin's time with the painting company in the early '70s, Benny tried his hand at a few small boards, but it was not till 1980 that he began painting more regularly for Papunya Tula Artists. In the early '80s, he became actively involved in planning the return to Pintupi homelands and travelled to Adelaide and Darwin for meetings about putting down a bore at Kintore and building a clinic and housing at the new settlement. Benny's Dreaming starts at Pukurru north-east of Kintore on the edge of Anmatyerre country, and travels south-west through Kintore to the site of Pinpirnga, a rockhole due west of Alice Springs for which he is the key 'kurdu' (keeper/owner). He has an outstation near this site. It is associated with the bandicoot, which was plentiful in these areas but is now almost extinct. Benny often paints Wintaru (Bandicoot) Dreamings for this area. He is married with four sons and two daughters and lives in Kintore.

BERGER, MAY

May Berger was born in 1935 in Alice Springs, where she has lived all her life. Her language/tribe is Arrente. For the past few years, she has been enrolled in Management and Home Management courses at the Institute of Aboriginal Development in Alice Springs. Through her contact with IAD, she began painting in the early '90s. She was inspired by watching other Alice Springs's resident artists. She has sold her work through the Gondawona Gallery in Alice Springs, and Jukurrpa artists' co-operative

based at IAD. She participated in the Jukurrpa exhibition 'Crossroads' at the Araluen
Arts Centre in 1991.

BETTY NAPANANGKA

Born in Willowra, where she has lived all her life. She is a Warlpiri/Anmatyerre speaker
and her principal Dreamings are Warkilpirri and Malpa (Bush Beans). She began painting at the end of the '80s when materials became available in Willowra through the
CDEP adviser, also painting coolamons and digging sticks. She is actively involved in
the ritual life of the Willowra community: 'I usually get involved in the ceremonies —
initiations and other important ceremonies — which is very important to me.'

BILLY PETYARRE

Billy Petyarre began painting later than most of the women did at Utopia — in 1989.
He was, however, one of the first people at Utopia to begin carving, and is now one of
the leading sculptors of the distinctive human and dog figures produced by Utopia
artists. A strongly traditional man, Billy Petyarre is also a dedicated artist, painting his
first solo exhibition in 1991 for Utopia Arts in Sydney. He is married to Mary Kemarre,
who also paints. They live in the Ngkwarlerlaneme community. Collections: National
Gallery of Victoria

BIRD, ADA PETYARRE

Born on the old Utopia station at Atnangkere c.1930, Ada Bird is an Anmatyerre
speaker, and one of the senior women at Utopia. Her country is Atnangkere and she
paints the Angertla (Mountain Devil Lizard), Engcarma (Bean), Unyara (Emu),
Annlara (Pencil Yam), Kadjera (Grass Seeds) and Elaitchurunga (Small Brown Grass)
Dreamings which she shares with GLORIA Petyarre, EMILY Kngwarreye, Myrtle Petyarre, Nancy Kemarre, Kathleen Petyarre, Violet Petyarre and Jeanna Petyarre. She
lives at Mulga Bore (Akaye Soakage) and has been involved with the Utopia Women's
Batik group since its inception in the late '70s. Her batiks are held in major collections
in Australia and overseas. The German filmmaker Wim Wenders acquired one of her
batiks and gave the artist a role in one of his films, partially shot in Central Australia.
She began painting in 1988 with CAAMA's Summer Project. In late '89 the National
Gallery of Australia in Canberra acquired a major canvas, and addition of her works to
many public and private collections followed. In 1990 Ada had her first solo exhibition
at Utopia Art in Sydney. Her work features on the cover of *Utopia — A Picture Story*,
A. Brody (Heytesbury Holdings, Perth, 1990), a publication based on an exhibition of
88 works on silk by the Utopia artists which toured Eire and Scotland; and in *The Art of
Utopia*, M. Boulter (Craftsman House, Sydney, 1991). She incorporates both traditional
designs and representational elements in her paintings and uses linear patterns which
are increasingly distinctive of her work. She has two daughters, June and Hilda, and
four sons, Colin, Steven, Paddy and Ronnie.

BIRD, JUNE NGALE

Born at Waite River, June Bird is the daughter of Ada BIRD Petyarre. An Anmatyerre speaker, her country is Mulga Bore, and she paints Tapalya (Bush Plum), Endunga Tichna and Alpira Dreamings. She has been producing batiks since 1978 and began painting with the Summer Project in 1988. She lives at Mulga Bore (Akaye Soakage).

BIRD, LYNDSAY MPETYANE

Lyndsay Bird Mpetyane (or Tjampijinpa to his Western Desert acquaintances) was born on Bushy Park Station c.1935. He takes his European surname from the name of the station owner at Bushy Park, Jim Bird. His Aboriginal name is Artola Art Nanaka Yunga Areteca. In his younger days, Lyndsay was a stockman, mustering sheep and droving cattle. An Eastern Anmatyerre speaker, Lyndsay's traditional country is Aremela, south of Mulga Bore. He is custodian of a Snake story which starts at Harper Spring (Erutakuna). The snakes grew up there and were friends. They travelled to Ti-Tree, Aileron, Bushy Park, Aremula and Elgoanna. Elgoanna is a very important site, with connections to Wood Green, Harper Springs, Woola Downs and Adelaide Bore. Alcoota Creek is the border for Lyndsay's part of the story. His Dreamings are Charpa (Honey Ant), Utnea and Enmalu (different kinds of snakes), Elcudjera (Prickle), Ulkuta (Perentie or Lizard), Kwata (Lizard's Egg), Ulumba (White Tree), Arake and Encelcha (the fruit of the bush plum tree and the tree itself). He also paints the Dreaming for a Green Grub which lives in this plum tree, and a Kangaroo story which belongs to Ronny Price. He lives at Mulga Bore (Akaye Soakage) on Utopia station with his wife Mavis Petyarre and their three daughters Kavean, Jessica and Rosy Ngale. Mavis also paints her Arangua (Flock Pigeon) and Endunga (Bush Plum) at Akaye Soakage Dreamings occasionally, as do her sisters, Janet and Pansy Petyarre. Mavis and Pansy's paintings were included in the Summer Project show. They have all been painting since 1987, a year before some of the other Utopia artists. Lyndsay employs a wide variety of painting techniques in his work, often on the same canvas. He had his first solo exhibition at Utopia Art in Sydney in 1989. Collections: National Gallery of Australia, Canberra

BIRRELL, JEANNIE NAPURRURLA

Place of birth Yirningarra and born in the late 1920s. Her language/tribe is Warlpiri, her country Mungkurlurpa and her Dreamings are Marlujarra, Wintiki and Warnarri. She started painting in 1986. She was married to old Jack Birrell Jungarrayi, who passed away. She lives at Lajamanu.

BIRRELL, JENNIE NAMPIJINPA, see HARGRAVES, Jennie Nampijinpa

BLACKSMITH, PETER JAPANANGKA (c.1915–91)

Born at Winneke c.1915, Peter Blacksmith's land at Parnta, an old outstation 80 km south-west of Lajamanu, was the closest Warlpiri land to Lajamanu. (He was not strictly

Warlpiri, but belonged to the related group Katurrngarruru.) His country also included Kiliki (Winneke Creek) and his Dreamings were Warna (Snake), Yarla (Wild Yam) from Lulju and Kanta (Bush Coconut). He started painting in 1986 for the Traditional Painting course and was a well-known painter at Lajamanu. His painting *Warna Jukurrpa* — Snake Dreaming — featured on the cover of the *Mythscapes* (National Gallery of Victoria, 1989) catalogue. He died in September 1991, a very old man by local standards, much loved for the sweetness of his disposition. Collections: National Gallery of Victoria

BOKO, EILEEN
A Pitjantjatjara speaker from the Peterman Ranges, she now lives in Alice Springs and is in her mid fifties. Eileen Boko began painting on canvas in mid 1986 with the original Jukurrpa group. Her works are characterised by very fine dotting and often depict intricate stories of Homesick, Seven Sisters and Bush Cherry Dreamings. Though still active in the Jukurrpa organisation, she seldom paints now because of failing eyesight.

BOKO, PATRICIA
Born at Titjikala (Maryvale) in 1963, Patricia Boko is a Pitjantjatjara speaker who lives with her husband and four children in Alice Springs. She works as a translator/interpreter at the Institute of Aboriginal Development Language Centre. She was taught to paint by her mother, Eileen BOKO, her maternal grandfather's Dreamings (Snake, Homesick) from the Petermann Ranges. She has participated in exhibitions in Alice Springs and Canberra and sold her paintings through Jukurrpa artists' co-operative and the CAAMA shop.

BOOTJA BOOTJA, SUSIE NAPANGATI
Born 'in the bush' c.1932, Susie Bootja Bootja is a senior woman in the Balgo community. As well as doing her own paintings, she enjoys working with other painters, and frequently helps on the paintings by her husband, Mick GILL. A Kukatja speaker, her country lies around White Hills and Helena Springs (Kurtal). She usually paints Water Dreamings. She has been painting for Warlayirti Artists since 1987. Bootja Bootja has a bold, colourful style which serves to give a powerful statement of her country and its many major water sources. She lives and works at Balgo. Collections: Holmes à Court

BRANDY TJUNGURRAYAI
Also cited as: Brandy Tjungarrayi
Born 'in the bush', probably near Jupiter Well, c.1930, Brandy is a Pintupi speaker who usually lives at Mulan and Christmas Creek. His country lies around Nyilla (Jupiter Well) and he usually paints Tingari stories and Emu Dreamings. He started painting in 1985 at Balgo and now sells his work through Warlayirti Artists. Brandy enjoys working on large canvases where his simple, yet dramatic designs have their maximum impact. A quiet man, steeped in Aboriginal Law, his works evoke something of the majesty and mystery of the men's ceremonial life. Collections: Art Gallery of WA.

BRISCOE, TEDDY MJNBA JAMPIJINPA

Born in 1943 of the Anmatyerre tribe, Teddy Briscoe is one of the senior initiated men at Mt Allan. His country is Mt Allan/Napperby. His Dreamings include Dingo, Kangaroo, Women's and Grass Seed. He and his son, Michael ROSS Jangala, both live on Teddy's outstation, one hour's drive to the east of Mt Allan at Pulardi, a Dingo Dreaming site. Though an occasional painter, he has work in collections both in Australia and overseas.

BROGAS TJAPANGATI
Also cited as: Bruce Brogas Japangardi/Jabanardi, Brogus Tjapangati

Born at Haasts Bluff 10 November 1949. The name Brogas by which he is usually known was also his grandfather's. Began painting on canvas in 1982 after watching older artists like Clifford POSSUM (who taught him to carve long before he took up painting), Billy STOCKMAN, Tim LEURA and Dinny NOLAN as a young man growing up in Papunya. He later worked at Papunya school, giving 'manual training' classes in the carving of snakes and goannas. In recent years, he has lived for long periods in Alice Springs and Papunya at different times, and lately in Hermannsburg, where his wife's family lives. His father's country lay around the region of Kunatjarrayi and Pikilyi, his mother's around Ilpilli, Kalimpinpa and Tjikarri. His paintings depict the Witchetty Grub and Water Snake Dreaming pertaining to Kunajarrayi, Parrot, Rock Wallaby and Women's Dreaming stories across these areas. Major commissions include the Queensland Art Gallery.

BROWN, DINNY TJAPANANGKA

Born 'in the bush' near Lake Gregory c.1935, Dinny Brown was one of the first people in the Mulan community to begin painting there in 1989 for Warlayirti Artists. A Walmatjari speaker, the artist is one of the senior men of the Mulan community, who puts a lot of his wide personal experience of Men's Law into his paintings. The artist's country is around Lake Gregory and his principal Dreaming is Water. He is a quiet reflective man whose poor eyesight prevents him from painting a great deal.

BROWN, FRANK JANGALA

Born in 1965, Frank Brown is an Anmatyerre speaker. His country is Mt Allan and he paints Bush Onion Dreaming. He is married to Karen DIXON, also of Mt Allan.

BROWN, JEANNIE NAKAMARRA

A Luritja speaker, Jeannie Brown was born at Haasts Bluff in the late '40s or early '50s, and now lives in Papunya. Unlike most of the early women painters who first worked on their husband or other male relatives' paintings, Jeannie taught herself to paint in about 1980, after watching other artists painting at the settlement, some years before her husband, Theo BROWN, began painting. The Dreamings she paints lie around the Haasts Bluff area and include Napaltjarri Women Dancing and the Munni Munni story. The couple have a son, Edward. Collections: Holmes à Court

BROWN, JIMMY TJAMPITJINPA

Born near Yumari, west of Kintore across the WA border, Jimmy grew up walking the bush until he was ten or twelve years old, when the family was brought in to Papunya in the late '60s by Jeremy Long's Welfare Branch patrols. He was one of those involved in the early Pintupi exodus to Yai Yai, an outstation of Papunya. Though a relatively young man, he is currently Chairman of the Kiwirrkura Council, a position which he is said to have earned by having looked after the area around Kiwirrkura for two seasons on his own. He began painting for Papunya Tula Artists at Kiwirrkura and described himself when interviewed in 1989 as 'still learning' to paint on canvas. His work depicts Tingari stories from around Yumari.

BROWN, LENA NUNGARRAYI

A Warlpiri speaker, Lena Nungarrayi Brown lives at Yuendumu and sells her work through Warlukurlangu Artists. The Dreamings she paints include Yarringkanyi (Mt Doreen), Wakulyarri (Striped Rock Wallaby) and Janmarda (Bush Onion). In 1990 she won the Patron's Award at the Darlington Arts Festival in Western Australia. Her work has been shown in Warlukurlangu exhibitions in Darwin and Perth and at Albert Hall in Canberra. Collections: South Australian Museum, Australian Museum, Musée National des Arts Africain et Oceaniens, Paris

BROWN, MARY NAPANGARDI

Born at Mt Doreen c.1955, Mary Brown is a Pintupi speaker. She lives at Nyirrpi. She paints Bush Tomato Dreaming for her country, which is east of Lake Mackay. Having painted since the late '80s, when she joined other Nyirrpi artists in 1989 in doing a painting on the school wall. She is Pauline GALLAGHER's sister.

BROWN, MEGGERIE NAPANANGKA

Born at Yuendumu in 1965, and a Warlpiri speaker, Meggerie Brown's country is Mt Theo and her Dreamings are Bush Tomato and Bush Banana. She lives in Yuendumu, has connections with Willowra community, but works with the Jukurrpa group based in Alice Springs. 'When I was fourteen, I used to watch the old women painting at the Warlukurlangu Gallery at Yuendumu. My mother showed me how to paint my Dreamings. I sold my first painting when I was about seventeen.'

BROWN, PEGGY NAPANGARDI

Born at Coniston Station c.1945 of the Anmatyerre tribe, Peggy Brown is the daughter of Mt Allan headman FRANK Japanangka. When she was a young girl, she was taught to paint by her grandfather and by Clifford POSSUM Tjapaltjarri. Her country is also Mt Allan, and she paints the Yuelamu Honey Ant Dreaming. She now lives in Alice Springs, where has sold her works through the Corkwood Gallery and Jukurrpa artists' co-operative.

BROWN, PRISCILLA NAPANANGKA

Born at Yuendumu in 1972, Priscilla Brown is a Warlpiri speaker whose traditional country is Mt Theo. She has been painting since she was eleven years old, after watching her mother painting at Yuendumu and asking her about her own Dreaming. She sold her first painting to Warlukurlangu Artists. She paints Bush Banana, Bush Goanna and Bush Tomato Dreamings. She lives in Yuendumu and has connections with the community at Willowra, but usually works with the Jukurrpa group in Alice Springs.

BROWN, SHEILA NAPALJARRI

Born c.1940, Sheila Brown is one of the senior Warlpiri women of the Yuendumu community whose interest in rendering traditional women's designs in western materials was one of the driving forces behind early experiments with canvas at the settlement. Her work was included in the first exhibition of Yuendumu paintings at the Araluen Arts Centre in Alice Springs in October 1985. She paints Ngarlkirdi (Witchetty Grub), Yiwarra (Milky Way) and Karntajarra (Two Women) Dreamings from the Kunajarrayi area of her heritage country. Since the mid '80s, she has shown in numerous exhibitions of Warlukurlangu Artists in cities all around Australia. Collections: many public and private collections, including the Christensen Fund and the South Australian Museum

BROWN, THEO TJAPALTJARRI

Born in the early '40s, Theo Brown was one of Papunya's volatile young men when painting began at the settlement in 1971. He subsequently lived at Umbungurru outstation near Glen Helen station, which for a decade in the late '70s and early '80s was also Clifford POSSUM's place of residence. He now lives in Papunya with his wife, Jeannie BROWN. He began painting for Papunya Tula Artists around 1984. His work was immediately distinctive for its lighter yellow ochre backgrounds and smoky effects — possibly connected to the failing eyesight which now prevents him from painting. The artist's mother's country lies around Mereenie in the Mt Zeil area, and he is of the Western Arrente language group. His paintings depict Witchetty Grub, Lizard, Katjutarri (a small edible tuber — another of his mother's stories) and a small blue butterfly associated with the site of Lukarrya, a hill west of Narwietooma station in his father's country. His work was shown in the USA in the Asia Society's 'Dreamings: Art of Aboriginal Australia' exhibition and in many group shows of Papunya Tula Artists. Collections: private and public collections, including the Flinders University Art Museum and the South Australian Museum

BROWN, TOBY TJAMPITJINPA (c.1920–1986)

An old man in his late sixties when he died at Hettie Perkins Home in Alice Springs in the mid '80s, the artist spent the last decade of his life living in fringe camps around Alice Springs and was an important figure in campaigns to improve their amenities. How long after coming to live in town he continued to paint for Papunya Tula Artists is uncertain. Most of his paintings seem to date from the mid to late '70s. A commemorative mural which he painted in a simplified Western Desert style on the wall of a new amenities block that was won through these struggles suggests that he may have been one of the earliest 'town painters'. A member of the Anmatyerre language group, his country lay around Anumba — Wallaby Springs — on Napperby Station. His paintings depict Kangaroo, Euro, Mulga Seed, Snake and other Dreamings from this region. Collections: University of WA Anthropology Museum, Flinders University Art Museum, SA Museum, Kelton Foundation etc.

BULLEN, ANDREW TJAPANGATI

Born 'in the bush' around Docker River near the SA/NT/WA border. As a young boy in the late '40s, Andrew Bullen came in with his family to the country around the newly established ration depot of Haasts Bluff, hundreds of miles north-east of their traditional country. He received no European schooling, and as he grew to manhood, the group moved across to camp at the site of present day Papunya, within reach of the Haasts Bluff ration drops. Later he did stockwork, mustering cattle south of Haasts Bluff around Dirty Water Creek. He was employed in Papunya as a health worker when he began painting for Papunya Tula Artists in 1980. Since then he and his wife, Barbara Maka, also a health worker, have lived and worked at Kintore and one of the Docker River outstations. His wife is now a health worker at Mt Leibig, where they reside with their daughter Sylviana. The artist's father was of the Pitjantjatjara language group and his country lay around Docker River. Andrew Bullen's paintings usually depict Kangaroo and Native Tobacco Dreamings from this area, and a Man's Dreaming story which he received from his mother and uncle. Collections: Flinders University Art Museum

BURNS, PAMPIRRRIYA (sometimes MARGARET) NUNGARRAYI

Born at Yatujungurlu (Kurlurrngalynypa) in 1936, her tribe/language is Warlpiri and her country Kurlurrngalynypa. She can also work on the Kiriwarrankurra Jukurrpa (Dreaming). Her own Dreamings are Witi and Ngarrka. She lives at Lajamanu. Works with her husband, Toby Jangala and started painting in 1986 in the Traditional Painting course. An impressive figure of a woman, her paintings are unusually symmetrical and 'neat' amongst the work of the older artists at Lajamanu.

BUSH, GEORGE TJANGALA

Born around Mayilnpa, just out of Alice Springs, c.1940 into a Luritja/Anmatyerre speaking family, George Bush was a member of the original group of artists in Papunya in the early '70s. At the time, he was living in Papunya working as a police tracker. For some time in the early '80s he lived on a remote outstation in his wife's country out towards the WA border, but currently divides his time between Papunya, where he still paints for Papunya Tula Artists, and Alice Springs, where he occasionally paints for the Centre for Aboriginal Artists. His Dreamings are water snakes, spider, various plants and other types of bush tucker. Collections: Holmes à Court

BUTLER, SALLY NAPURRULA

A Luritja speaker, Sally Butler was born at Papunya and started painting when she began the IAD literacy course in 1986. Has connections with the Tjukula community, between Kintore and Docker River near the NT/SA/WA border, but usually works with the Jukurrpa group in Alice Springs.

BYE BYE NAPANGATI

Born 'in the bush', probably in the Stansmore Range area in the mid '30s, Bye Bye is a Kukatja speaker and a leader of the Women's Law in the Balgo community. The stories of this Law fill her canvases, usually Tingari Dreamings. Her country lies around the Stansmore Ranges, Point Moody and Yagga Yagga. Married to artist SUNFLY Tjampitjin, she has been painting for Warlayirti Artists since 1986. The artist often produces surprisingly imaginative designs and has generally resisted the tendency of many other women artists at Balgo to use brighter colours. Collections: Art Gallery of Western Australia, National Gallery of Victoria

C

CAMERON TJAPALTJARRI

Born at Haasts Bluff in the early '50s. His family were amongst those who set up camp in this area after walking in from Pintupi country hundreds of kilometres to the west. The area around the region of Perentie — the Lizard Dreaming mountain which lies alongside Kintore — was his father's country. He started painting at Kintore in about 1987 under the instruction of his older brothers, Old Mick NAMARARI Tjapaltjarri and BENNY Tjapaltjarri, both of whom began painting in Papunya in the early '70s. Stories depicted in Cameron's paintings relate to the Tingari cycle and include a Bandicoot Dreaming story around Desert Bore and a Wallaby Dreaming which passes through the site of Ajunti, moving north-west to finish up at Jungyn, a Wallaby and Budgerigar Dreaming site north-west of Nyirrpi often depicted in Charlie EGALIE's paintings. Collections: Holmes à Court

CAMPBELL, DINI TJAMPITJINPA

Born in the early '40s in Pintupi country west of Kiwirrkura, across the WA border near Jupiter Well. He grew up 'in the bush' with his family, and had already been initiated when the group walked into the Catholic mission settlement of Balgo in the late '50s. While living at Balgo, Dini did stockwork and wood carting. While visiting relatives in Papunya, he would have observed the old men painting during the '70s. His older brother, ANATJARI Tjampitjinpa, was one of the original group of Papunya artists. During one of these visits in 1981, Dini had his first experience of painting on canvas as one of the team of men who assisted Uta Uta Tjangala on the monumental canvas depicting events at the site of Yumari which has since travelled the world as part of the Aboriginal Arts Board collection. Painting started up at Balgo Adult Education Centre around this time, moving quickly from Christian themes to paintings of artists' country, and developing distinctive regional styles. He does not appear to have painted at Balgo during this period, but the influence of these Balgo styles (e.g. linked dotting) was evident in the paintings which he produced for Papunya Tula Artists after moving from Balgo to Kintore in the early '80s. He paints the stories of the Tingari cycle in his country round Lake Nyaru and Walatju. Married with two young children, he is one of the most dedicated artists currently working out of Kintore. Collections: National Gallery of Victoria, Supreme Court of NT, Darwin. Exhibitions: John Weber Gallery, New York, 1989, solo exhibition Gallery Gabrielle Pizzi, 1990

CAMPBELL, GORDON TJAPANANGKA (10/4/1941–1986)
Also cited as: Gordon Egalie Campbell Tjapanangka

Following his father's death, when Gordon was only a 'little baby in a coolamon', he was raised by a relative, whose surname he adopted. He was related to the artist Charlie EGALIE through his natural father, a Western Arrente man known as Tululu Egalie, whose name he kept as a middle name. His mother was Warlpiri/Anmatyerre. He attended the Old Bungalow School for Aboriginal children in Alice Springs. At the age of nineteen he left to go droving. After a period of working on Narwietooma station, he travelled from the Kimberley to the Sunshine Coast as a stockman before settling in Papunya, where he lived till his untimely death in the mid '80s. A highly intelligent and articulate man who spoke seven or eight languages including English, he gave his language group as Western Arrente/Anmatyerre/Warlpiri. He arrived in Papunya in 1972 and observed the development of the painting movement from that point. He began painting for Papunya Tula Artists after passing through the ceremonies which make one a man and thus qualified to paint. In this period he was taught by Tim LEURA Tjapaltjarri and later by his cousin, Paddy CARROLL Tjungarrayi. His traditional country was Kunajarrayi, to the west of Mt Wedge, and his paintings depict Rain, Kangaroo and Bush Fire Dreamings from this area. He and Michael NELSON Jagamara were close friends. He was related to the Pintupi artist PINTA PINTA by marriage, his mother-in-law being Pinta Pinta's sister. His wife Susaleen also paints. Her work is included in the Museums & Art Galleries of NT. Collections: Holmes à Court

CAMPBELL, NANCY NAPANANGKA
Born at Six Mile, Ti-Tree in 1961, Nancy Campbell is a Warlpiri speaker, with no close relations among the other Anmatyerre artists at Napperby, where she lives. Her country lies around Anningie and Ti-Tree. Her principal Dreamings are Louse and Kangaroo. She has been painting since 1986. Her work has been exhibited in several state capitals.

CARROLL, PADDY TJUNGARRAYI
Also cited as: Paddy Carroll Tjungurrayi, Paddy Carroll Jungarai
Country and birthplace Yarrungkanyi, north-west of Yuendumu, c.1927 or earlier. Paddy Carroll's father was Warlpiri/Anmatyerre, and his mother Luritja/Warlpiri, her country being the site of Winparrku near Haasts Bluff. Paddy grew up in this area, the family coming in to Haasts Bluff and Yuendumu to collect rations of bread and tea. His father was shot by Europeans in the Coniston massacre of 1928. Paddy knows little of his father's country; his mother refused to speak of it after the murder. Two of Paddy's brothers also fled to Queensland. The three finally met up again when Paddy was a young man in his early twenties and they found themselves in the same army unit stationed in Elliott near Darwin during World War II. Jimmy KITSON, a leading ceremonial figure in the Willowra community, is also Paddy's brother. After the war, Paddy lived in Alice Springs and Darwin, working across the country as a carpenter and stockman. He worked for thirty years at Narwietooma station, droving cattle across the Tanami and helping to lay telegraph lines in remote areas. He began painting in about 1977 when John Kean was running Papunya Tula Artists and Paddy and his family were living at Three Mile Bore, an outstation of Papunya. David CORBY was probably

influential in his starting to paint. Paddy's extensive ceremonial knowledge is indicated by the range of Dreaming stories depicted in his paintings, which include: Witchetty Grub, Wallaby, Yala (Bush Potato), Possum, Goanna, Woman, Man, Malyippi (Sweet Potato), Wapiti (Sweet Potato), Yawalyurra (Bush Grapes), Mukaki and other Bush Tucker stories, Carpet Snake, and Ngatijirri (Budgerigar). For a time, he lived at Inapanu outstation, near Mt Lori, and sometimes in Papunya. He came to Sydney in 1981 with Dinny NOLAN to make the first sand painting to be seen outside the Western Desert — in the grounds of the SH Ervin Gallery. His paintings were part of 'Painters of the Western Desert', Papunya Tula Artists's first three man show with Clifford POSSUM and UTA UTA Tjangala in the 1984 Adelaide Festival of Arts, attended by all three artists. He was one of five Papunya Tula artists invited to submit designs for the mosaic for the new Parliament House in Canberra. He painted the concentric circles included in the design of the Bicentennial $A10 note issued in 1988. In 1989 he travelled to Brisbane with Anatjari Tjampitjinpa for an exhibition of Papunya Tula Artists at the Queensland Art Gallery. In 1991 he travelled to America with Dinny Nolan Tjampitjinpa, visiting colleges and Native American communities on a tour organised by poets Billy Marshall-Stoneking and Nigel Roberts. Paddy Carroll once remarked to a journalist puzzling over the meaning of a painting's iconography that 'We have had to learn your language, now it is time you learned ours.' Paddy and his second wife, Ruby Nangala, now live in their new house at Three Mile outstation, just north of Papunya. Collections: Art Gallery of South Australia, National Gallery of Australia, Canberra, Parliament House, Canberra, Australian Museum, Sydney, University of Western Australia Anthropology Museum, Holmes à Court, Flinders University Art Museum, Broken Hill Art Gallery etc.

CASSIDY TJAPALTJARRI
Also cited as: Cassidy Stockman Japaljarri, Cassidy Japaljarri, Cassidy Possum Tjapaltjarri

Born on Napperby station in 1923, Cassidy Tjapaltjarri is one of the most flamboyant figures in this small community, and in the media coverage of the Napperby artists' first exhibition at the Hogarth Galleries in Sydney was identified as leader and spokesman for the painting group. Now a pensioner, Cassidy is elder of the Anmatyerre tribe. His traditional country is Red Hill and Napperby. He paints Caterpillar and Goanna Dreamings for this area and also Bush Tucker Dreamings from his grandfather's country around the Mt Allan area. 'This Dreaming is about the place where I was born. This waterhole and this emu track are part of my Dreaming. It takes me two weeks to make. One day my painting will make Napperby number one. I show all the young fellas what we Aboriginal people can do for ourselves.'(*Sydney Morning Herald*, 11 July 1987)

CHARLES, BARBARA NAPALTJARRI
Also cited as: Barbara Charles Nabaljari

Born on Napperby station c.1959, Barbara Charles and her husband, Michael TOMMY Tjapangati, are both Anmatyerre speakers. Barbara's country lies south of Twenty Mile

Bore, on both Napperby and Coniston stations. Her paintings usually depict Snake and Witchetty Grub Dreamings from this area, which she shares with her sister Rachel. She started painting in 1983 at Napperby station. She sometimes painted for Yuelamu Artists while visiting relatives in Mt Allan. In recent years she and her husband have moved from Napperby and taken up more or less permanent residence at Mt Allan. Her work has been shown in several capital cities.

CHARLIE TJAPANGATI

Born 'in the bush', at Palinpalintjanya, north-west of Jupiter Well, c.1949, Charlie Tjapangati was a young man already initiated when Jeremy Long brought his family into Papunya with one of the last of the Welfare Branch patrols in about 1964. At Papunya he worked for rations on the construction of buildings at the settlement. His country lies in Pintupi territory across the WA border and west of Jupiter Well — near Puntatarpa. He began painting for Papunya Tula Artists in about 1978, having observed the older men painting while living in West Camp, Papunya. He accompanied Billy STOCKMAN and Andrew Crocker to America for an exhibition of the paintings in the 'Mr Sandman Bring Me a Dream' collection, which was the initial purchase of Western Desert art by the Holmes à Court collection. Stories from the Tingari cycle are the usual subject of his paintings. He moved to the newly established Pintupi settlement of Kintore in 1982. Collections: public and private collections, including Richard Kelton, Holmes à Court and National Gallery of Australia, Canberra

CHISOLM, CHARLIE JANGALA (d.)

Born in approximately 1945, Charlie Chisolm was an Anmatyerre speaker whose traditional country was Yuelamu. He lived sometimes at Santa Teresa, sometimes at Mt Allan and sometimes at Napperby. He painted the Dreamings for Yuelamu (Honey Ant) as well as Bush Potato. He was the brother of Mary ALLAN Nangala and Jack COOK. He also had Warlpiri connections and had painted at both Yuendumu and Napperby. He had been selling his paintings through Mt Allan since at least the mid '80s, sometimes painting his ground sheet when no other materials were available to work on. One of his paintings is included in the Alice Springs Museum/Art Gallery. He died in the early '90s.

COCKATOO, KITTY PULTARA
Also cited as: Kitty Cockatoo Napaltjarri — the first being her Anmatyerre skin name, and the second her Warlpiri one

Born at Napperby in 1952, Kitty Cockatoo has lived on Napperby station for most of her life. She is the older sister of JESSIE Napaltjarri and Kitty PULTARA (they all have the same mother) and has been painting since 1986. Her paintings show Lightning and Bush Plum stories of the Napperby area and Central Mt Wedge station.

COLLINS, ANDREW JANGALA

Born in 1950, Andrew Collins moved at the end of the '80s to the settlement of Ti-Tree along with his brother Jack COOK, their wives, Elma Ross and Anne Cook, and a number of other artists from Mt Allan. His traditional country is Mt Allan, and he paints Yuelamu, Women, Water and Kangaroo Dreamings for this country. An Anmatyerre speaker, he is married to Elma Ross Napanangka, who also paints occasionally.

COLLINS, BERYL NANGALA

Born in 1960, Beryl Collins is an Anmatyerre speaker. Her traditional country is Ngarliyikirlangu and also Yuelamu. She paints Women, Emu and Honey Ant Dreamings. She is married to Alby STOCKMAN Japanangka and lives at Mt Allan.

COLLINS, CONNIE NUNGARRAYI

Born at Yuendumu in 1962, and a Warlpiri speaker, Connie Collins has been living in Alice Springs since she was a child. She paints Kangaroo Dreaming from her father's country, Pirrpirrpakarnu, which lies on Mt Doreen station, west of Yuendumu, and she is attending an Institute of Aboriginal Studies Bridging Course.

COLLINS, IMPANA

A Pitjanjatjara speaker who lives in the Mutitjulu community, Uluru — where she was probably born. When she was growing up, she spent some time at Areyonga. Like some other Mutitjulu painters (e.g. KUNBRY), Impana is also very proficient at wood carving. She remembers learning to carve as a teenager to sell artefacts to the tourists who came to the Rock. She was taught this skill by other members of her family. As a young girl, she worked with Kunbry taking tourists on camel rides around the Rock and selling 'punu'(artefacts) at the Red Centre Motel. Impana was one of the first women to start painting in the Mutitjulu community, in 1986. Common subjects of her paintings are Liru and Kuniya (two different kinds of snake) Dreamings, Women's Inma (song and dance), the Yulara waterhole and a place near Uluru called Mantaroa. Most of her paintings are small because she recognises that it is easier for the tourists to fit them into their suitcases or cars, but she has done larger paintings for Maruku Arts and Crafts. Collections: Museum of Victoria, Osaka Museum, Japan

COLLINS, RUBY NAKAMARRA

Born in the late 1940s, Ruby Collins shares the country of Wapurtali with Bessie SIMS. Both paint Ngarlajiyi (Bush Carrot) Dreaming for this country. Ruby has been painting for Warlukurlangu Artists since the mid '80s. Her work rarely deviates from the earth colours of the traditional palette or classic renditions of the Dreaming designs. A Warlpiri speaker, she lives at Yuendumu.

COOK, ANNE NUNGARRAYI

Born c.1940, and an Anmatyerre speaker, Anne Cook's traditional country is Mt Leichhardt. She paints Women and Bush Potato Dreamings. She is married to Jack COOK and is a sister of Teddy Jungarrayi. She has family connections at Ti-Tree, where she lives when not at Mt Allan.

COOK, JACK JANGALA

Born c.1935, Jack Cook is an Anmatyerre speaker whose country is Ngarliyikurlangu and who paints Emu Dreamings. One of the senior men at Mt Allan, he often delegates his children to paint his stories. He is married to Anne COOK and ROWENA Nungurrayi and has family at Ti-Tree with whom he sometimes stays. He speaks excellent English, which he learnt from having been brought up with D.D. Smith, manager of Mt Allan station for many years.

COOK, LISA NAMPIJINPA

An Anmatyerre speaker, Lisa Cook is the daughter of Jack COOK Jangala and Anne COOK Nungarrayi. Born in 1972, she paints Honey Ant and Emu Dreamings for her country, Mt Allan, where she lives.

COOKE, HENRY (PARTI-PARTI) JAKAMARRA

Born at Yumurrpa ('where the yams grow') in 1922, Henry Cooke lives at Lajamanu. His country is Yumurrpa and he can paint the Yarla (Wild Yam), Warna (another type of yam) and Marlu (Kangaroo) Dreamings. He began painting in 1986 in the Traditional Painting course.

CORBY, DAVID TJAPALTJARRI (c.1945–1980)

Though still a young man, the artist joined his older brother, Charlie EGALIE, in the original group of 'painting men' at Papunya at the beginning of the '70s. Though his country lay around Tjunti, north-west of Vaughan Springs station in Warlpiri territory, he lived in Papunya and was a dedicated worker for his people before his untimely death. His paintings were unusual in the early days of the painting movement for the signatures they bore. He painted Budgerigar, Wallaby, Emu and Witchetty Grub Dreamings. In 1979 David Corby and Turkey TOLSON were artists-in-residence at Flinders University, and the Flinders University Art Museum holds many of the paintings which the artists completed during the residency (see *Dot and Circle: A Retrospective Survey of the Aboriginal acrylic paintings of Central Australia*, [ed. J. Maughan & J. Zimmer, RMIT, 1986]) Collections: Museums & Art Galleries of NT, Flinders University Art Museum

CORBY, NATALIE NUNGARRAYI

Born in Papunya 18 September 1967, Natalie Corby is the daughter of Charlie EGALIE, who joined Papunya Tula Artists in 1972 and taught her to paint in the early

'80s. She was one of the first women in Papunya to begin painting in her own right, and with almost a decade of painting now behind her, she is one of the most experienced women artists in the Western Desert style. She belongs to the Warlpiri language group and usually paints her father's stories and sometimes stories involving women's corroborees and dancing.

COWBOY LOUIE PWERLE

Born c.1941 at the sheep camp on Old McDonald station, and an Eastern Anmatyerre speaker whose traditional country lies on the western side of the Sandover River on Utopia station, stretching west onto Mt Skinner station. He is the younger brother of LOUIE Pwerle, and custodian of a secondary series of Dreaming sites over the same area, the great variety of which can be seen in his paintings. The name 'Cowboy' comes from his reputation as a stockman and his 'flashy' dressing. Married to sisters Carol and Elizabeth Kngwarreye, he lives most of the time at Mosquito Bore (Lytntye), but also spends time at Boundary Bore on the western boundary of Utopia land and Soakage Bore (Atnarare), south-east of Lytntye. His work has been shown in several exhibitions mounted by Delmore Gallery in Adelaide, Melbourne, Brisbane. Collections: National Gallery of Victoria

D

DAISY NAPANGARDI

Though she usually lives at Napperby, Daisy's heritage country is Yuelamu, and she paints Yuelamu (Honey Ant), Little Snakes Underground and Bush Tucker Dreamings. Her father is FRANK Japanangka, one of the most senior men at Mt Allan. She was born in 1955 and is an Anmatyerre speaker. She lives at Mt Allan and is married to another Mt Allan artist, DENNY Jampijinpa.

DAISY (PURLPURLNGALI) NAPURRURLA

Born at Karangula in 1928, her tribe/language is Warlpiri and her Dreaming is Ngarlu. She is very high up in the women's business at Lajamanu and in the dancing too, and started painting in 1986. She lives at Lajamanu. Collections: National Gallery of Victoria

DANIELS, BARNEY TJUNGURRAYI

Born at Haasts Bluff in the mid '50s ('ration time'), Barney Daniels received some European schooling at Mungana, a settlement about five miles (8 km) out of Alice Springs. He spent five years in Western Australia working as a stockman at Halls Creek station, then returned to his traditional country at Haasts Bluff and continued droving work on the government cattle station which had been established there, before starting to paint in the mid '80s. He began on small boards, which he sold to the Centre for Aboriginal Artists. He paints Rainbow Snake, Blue Tongue Lizard, Bush Fire, Centipede, Witchetty Grub/Snake and Bush Tucker Dreamings. He describes himself as self-taught. He was one of the pioneers of the style of stippled brushwork backgrounds which is still distinctive of his canvases. He describes his language/tribe as Luritja/Pintupi, though his mother was an Anmatyerre woman from Napperby and his father Warlpiri. He was commissioned by the Australian Bicentennial Authority to paint furniture, including a desk and a TV set, for the touring 1988 Bicentennial exhibition, which also included a life-size sculpture of the artist, one of 20 Australians so represented. In recent years, he has sold mainly through the Gondawana Gallery and other Alice Springs outlets. When interviewed for this dictionary, he was living at Morris Soak in Alice Springs. Collections: Flinders University Art Museum, Langbeach Museum, California. Exhibitions: Gauguin Museum, Tahiti, Feb '88, Tin Sheds, Oct '88. Reference: *Aboriginality*, J. Isaacs (UQP, 1992)

DANIELS, CAROL NAMPIJINPA

Born in Yuendumu c.1960, Carol Daniels is a Warlpiri speaker. She lives at Yuendumu, but also has family connections with the Mt Allan community. She paints Fire and Bush

Potato Dreamings. She started painting in about 1985: 'I was watching my uncles painting and my sister told me the Dreamtime story to make a painting.' She has recently been working with the Jukurrpa group in Alice Springs.

DANIELS, DOLLY NAMPIJINPA
(formerly GRANITES)

Born c.1931 at Mt Doreen, and a Warlpiri speaker, Dolly Daniels is 'boss' for the Yawulyu or women's ceremonies at Yuendumu. Her Dreamings are Warlukurlangu (Fire), Yankirri (Emu), Watiyawarnu (Acacia Seed), Yumpulykanji (Burrowing Skink) and Ngapa (Water). She has been exhibiting with Warlukurlangu Artists since the first exhibition of Yuendumu paintings in 1985 at the Araluen Arts Centre in Alice Springs, in exhibitions around Australia including Perth, Melbourne, Adelaide, Sydney, Darwin and Brisbane. In 1987 her work was also included in special 'Karnta' (Women's) exhibitions in Adelaide, Sydney and Fremantle. She was part of the South Australian Museum's 'Yuendumu — Paintings out of the Desert' project and exhibition in March 1988, 'Mythscapes' at the National Gallery of Victoria in 1989 and 'L'été Australien' at the Musée Fabre, Montpellier, France in 1990. She travelled to New York as part of a party of Warlpiri artists who attended the 'Dreamings: Art of Aboriginal Australia' exhibition. Her impressions of the visit are recorded in the film *Market of Dreams*. In 1991 she exhibited a collaborative work with Anne Mosey in 'Frames of Reference: Aspects of Feminism and Art', part of the Dissonance program celebrating 20 years of women's art in Australia. Dolly also collaborated with Anne Mosey on an installation for the 1993 Biennale of Sydney. A leading personality in the Yuendumu community, Dolly is co-Chairperson (with Bronson NELSON, of Warlukurlangu Artists, Chairperson of the Yuendumu Women's Centre, a member of the Warlpiri Media Association and, with Lucy KENNEDY and Bessie SIMS, one of three women on the Yuendumu Council. Collections: National Gallery of Victoria, South Australian Museum, Australian Museum, Sydney. References: Ryan, J., *Mythscapes* (NGV, 1989); Crossman, S. & Bardou, J-P., *L'été Australien* (Musée Fabre, Montpellier, 1990)

DANIELS, LESLIE JAMPIJINPA

Born in about 1945, Leslie Daniels is a Warlpiri speaker. His traditional country is Mt Wedge and Yuendumu, and he paints Snake, Fire, Thunderstorm, Kerrinyarra (Mt Wedge) and Honey Ant Dreamings. He is married to Emily ANDY Napaljarri, whose family connections to the painting movement go back to the early '80s in Papunya. Lives at Mt Allan.

DANIELS, ROBIN NAPALJARRI

Born at Yuendumu, c.1960, her language/tribe is Warlpiri and she lives at Lajamanu. Her country is Kunajarrayi, and her Dreamings are Ngalyipi (Bush Medicine Vine), Laju, Warna, and Yarla. She started painting in 1987.

DAVEY, JILLIAN

Jillian Davey was born 'in the bush' in 1954 at Wina, by a rockhole south-west of Kata Tjuta (the Olgas), near her father and grandfather's country. Both parents were Pitjant-jatjara speakers. Her mother's country is closer to Ernabella, and the family moved to the mission, which had been established in 1936. Jillian grew up at the Ernabella mission and attended Ernabella school. It was at the school that Jillian first started drawing with crayons. Her designs were very much based on what by that time were already identifiable as 'Ernabella shapes', 'doodlings' which have their origin in the drawings of the older women. After school, Jillian began painting and weaving with Ernabella Arts Inc. and in 1975 went to Indonesia to study batik. However, her preferred medium continued to be watercolours, and later, acrylics. Jillian's work has been exhibited widely and in 1985 she designed the South Australian Electoral Commission poster. In 1988 she began exploring the rich subject matter of Tjukurrpa (the Dreaming) with acrylics on canvas. Her painting of *Kutungu* — her father's country — was selected for the Tandanya Calendar Collection of 1990. Jillian lives at Ernabella with her family. She has one daughter, Rita.

DAVID, TOMMY

Born at Wayarria in 1935, he grew up at Wankari. He thinks he was a 'little bit crazy' then. He could listen to his parents, but he still behaved like a little boy. Afterwards his mother took him to Areyonga. There he went to school to learn how to get a job. After that he went to Ammonguna and got a job there. [Interviewer's paraphrase of Tommy David] He paints pictures of Kunia (Carpet Snake) and 'one girl's footprints when she came from the cave'. Sometimes Tommy paints snakes and different tracks. He says he's an artist 'in a small way'. He paints his own Dreaming, not those of anybody else. He now lives at Kaltukatjara community, Docker River. He knows artists at Kintore, including Johnson (John John) BENNETT, and Ronnie Allen, Bill Edimintja and Eddie Edimintja (EDIMINJA) at Docker River, though these last two paint very little now because of poor eyesight. Tommy is an evangelist in the Lutheran Church at Docker River.

DEMPSEY, (YOUNG) TIMOTHY TJUNGURRAYI

Born at Haasts Bluff c.1941, he is the older brother of Barney DANIELS, with whom he shares this country, which is close to their mother's country in the Papunya/Napperby area. Their father was a Warlpiri speaker from the Lajamanu area, giving the brothers two widely separated heritage countries in these regions. The artist gives his tribal affiliation as Luritja. Timothy received some schooling at Narwietooma station. He worked as a stockman then as a mechanic on bore maintenance before settling in Papunya in the early '60s, helping in the transfer of people from Haasts Bluff to the new settlement. At Papunya, he was introduced to painting in 1985 by watching Clifford POSSUM, with whom he shared a camp. He is also related to artist Mary DIXON. He lives near his traditional country on 'Five Mile' outstation near Papunya and paints Centipede, Spear

Ceremony, Barking Spider and Hunting for Kangaroo Dreamings, and paints occasionally for Papunya Tula Artists as well as the Centre for Aboriginal Artists. He is married to Epingka Nangala and they have three daughters and a son. Epingka paints the Women's Dreaming for her country at Haasts Bluff, and has been producing occasional paintings since the mid '80s.

DENNY JAMPIJINPA

Born in 1950, Denny Jampijinpa is an Anmatyerre speaker whose traditional country is Mt Allan. He is a 'bush doctor': traditional Aboriginal medicine man. The Dreamings he can paint are Snake, Bush Tucker, White Creek Wallaby, Scrub Turkey, and Honey Ants from White Creek. He is married to DAISY Napangardi, and now lives at Nyirrpi. He began painting in about 1987.

DICKSON, BERTHA NAKAMARRA

Born in Yuendumu in the 1950s, Bertha Nakamarra Dickson now lives in the Hidden Valley town camp of Alice Springs. When she was living at Yuendumu, her aunt, Ruby Napurrurla, taught her painting. Bertha's country is situated near Mission Creek and she paints Warna (Snake) and Yawakyi (Bloodberry) Dreamings, which belong to the Jupurrurla/Napurrurla and Jakamarra/Nakamarra skin groups. Together with her husband, Andrew Japaljarri SPENCER, Bertha worked for HALT (Healthy Aboriginal Lifestyle Team) in 1989/90. HALT's aims were to educate Aboriginal people about the dangers of alcohol and drug abuse, diseases related to unhealthy nutrition, lack of hygiene etc. During that time, they produced a series of paintings in the traditional Western Desert style but dealing with these contemporary issues. Bertha has close connections with the Warlpiri communities of Yuendumu, Lajamanu and Willowra. She started with the IAD Literacy Course in 1992, and sells her paintings through the Jukurrpa artists' co-operative. Monica Nakamarra DOOLAN is her sister.

DIXON, BEATRIX NANGALA

Born in Alice Springs in 1960, Beatrix Dixon is the daughter of Kitty PULTARA and niece of Clifford POSSUM. Glenda Briscoe, who also paints occasionally, is her cousin. An Anmatyerre speaker, Beatrix's traditional country lies around No. 1 Bore on Napperby station. She paints Emu, Dingo and Kangaroo Dreamings associated with No. 1 Bore, and began painting in 1986. She lives at Napperby. Her work has been exhibited in several national capitals, the USA and the UK.

DIXON, COLIN TJAPANANGKA

Born in 1954 in Warlpiri country at Mt Doreen station, Colin Dixon spent his early years both on Mt Doreen station and at Yuendumu, receiving some schooling in both places. He and his wife Mary DIXON began painting for Papunya Tula Artists in the mid '80s when the company began making regular trips to Mt Leibig, a settlement about 50 km north-west of Papunya, where the couple had been living for many years.

The artist's country from his father's side lies around Tjanyinki. His principal stories are Women Dreaming, Man Dreaming, Honey Ant Dreaming and Two Young Men. His mother's country is from Pilinyanu, also west of Mt Doreen station and also Warlpiri territory. Colin's works were included in the Stockmen's Hall of Fame, Longreach, Queensland and World Expo '88 in Brisbane. Colin and his wife, Mary Dixon, sell their work through the Centre for Aboriginal Artists in Alice Springs, and a variety of other outlets as far north as Katherine, and still occasionally through Papunya Tula Artists. Colin Dixon's work was included in an exhibition at the Gauguin Museum, Tahiti, in 1988. He also travelled to America in 1988 for the exhibition 'Central Desert Art' which opened the Caz Gallery in Los Angeles. Collections: Art Gallery of South Australia

DIXON, FABIAN JAPANANGKA
A Warlpiri, he lives at Lajamanu, and began painting in 1987. He worked in the health clinic at Lajamanu for about eight years. He was trained as a Nungkayi (Aboriginal healer) — while he worked in the western health system.

DIXON, HARRY JAPANANGKA
An Anmatyerre speaker, Harry Dixon was born in 1951. His heritage country is Mt Allan and Mt Traeger. He paints Honey Ant, Water, Snake and Bush Fire Dreamings for this country. He is married to Lucy DIXON Napurrurla and lives at Mt Allan.

DIXON, IRIS NAPANANGKA
Born at Mt Doreen c.1950–5, her tribe/language is Warlpiri, and her country Janyinki/Mina-mina. Her Dreamings are Mardukuja-mardukuja (Kana), Warna, and Ngalyipi (Bush Medicine Vine). She lives at Lajamanu, and works with her husband Tim KENNEDY. Started painting in 1986.

DIXON, KAREN NUNGARRAYI
Born in 1960, of the Anmatyerre tribe, her country is Mt Allan and she paints Bush Onion Dreaming. She is married to Frank BROWN and lives at Mt Allan.

DIXON, LUCY NAPURRURLA
Also cited as: Lucy Napurrula
Lucy Dixon's tribe is Anmatyerre/Warlpiri, and her country is Willowra. She paints a Yala Dreaming from this area, also Lightning, Women's, Honey Ant and Mt Denison Bush Potato Dreamings. She is married to Harry DIXON and lives at Mt Allan.

DIXON, MARY NUNGARRAYI
Born near Town Bore Creek, east of Papunya in the year the settlement was officially opened — 1960 — Mary Dixon identifies Warlpiri as her language group but nominates the area around Haasts Bluff where she grew up as her country. She moved to Mt Leibig settlement when it was established, closer to Warlpiri country. She and her

husband, Colin DIXON, have four children. The artist Maudie PETERSEN is her sister. Mary started painting in the mid '80s when Papunya Tula Artists began making regular trips to Mt Leibig to service the artists living there. Mary often paints Witchetty Grub Dreaming and a Milky Way Dreaming concerning the origins of Venus, Orion and the Pleieades. Her work was included in exhibitions mounted by the Centre for Aboriginal Artists at the Gauguin Museum, Tahiti in 1988 and at the Chapman Gallery, for which Mary travelled to Canberra. She has been included in a number of publications based primarily on the work of the painters operating through the Centre for Aboriginal Artists. Collections: Art Gallery of South Australia, Holmes à Court, Wollongong City Art Gallery

DIXON, MATALA
Born on 1 July 1948 at Docker River, Matala Dixon is a Pitjantjatjara speaker who lives at Mutitjulu community, Uluru. Her country is the Petermann Ranges, for which she paints Papa (Dog), Tjerla (Honey Ant) and Kuniya (Carpet Python) Dreamings. She is married to Ross Dixon, also a painter. They have two daughters, Monica and Ruth. Matala has been painting since 1983 and sells her work through Maruku Arts and Crafts.

DIXON, MINNIE NAPANANGKA
Born at Willowra c.1940, Minnie Dixon's traditional country is Willowra, for which she paints Goanna, Bush Onion, Bush Tomato, Bush Bean and Bush Potato Dreamings. She lives in Willowra but has connections to the communities in Ti-Tree, Yuendumu and Lajamanu. She began painting in 1985, learning from other artists in her family.

DIXON, TIGER JAPANANGKA
Tiger Dixon was born in 1937 and belongs to the Anmatyerre language group. He is one of the senior men in the Mt Allan community and the brother of FRANK Japanangka, traditional owner of Mt Allan. His country is also Mt Allan, and he paints Bush Banana and Yuelamu Dreamings.

DIXON, VALDA NAPURRURLA-NANGALA
Born at Lajamanu in the mid '50s, she is about thirty-five years of age. For reasons too complex to explain here, Valda (pronounced 'Velda') has two skin names. She is of the Warlpiri tribe/language, and her country Waylilinpa. Her Dreamings are Watiyuwarnu (Trees), and Warlukurlangu (Fire). She started painting in 1987, and lives at Lajamanu.

DON TJUNGARRAYI
Born at Yupurirri, south of Newhaven station c.1939. After the establishment of the combined mission and government settlement at Yuendumu, he attended the mission school at Yuendumu, was initiated near Haasts Bluff and later worked as a stockman and fencing contractor at the nearby stations of Narwietooma, Hamilton Downs and

Napperby before marrying and moving to Papunya, where he had a job in the communal kitchen. He was taught to paint by Paddy CARROLL, whom he knew from his days as a stockman. In the late '70s he was living with Paddy at Three Mile Bore (during John Kean's time of running the Papunya Tula Artists). He has painted steadily since that time and his work is included in many public and private collections. His wife ENTALURA is also an artist, one of the most senior women painting for the Papunya company. They have one son, one daughter and four grandchildren. His sister, Maggie Nungarrayi, is now painting at Mt Allan. The artist describes himself as belonging to the Warlpiri/Luritja tribe or language group. His country from his mother's side lies around Kerrinyarra — Mt Wedge. Don's mother is OLD MICK Tjakamarra's sister. Their country is Winparrku. Old Mick helped to raise Don after his father's death. Don's Dreamings include Rainbow, Barking Spider, Possum, Eagle Hawk, Budgerigar, Wallaby, Witchetty Grub, Carpet Snake and Kangaroo, many of which he holds in common with Paddy Carroll. In 1986 he won the Alice Springs Art Prize. Collections: Holmes à Court, Victorian Arts Centre, Wollongong City Art Gallery

DOOLAN, MONICA NAKAMARRA

Born in Yuendumu in 1956, Monica Nakamarra Doolan is a Warlpiri speaker. She did her first paintings while attending a teachers' training course at Batchelor College in 1989. She paints Warna (Snake), Yawakyi (Bloodberry) and Ngurlu (edible seed used for damper) Dreamings from the country round Mission Creek. She occasionally helps her mother, Liddy Napanangka WALKER, and her maternal aunties with their paintings. Most of her maternal relatives live at Lajamanu and Yuendumu, though Monica herself now lives in Alice Springs. Bertha Nakamarra DICKSON is one of her sisters.

DOONDAY, BILL TJAMPITJIN

Born 'in the bush' in the area near the Stansmore Ranges c.1930, Bill Doonday is a Ngarti speaker. His country is Mangkai (the Stansmore Ranges) and his principal Dreamings belong, like those of most of his Pintupi countrymen further to the east, to the Tingari cycle. He also paints Emu Dreamings. He began painting for Warlayirti Artists in 1989. Bill Doonday's work is typical of the work of the other men working out of the Mulan community near Balgo, WA. It shows more figurative elements than one would find in the work of the Kukatja artists at Balgo itself. There may be traditional reasons for this; the artist does not connect it to European influences. His work is full of references to Men's Law.

DORA NAPALJARRI

Born at Willowra, where she still lives, Dora Napaljarri is a Warlpiri speaker, and her country is Rabbit Bore (Patirlirri). Her main Dreaming is Ngatijirri (Budgerigar).

E

EDIMINJA, EDDIE TJAPANGATI
Also cited as: Eddie Edimintja/Edaminja/Edeminja/Etaminja

Born at Ulpunyali, west of Watakarra (Kings Canyon) in 1916, Eddie's language is Pitjantjatjara. His country is Walu, east of Tjuninyanta. His Dreaming belongs to Tjungku, between Tjuninyanta and Walu, in the Petermann Ranges area. Eddie now lives in the Kaltukatjara community, Docker River. His father's country is Patanu, west of Walu. Eddie used to work on Middleton Downs station, and on Middleton Ponds for Bob Buck, who was 'like a father' to him. He also worked on Wallahra Ranch for Bob Liddle when he was a boy, and as a stockman on Orange Creek station. He was a stockman at Haasts Bluff and helped take a mob of horses from Maryvale to Haasts Bluff. Eddie first started painting at Papunya in the mid '70s after he stopped working on stations. An associate of LIMPI Tjapangati, with whom he lived at Haasts Bluff during the mid '80s. During this period his work shows the influence of Limpi's style. For a time in the late '80s he lived at Tjukula, between Docker River and Kintore. He also knows Mick NAMARARI (Ngamarari) Tjapaltjarri, who paints the Dreaming of the place called Manpi. Eddie paints The Two Women Dreaming and the Three Men Lying Behind Windbreaks. He knows many other artists, too many to tell. Because of failing eyesight, his two sons Rex and Donald Eddie help him with the painting now. His paintings have been exhibited and bought in Adelaide and Alice Springs. Collections: Museums & Art Galleries of NT, SA Museum

EGALIE, CHARLIE TJAPALTJARRI

Born at Pikilyi (Vaughan Springs), north-west of Mt Leibig around Waite Creek c.1940, Charlie's language/tribe is Warlpiri/Luritja. He received some basic European schooling at the mission school in Yuendumu, and was initiated near Haasts Bluff. He worked as a stockman for seven years on the station at Haasts Bluff and later in Queensland. After marrying his wife, Nora Nakamarra, he worked on Narwietooma station for another seven years. Charlie and his wife came to Papunya in the very early days of the settlement — when there were only a couple of houses built. They have two sons and two daughters, of whom Natalie CORBY has been painting since the early '80s under her father's instruction. Charlie Egalie now lives with his family at Mt Leibig, where his mother and father have settled closer to their country round Kunajarrayi. Though he is represented in Geoffrey Bardon's book on the beginnings of the art movement, Charlie himself dated his painting from Peter Fannin's time running Papunya Tula Artists — about 1972. Billy STOCKMAN, KAAPA Tjampitjinpa and Johnny WARANGKULA guided him in the beginning. His paintings depict Woman, Sugar Ant, Budgerigar, Wallaby, Bushfire and Man Dreamings at sites across this region.

Paddy Japaljarri SIMS, one of the leading Yuendumu artists, is a close relative of Charlie's. Nora Egalie Nakamarra has occasionally painted stories of her country at Kunajarrayi since her husband showed her how to paint in 1989. Charlie Egalie's painting of Budgerigar Dreaming was used for the front cover of Nadine Amadio's *Wildbird Dreaming*. The artist travelled to Sydney for the book launching and also represented Papunya Tula Artists at the opening of the National Gallery of Victoria's 'Face of the Centre' show in 1985. Collections: Holmes à Court, Art Gallery of WA, National Museum of Australia, Canberra, University of WA Anthropology Museum, SA Museum, Peter Stuyvesant etc. Reference: Amadio & Kimber, *Wildbird Dreaming* (Greenhouse Publications, 1988)

EGAN, BETTY

A Wadjarri speaker originally from Yullalong Station in WA, Betty Egan's traditional country lies around the Murchison River. Now in her thirties (born c.1955), she lives and studies in Alice Springs. Her painting was highly commended in the 1989 NT Art Award, one of Jukurrpa's early successes which helped to consolidate the group. She has sold works to Oroton to be made into silk scarves, and her painting *Murchison River Dreaming* was acquired by the National Gallery of Australia from the '89 Jukurrpa exhibition at the Araluen Arts Centre.

EGAN, JEANNIE NUNGARRAYI

Born in 1948 and a Warlpiri speaker, Jeannie Egan is one of the younger women painters at Yuendumu who joined the group of senior women painting at Yuendumu in 1987. She rapidly emerged with a distinctive style of strong narrative elements, boldly outlined in basic earth colours. In September 1987, only a month after she first exhibited with Warlukurlangu Artists at the Reconnaissance Gallery in Melbourne, she won the National Aboriginal Art Award and the Rothman's Foundation Award for the best artwork in introduced media. Since then, her work has been included in many exhibitions of Warlukurlangu Artists in capital cities around Australia. Her Dreamings are Wanakiji (Bush Plum), Yarumayi (White Ochre), Miinypa (Native Fuschia) and Parlukurlangu (Giant). Her 1987 painting of the Goanna Dreaming at the site of Yarumayi was included in 'Images of Religion in Australian Art' in 1988–9 and in 'Mythscapes' in September 1989, both at the National Gallery of Victoria. Her work is also reproduced in *Contemporary Aboriginal Art: from the Robert Holmes à Court Collection*, (ed. A. Brody (Heytesbury Holdings, Perth, 1990). She has completed a major trilogy setting out the entire Milky Way Dreaming narrative. She also worked on a 7 x 3 m canvas by 42 of Yuendumu's artists commissioned by Prof. H. Antes of Berlin, which formed part of the 1993 touring exhibition 'Aratjara — Australian Aboriginal Art'. Collections: National Gallery of Australia, Canberra, National Gallery of Victoria, Art Gallery of New South Wales, Art Galleries & Museums of Northern Territory, Akademie Der Kunst, Berlin, Christensen Fund, Holmes à Court, Musée des Arts Africains et Oceaniens, Paris, many private collections in Australia and overseas

EGAN, MATTHEW JAMPIJIMPA

Born at Ngapa, Matthew Egan is a Warlpiri speaker who lives at Yuendumu and paints for Warlukurlangu Artists. His Dreamings include Warlukurlangu (Fire) and Ngapa (Water). His work was shown in exhibitions of Warlukurlangu Artists in Melbourne and the Gold Coast in 1992.

EGAN, REBECCA NAMPIJINPA

Born on 1 August 1962 at Watiyakurlangu, south of Yuendumu, Rebecca is a Warlpiri/ English speaker and grew up at Yuendumu. Her Dreamings are Pama (Sandflies), Ngapa (Water), Warlukurlangu (Fire), Watiya Kurlangu (Mulga Tree) and Yankirri (Emu). She moved to Adelaide in 1986 and began painting in 1987, driven by home-sickness for the country she had left behind. She sent messages to her family to find out her Dreamings so she could paint them and ease the pain of separation. She paints from her childhood memories of the women painting their bodies and dancing boards for ceremonies. She sold her work through galleries in Adelaide. She also visited schools in Adelaide showing her paintings and talking about her Dreamings. In 1991 she returned to Yuendumu to obtain the approval of senior Nampijinpas/family members at Yuendumu for her paintings. She later won the Kings Canyon Frontier Lodge NT Art Competition and waas resident artist at the Corkwood Gallery.

EGAN, TED JANGALA

A Warlpiri speaker, Teg Jangala Egan lives in Yuendumu. His Dreamings include Warlukurlangu (Fire) and Ngapa (Water). His work has been shown in exhibitions of Warlukurlangu Artists in Melbourne and Sydney since 1990. Collections: Museum of South Australia

EILEEN NAPANANGKA

Born at Umbungurru near Papunya in 1957, Eileen is a Luritja speaker, whose traditional country is Jay Creek, near Hermannsburg. She paints Emu, Bush Onion and Rainbow Dreamings and has been painting since 1986 under the watchful eye of her mother-in-law, Kitty PULTARA, at Napperby, where she now lives.

ELMA NAPANANGKA
Also cited as: Elma Napanungka

Born in 1950 of the Anmatyerre tribe, Elma's heritage country is Nharliyikurlangu and she paints Water and Emu Dreamings. She is married to Andrew COLLINS and lives at Mt Allan.

EMILY KAME KNGWARREYE

Born c.1910 at Alhalkere (Soakage Bore) Utopia Station, Emily is an Eastern Anmatyerre speaker and senior artist at Utopia. Her country is Alhalkere and her Dreamings include Sand Goanna, Wild Orange, and Emu. Emily first saw white people as a young girl aged about nine. She worked in her younger days as a stockhand on pastoral properties in this area (see *The Art of Utopia*, M. Boulter) at a time when Aboriginal women on the stations were usually only employed as domestics — suggesting the forceful independence of her personality. Emily was the adopted daughter of Jacob Jones, a very important lawman in the Alyawarre community, and is a leader in the women's ceremonial business at Utopia. From the time she painted her first canvas for 'A Summer Project 1988–9', the work of Emily Kame Kngwarreye has received widespread acclaim and recognition. Emily found in acrylics and canvas a medium more suited to the bold immediacy of her style than the more laborious production processes of batik, in which she had been working for the preceding decade and exhibiting with the Utopia women in exhibitions in Australia and abroad since 1977. Her technique is highly individual with under-drawings covered by layers of dots. Her pleasure in working as an artist is reflected in her powerful colours and her energetic and expressive compositions. In 1990 Emily's work was shown in two highly successful solo shows in Sydney, as well as the Art Gallery of NSW's 'Abstraction' show. Later that year she participated in the CAAMA/Utopia artists-in-residence program at the ICA, Perth. (Reference: Batty, P. & Sheridan, N., *Utopia Artist in Residence Project* [Holmes à Court Foundation, Perth, 1990]). Several more solo shows have followed: Gallery Gabrielle Pizzi, Melbourne (1990, 1991) and Utopia Art, Sydney (1991, 1992). Her work was rapidly acquired by major public and private collections in Australia and overseas and is keenly sought after by other buyers. In three years, she has been represented in 48 group exhibitions around Australia and the world, including Ireland — 'A Picture Story', Royal Hibernian Gallery, Dublin; Russia — 'Aboriginal Paintings from the Desert', Union Gallery, Moscow, 1991 and touring St Petersburg, Ukraine, Minsk Byelorussia, Riga Latvia; USA — 'Contemporary Aboriginal Art', Harvard University and touring USA and Australia; Japan — 'Aboriginal Art from Australia', National Museum of Modern Art, Tokyo, 1992 and 'Crossroads Toward a New Reality', National Museum of Modern Art, Kyoto and Tokyo etc. She is the most lauded painter of the Utopia art movement to date, and one of the best known of the desert artists, painting with an undiminished energy which belies her years. In 1992 she was awarded an Australian Artists Creative Fellowship. In 1993 she exhibited in the Joan and Peter Clemenger Triennial Exhibition of Contemporary Australian Art at the National Gallery of Victoria and featured in 'Aratjara — Australian Aboriginal and Torres Strait Islander Art' touring Dusseldorf, London and other European Galleries. Collections: Holmes à Court, National Gallery of Australia, Canberra, Art Gallery of New South Wales, Art Gallery of Western Australia, National Gallery of Victoria, Queensland Art Gallery, Benalla Regional Art Gallery, Araluen Arts Centre, Alice Springs, Auckland City Art Gallery, New Zealand, Artbank, Carnegie, ATSIC etc.

EMILY NAPALJARRI, see ANDY, Emily Napaljarri

ENTALURA NANGALA

Born at Alumburra, a spring just south-west of Papunya c.1929, Entalura was among the people moved across to Papunya from the settlement at Haasts Bluff at the beginning of the '60s. She began painting in the early '80s during Andrew Crocker's time of running Papunya Tula Artists, having gained her early experience of the medium of paint on canvas through working on the backgrounds of her husband DON Tjungarrayi's paintings. A Warlpiri speaker, Entalura lives at Papunya with her husband and until recently her daughters, Ada and Nora ANDY Napaljarri, both of whom also paint. Entalura's paintings depict Bush Fire, Bush Onion, Honey Ant, Water, Black Plum and Two Women Dreamings from the Papunya area. Collections: National Gallery of Australia, Canberra

EUBENA NAMPITJIN

A senior woman of the Mulan/Balgo communities, Eubena was born 'in the bush' about 1930 or earlier, in the area near Well 33 on the Canning Stock Route. Eubena paints Tingari stories for the lands around the Northern Canning Stock Route, including the Nyilla Rockhole, north of Jupiter Well, where the artist spent much of her youth. These include the Kangaroo Dreamings of Warntartarri and Wuntaru/Yintarnyu. She began painting in 1986. She usually works with her husband, WIMMITJI Tjapangati, and as such their works are often extremely similar. Her daughter, Emma GIMME, sometimes assisted on her mother's canvases. Eubena's canvases exhibit a strong sense of country and have a sense of timeless tradition and are full of mythological associations. Collections: Holmes à Court, National Gallery of Victoria

EUNICE NAPANGARDI

Born at Yuendumu in the early '50s, Eunice is Luritja/Warlpiri, and is the sister of PANSY and Alice Napangardi and Rene ROBINSON Napangardi, with whom she shares many of the Dreamings they paint. One of the first women painters: to judge from stylistic similarities, she worked on her 'old bush husband' KAAPA Tjampitjinpa's 'town paintings' for several years in the early '80s, emerging in the late '80s as an artist in her own right and one of the Centre for Aboriginal Artists' leading painters. Her work is included in the Stockmen's Hall of Fame and she was one of three women selected for a special furniture painting project for the Bicentennial Travelling Exhibition. Her work also featured in the 'Tjukurrpa' Exhibition at the Blaxland Gallery c.1989. In 1991 she exhibited again at the Aboriginal Arts Australia Gallery in Sydney with MAXIE Tjampitjinpa, travelling to Sydney for the opening. She has also completed two major commissions: for the new Alice Springs airport, which opened in December 1991, and for a travelling exhibition that started in Washington in 1992. She also exhibited in Brisbane with Pansy Napangati in a two women show. Collections: Wollongong City Art Gallery, Federal Airports Corporation, Richard Kelton etc.

EVANS, KITTY NAKAMARRA

Born at Mt Allan in 1951, Kitty's Dreamings are Yowagi (a small bird), Witchetty Grub, Bush Potato and Bush Bean. These Dreamings were all given to her by her mother. She also paints a Men's Initiation given to her by her father, now deceased. She began painting for Corkwood Gallery in 1988. Some of her activities are at the 'tourist end' of the market: e.g. 12 months painting in the foyer of the Sheraton Hotel for six nights a week; painting a 'Bush Tucker Dreaming' on a car belonging to a German travel agent. During the tourist season she and her young son do traditional dancing for one of the tours. However, she is also represented in the Art Gallery of South Australia and has twice shown in the annual 'Women of the Western Desert' exhibitions in Perth, and has sold her work to overseas collectors. She lives in Alice Springs with her son and husband.

F

FENCER, ANDY JAPANANGKA

Details of Andy Fencer's birth are sketchy, but he is a very old man, perhaps over seventy years of age. He is of the Warlpiri language and tribe and his country is Yarungkanyi, out near Perunta, an outstation of Lajamanu. He lives at Lajamanu, and started painting in 1986.

FLEMING, ROSIE NANGALA

A senior woman in the Yuendumu community, and founder of the Warlpiri Women's Museum at Yuendumu in the '70s. Now in her sixties, she is senior custodian of a Bird Dreaming which she often depicts in her paintings, as well as Water and Butterfly Dreamings. She is a close friend of Peggy POULSON, and the two often paint together. She had been doing carving and other kinds of crafts (e.g. seed necklaces and mats) for many years, selling through the Centre for Aboriginal Artists in Alice Springs, but when the opportunity arose in 1988, she began painting seriously. Her work was shown in the Centre's exhibition at the Blaxland Galleries in the same year, and she has since painted a major commission for Telecom. She travels back and forth between Alice Springs and Yuendumu, living in both places.

FORREST, BETTY NAPANANGKA

Born at Mt Coniston in about 1947, Betty Forrest is Anmatyerre/Warlpiri. Her country is Redbank and she paints Goanna, Bush Beans and Bush Plum Dreamings. She lives at Willowra and has been painting since 1989. She is married to occasional painter Teddy Long and related to other artists in the Willowra community.

FORRESTER, JANET NALA

Born c.1954, Janet Forrester is a Luritja speaker, who began painting in the late '80s with the Jukurrpa group, based at IAD, Alice Springs. Her work was included in a major exhibition of the Jukurrpa artists at Araluen Arts Centre in 1989, and in several subsequent Jukurrpa shows, though in the past few years, she has mainly sold her work through galleries in Alice Springs. She has connections to the community at Ernabella, but mostly lives in Alice Springs. Collections: National Gallery of Australia, Canberra

FRANK, CAROL NAPANGARDI

Born in 1965, Carol Frank is an Anmatyerre speaker. Her father, FRANK Japanangka, is one of the most senior men in the Mt Allan community. Her heritage country is Yuelamu and she paints Honey Ant and Witchetty Grub Dreamings for this area. She lives at Mt Allan and is married to Desmond TILMOUTH, who also paints.

FRANK JAPANANGKA

Born 'in the bush' near Yuelamu in the 1920s, Frank (or Franky) Japanangka is keeper of the Yuelamu site and a leading figure in the Mt Allan community. He worked as a stockman in earlier years. An Anmatyerre speaker, his country is Yuelamu and he paints Honey Ant and Witchetty Dreamings for that country. He does not paint a great deal, but said of the Mt Allan Museum and Art Gallery, 'Since we thought of this place — so they never sell this country — long time I been painting.' His daughters, Carol FRANK and Peggy BROWN, and several of his nieces whom he raised are also painters. In recent years, he has withdrawn from community politics to reside mainly on the outstation at Yulyipinyu, close to the western boundary of Mt Allan and adjacent to Japanangka/Japangardi Honey Ant Dreaming country.

FRED TJAKAMARRA

Born near Lappi Lappi (Hidden Basin), Western Australia, c.1925, Fred Tjakamarra is a Kukatja speaker. His country is Ngapakulangu, near Hidden Basin. He is one of a number of Tjakamarra men in Balgo community responsible for important Water Dreaming sites and associated rain ceremonies in this remote region. A senior man, he took to painting only in 1990, but has produced a large body of work for Warlayirti Artists in a short time. He paints Water Dreamings, his works always presenting a strong visual image and communicating also something of the artist's knowledge and authority in the community.

G

GALLAGHER, CAROL NAPANGARDI

Born c.1935 at Larlkapura, north of Yuendumu in Mudbra country. She is Mubra/Warlpiri and is responsible for a Women Dreaming and a Lukarrara (Seed) Dreaming. Carol has been painting for Warlukurlangu Artists since 1986 and has been included in many of their group exhibitions.

GALLAGHER, CHARLES JAMPIJINPA

Born at Nyirrpi in the 1920s, Charles Gallagher is a Warlpiri speaker who paints Emu, Butterfly and Women's Dreamings for his country around Nyirrpi. He lives in Nyirrpi and is married to Pauline GALLAGHER. He has been painting since the late '80s, and he did two of the paintings on the Nyirrpi school walls in 1989.

GALLAGHER, CORAL NAPANGARDI

Born c.1933, Coral Napangardi is a Warlpiri speaker. She lives with her husband, Jack Jampijinpa GALLAGHER, at Walilinypa, an outstation of Yuendumu. She paints Kanta (Bloodwood Gall or Bush Coconut) and Wardapi (Goanna) Dreamings and collaborates with her husband on Yankirri (Emu), Ngapa (Water) and the Warlu (Fire) for which she is kurdungurlu (manager) through marriage and her life experience. One of their early collaborative works, *Warlukurlangu Jukurrpa*, 1986, was purchased by the National Gallery of Australia. Coral has been painting since the mid '80s and has shown with Warlukurlangu Artists in Perth, Melbourne, Adelaide, Canberra, Sydney, Seattle, USA and Portsmouth, UK as well as in the 'Karnta' (Women) exhibitions in 1987 in Darwin, Adelaide, Sydney and Fremantle, and in the recent 'Flash Paintings' exhibition at the National Gallery of Australia in December 1991. She was one of 42 Yuendumu artists who worked on a 7 x 3 m canvas now touring Europe as part of the 1993 'Aratjara — Australian Aboriginal Art' exhibition. Collections: National Gallery of Australia, Canberra, Museum of South Australia, Christensen Fund, private collections

GALLAGHER, JACK JAMPIJINPA

Born c.1920 in the vicinity of Warlukurlangu, where his father was also born. He is Warlpiri and lives at Walilinypa, an outstation of Yuendumu, with his wife, Carol GALLAGHER. Walilinypa is in the area of Warlukurlangu, also associated with the Fire Dreaming which he paints, often in collaboration with his wife. Their *Warlukurlangu Jukurrpa* 1986 is in the National Gallery of Australia collection. He began painting for Warlukurlangu Artists in the mid '80s.

GALLAGHER, PAULINE NAPANGARDI

Born c.1950 at Yuendumu, Pauline Gallagher is a Warlpiri speaker. Her country is Yuendumu, and she paints Honey Ant Dreaming for this place. She lives at Nyirrpi, and is married to Charles GALLAGHER. She has connections with the Aboriginal communities of Yuendumu, Kintore, and those in Alice Springs. She did a painting on the Nyirrpi school wall in 1989 and probably began painting in the late '80s.

GEORGE TJANGALA (c.1925–1989)
Also cited as: George Jangala, George Tjangala Maxwell

Born c.1925 at a traditional 'borning place' called Lingakurra, a lake site in sandhill country to the south-west of Kintore past Docker River. In addition to Lingakurra, the artist also has rights in the country around Mitukutjarrayi and Marnpi — also in Pintupi territory. His family travelled eastwards from these regions, regularly walking in to collect rations from Haasts Bluff and later doing some work cutting timber and building stockyards for the cattle station established at Haasts Bluff. George also did some stockwork at Haasts Bluff before coming in to stay at the new settlement of Papunya in the '70s. However, it was not till Janet Wilson and Dick Kimber's time of running the Papunya Tula Artists company in about 1976 that George started painting, instructed by Turkey TOLSON, with whom he was living at the time at Brown's Bore outstation, south-west of Papunya. He moved out to Kintore in the early days of that settlement. He had an outstation at Ngutjulnga, just beyond the Woman Dreaming mountain which lies alongside Kintore. His paintings depict Hare Wallaby, Acacia Seed, Fire Shield-maker, Water, Bush Tucker including Mungilpa, the little grass seed used to make damper, Tumble Weed and Goanna Dreamings and Tingari Dreamings from around the region of Lingakurra. His work was shown in the Asia Society's Dreamings exhibition. A kind and gentle man, well-liked by everyone, he died in 1989. Collections: Art Gallery of South Australia, University of Western Australia Anthropology Museum, Museums & Art Galleries of NT etc.

GEORGE TJAPALTJARRI ('DR GEORGE')

Born south-west of Jupiter Well, his language group is Pintupi. He came out of the desert with his family in 1964. An Aboriginal doctor, he is attached to Kintore Clinic (hence 'Dr George'). His traditional country includes Karrinwara, west of Kintore, and Kilingya in Wenampa territory west of Jupiter Well. He paints for Papunya Tula Artists. Collections: National Gallery of Victoria, Museums & Art Galleries of NT

GEORGE TJAPALTJARRI ('JAMPU')

Born 'in the bush' around Walla Walla near Kiwirrkura, WA, c.1950. The family was brought in to Papunya with other Pintupi tribesmen by the NT Welfare Branch patrols in the late '60s. Soon afterwards his entire family were killed, and Jampu spent time at Balgo and Yuendumu before moving to Kintore soon after the establishment of the settlement there in the early '80s, and taking up a position as a community health worker. He now lives at Kiwirrkura, working for the health service there. He began painting for Papunya Tula Artists at Kintore about 1983 after watching the other artists at work and continued painting in Kiwirrkura. His country lies around Winparrku to the north of Kiwirrkura. His paintings depict Tingari stories from this area.

GEORGE TJAPANANGKA ('YUENDUMU GEORGE')
Born c.1938, George Tjapanangka spent his childhood in the area of Yurrituppa before his family had contact with Europeans. He has country at Marpurri, a soakage water close to the southern shore of Wilkinkarra. A Pintupi speaker, George began painting for Papunya Tula Artists in the late '80s and now lives at Kintore.

GEORGE TJUNGARRAYI
Also cited as: Tjungurrayi, Jungarai
Born 'in the bush' in Pintupi country across the WA border c.1947. He began painting in West Camp in Papunya about 1976 for Papunya Tula Artists, the same time as his older brother WILLY Tjungarrayi, and continued painting while residing at Yai Yai, Warawa, Mt Leibig and now Kintore. His ancestral country covers the sites around Wala Wala, Kiwirrkura, Lake Mackay, Kulkuta, Karku, Ngaluwinyamana, and Kilpinya to the north-west of Kintore across the WA border. He paints the Tingari stories for this region. Collections: Holmes à Court

GEORGINA NAPANGARDI
A Warlpiri speaker, her country is Mt Theo (Purturlu), and she lives at the Willowra community.

GIBBS, YALA YALA TJUNGARRAYI, see YALA YALA Tjungarrayi

GIBSON, BARBARA NAKAMARRA
Born at Yarturlu-yarturlu in 1938, her tribe/language is Warlpiri. Her country is Yarturlu-yarturlu (the Granites) and her Dreamings are Yawakiyi, Ngurlu, and Janganpa. She started painting in 1986 in the Traditional Painting course at Lajamanu. She lives at Lajamanu, where she has worked as a teaching assistant at Lajamanu School. She was the main informant for Barbara Glowczewski's book *Les Reveurs Du Desert*, where — under another name — she talks about her paintings.

GIBSON, BERYL NAKAMARRA
Born at Yarturlu-yarturlu c.1955, her tribe/language is Warlpiri and her country Yarturlu-yarturlu (the Granites). Her Dreamings are Yawakiyi, Ngurlu, and Janganpa. She started painting in 1986, and lives at Lajamanu, having worked as an assistant teacher at Lajamanu school in the late '80s.

GIBSON, KENNY TJAKAMARRA

One of the younger artists living at Balgo, Kenny Gibson was born in Yuendumu about 1959. A Warlpiri speaker, his country is near Jupiter Well, and his principal Dreaming is Wanayarra (the Rainbow Serpent). He began painting in 1986, and his work demonstrates a high level of talent and imagination. He has a neat, careful technique, and yet was one of the innovators in the early days of painting in the Balgo community. His works achieve a real sense of movement. He sells his paintings through Warlayirti Artists. Collections: Art Gallery of WA, the National Gallery of Victoria

GIBSON, NANCY NAPANANGKA

Born in the late '20s or early '30s at Lapi-Lapi (Lake Mackay), she is Warlpiri/Pintupi and paints her father's Dreamings, Kanakulangu and Ngalyipi (Snake Vine). Nancy started painting approximately 1988/9 and first sold her paintings through Warlukurlangu Artists at Yuendumu. Since the local store at Nyirrpi, where Nancy lives, stocks canvas and paint to supply local artists, Nancy sells her paintings through the store. Her children and daughter-in-law are also painters. She has family connections with the communities at Kintore, Balgo and Kiwirrkura.

GIBSON, PADDY JAPALJARRI

Born at Watijarra c.1927 and lives at Lajamanu. Paddy is a very old and dignified gentleman. His brother was Tony Japaljarri Gibson, who died in the late '80s. His language/tribe is Warlpiri, and his country Jarripiji (near the Granites), Purrkiji, and Yapakurlangu. His Dreamings are Jangunypa (Bush Louse), Pijarrpajarrpa (Marsupial Mole) and Mala. Paddy Gibson's work is much sought after by the market and he is recognised within the community as one of Lajamanu's leading painters. Collections: National Gallery of Victoria

GIBSON, SISTER NAKAMARRA

Born at Yumurrpa c.1936, her language/tribe is Warlpiri, her country is Yumurrpa, and her Dreamings are Yarla and Wapurti. She started painting in 1986 in the Traditional Painting course at Lajamanu, where she lives. Married to Paddy GIBSON Japaljarri, she is a very tall, imposing woman, who at one time worked for the hospital in Lajamanu — hence the name 'sister'. Collections: National Gallery of Victoria

GIDEON TJUPURRULA
Also cited as: Gideon Tjiparulla Jack

Born in the late '20s in the Gibson Desert at Pinarri, west of Kintore in the vicinity of Lake Mackay. He is Pintupi/Pitjantjatjara, and his Dreamings are Women, Rockhole, Mitukutjarrayi (Yuwalki) and Lake Mackay. He first saw Europeans at Ilpilli in about 1930. The family later moved eastwards to the fringes of European settlement, settling at Haasts Bluff in the late '40s. Gideon received some education in the Hermannsburg schoolroom, leaving to be initiated in the Glen Helen area and work as a stockman on

Glen Helen station. He began painting for Papunya Tula Artists at Haasts Bluff in about 1976, learning by watching other artists, especially Billy STOCKMAN and Tim LEURA. Gideon is one of a group of Eastern Pintupi artists who remained at Haasts Bluff after the move to Papunya at the beginning of the '60s. The group also included LIMPI Tjapangati, Old MICKININIE, Timmy JUGADAI (who initially taught Gideon about painting in acrylics), Eddie EDIMINJA and LIONEL Kantawara. Gideon is the only one of this group still painting in Haasts Bluff, where a new painting enterprise focused on the Women's Centre has emerged in the '90s, in which Gideon's wife, Eunice Napanangka JACK, is a leading figure. Collections: Holmes à Court, National Gallery of Victoria and Wollongong City Art Gallery, many public and private collections

GILL, MATTHEW TJUPURRULA

Matthew Gill's work has received much attention from non-Aboriginal people, in part because of his fascination, to a far greater degree than anyone else in the Balgo community, with non-traditional designs and techniques. He has, for example, combined the X-ray technique of Arnhem Land with his own desert motifs. Born at the old Balgo Mission in about 1960, he began painting in 1982. He usually paints Snake, Emu and Water Dreaming stories from the area surrounding Lake Lazlett. A Kukatja speaker, he lives either at Balgo or in the Nyirrpi community. He is the son of Mick GILL. In 1989 the artist spent three months living and painting in Japan. Former Warlayirti Artists coordinator Michael Rae described Matthew Gill as 'the most original and talented of all the younger artists at Balgo'. Collections: Holmes à Court, Donald Kahn Collection

GILL, MICK TJAKAMARRA

Born 'in the bush', probably around Lake Wills and Lake Hazlett c.1920, Mick Gill is one of several senior Tjakamarra men in the Balgo community who all come from the country surrounding Lappi Lappi or Hidden Basin (others include Alan WINDEROO and Albert NAGOMARA). The artist's country is Liltjin, south-east of Balgo. These men and their wives are all Kukatja speakers who live and sometimes work together. Mick Gill, who usually paints Water Dreaming stories for this site, started painting in 1985. His paintings are sold through Warlayirti Artists. His work is marked by the sense of controlled energy that he gets from his close, swirling lines. He talks of areas of country being the 'same' as parts of the body and his work conveys something of this feel. He is married to Susie BOOTJA BOOTJA. Collections: Art Gallery of Western Australia, National Gallery of Victoria

GIMME, ENA NUNGURRAYAI (c.1953–1992)
Also cited as: Ena Gimme Nungarrayi

Born 'in the bush' near the Canning Stock Route c.1953, Ena Gimme was a member of the Mulan community and a Kukatja speaker. She spent her early years in the area around Kinyu, north of the Canning Stock Route. Her traditional country was Kalliyangku, near the Canning Stock Route, and her main Dreamings are Tingari stories. The artist's work shared more in common with that of older Warlayirti painters than it did with that of her peers. Perhaps this shows the influence of her mother, EUBENA Nampitjin, on whose paintings she sometimes assisted. Ena Gimme began painting for Warlayirti Artists in 1989. She used layers of different coloured dotting to create 'rough' but dramatic works, often with a 'floral' look. Collections: National Gallery of Victoria

GINGER TJAKAMARRA

Born 'in the bush' in the mid '40s, Ginger began painting for Papunya Tula Artists in the early '80s. His country lies in Pintupi territory south-west of Kintore towards Kulkuta. He currently resides at New Bore outstation, west of Papunya. Collections: Holmes à Court, National Gallery of Victoria

GLADYS NAPANANGKA
Also cited as: Gladys Warangkula Napanangka

Born in a creek bed near Haasts Bluff c.1920, Gladys grew up in the bush around the Haasts Bluff area and was christened by the missionaries at Haasts Bluff. Her parents came from Warlpiri country north of Mt Wedge, but Gladys speaks and identifies as Luritja because of her affiliations with the Haasts Bluff community. Her first husband was OLD WALTER Tjampitjinpa, the former police tracker who, with UTA UTA Tjangala and OLD MICK Tjakamarra, oversaw the painting of the original mural on the Papunya school wall. After Old Walter's death in 1981, she married another member of the original group of painting men, Johnny WARANGKULA. Johnny's failing eyesight meant that Gladys often assisted him on the backgrounds of his paintings, employing the overdotting techniques for which his work is renowned. Gladys also paints in her own right; her work is represented in the Art Gallery of South Australia, and was included in World Expo '88. She paints Witchetty Grub and other Bush Tucker stories from her father and mother's country. She lives in Papunya, where she is one of the senior women of the community.

GLORIA PETYARRE
Also cited as: Gloria Tamerre Petyarre

Born c.1945, and an Anmatyerre speaker, her country is Atnangkere and her Dreamings are as for Ada Bird: Mountain Devil Lizard, Bean, Emu, Pencil Yam, Grass Seed and Small Brown Grass. She has four sisters who are also artists: Ada BIRD, Violet, Myrtle and Kathleen. She first gained recognition as an artist working in the medium of batik, exhibiting with the Utopia women in shows around Australia and abroad for a decade (1977–87) before taking up the medium of canvas, painting her first work for CAAMA's Summer Project exhibition. In 1990 she travelled to Ireland, London and India as a representative of the Utopia women, accompanying the 'Utopia: A Picture Story' exhibition (Tandanya, Adelaide, The Royal Hibernian Academy, Dublin Ireland, and Meat Market Gallery, Melbourne, 1991). In 1991 she had her first solo exhibition at Utopia Art in Sydney. Her work is based on the body paint designs for her Dreamings, at first showing clearly the designs painted across the women's breasts and shoulders in the ceremony. Since those early highly distinctive works, she has developed her painting to higher levels of abstraction, continually experimenting with line and colour. She says she prefers the greater freedom and control she finds with the medium of acrylic on canvas. Several of the works in her solo exhibition had no dots at all, but bands of brilliant colour whose optical effects have evoked comparisons with the British artist Bridget Riley. Gloria's husband, Ronnie Price Mpetyane, started painting in 1989 and does strong men's paintings in the dot style, as well as neo-western landscapes in vivid colours. They live at Mulga Bore (Akaye Soakage). Gloria's work features on the cover of *The Art of Utopia* (Michael Boulter), and has been included in major survey exhibitions including 'Flash Painting' at the National Gallery of Australia in 1992, the 1991 Art Gallery of New South Wales touring 'Aboriginal Women's Exhibition', and solo exhibitions in 1991 at Australian Galleries, New York and Utopia Art, Sydney. Collections: National Gallery of Australia, Canberra, Allen Allen and Hemsley, Museum of Victoria, Museums & Art Galleries of NT, Powerhouse Museum, Sydney, Westpac, New York, Gold Coast City Art Gallery, Holmes à Court, etc

GOODWIN TJAPALTJARRI
Also cited as: Goodwin Kingsley Tjapaltjarri

Born at Haasts Bluff in 1950, Goodwin spent his boyhood 'in the bush', walking around the Haasts Bluff area. The family came in to Papunya when the settlement was established in 1960 and Goodwin attended school there briefly. During the '70s he worked as a stockman at Haasts Bluff, Hermannsburg, Vaughan Springs, and Orange Spring near Jay Creek. Goodwin is close family to Old Mick NAMARARI, whose involvement with the painting movement from its beginnings must have been observed by Goodwin during his visits to Papunya during this period. In the early '80s he began to paint for Papunya Tula Artists, with instruction from Charlie EGALIE on the use of paint on canvas and Turkey TOLSON on the Dreaming stories which he was entitled to paint. Goodwin's traditional country is in Pintupi territory around Nyuuman, south-east of Kintore, where Old Mick Namarari has his outstation. He paints Dingo and Rock Wallaby stories from this area. Collections: Holmes à Court

GORDON, JULIE NAPURRURLA

Born at Yuendumu in 1971, Julie Gordon is a Warlpiri speaker. Her country is Mission Creek and she paints Snake, Witchetty Grub and Janganpa (Possum) Dreamings. She lives at Yuendumu and has connections with the Willowra community, but has worked with the Jukurrpa artists' organisation in Alice Springs. Artist's statement: 'I was watching my family doing painting at Yuendumu and Willowra. I started painting at Mt Barkly and at Willowra. My mother taught me to paint from my grandfather and grandmother.'

GORDON, PALMER TJAPANANGKA

Born on Gordon Downs station c.1942, Palmer Gordon is a member of the Tjaru language group, and resides in Billiluna. His country lies near Lewis Creek and he often paints Muntun (Rainbow Snake) Dreaming stories. He began painting for Warlayirti Artists in 1987. While Balgo works are predominantly bold and stark, Palmer Gordon's canvases exhibit a hazy, suggestive look that may require several viewings to be appreciated. His dotting is light and spare and the design is convoluted and complex. His works have an 'organic' look that is probably an accurate reflection of the country they portray.

GORDON DOWNS, JOHNNY TJANGALA

Born c.1940 near Gordon Downs station, Johnny Gordon Downs is a Tjaru speaker whose traditional country is Mimintilli, near the Stansmore Ranges. His principal Dreamings are Tingari and Water. He lives in Balgo and began painting for Warlayirti Artists in 1989. This artist, more than any other at Balgo, has stripped down his imagery to its simplest elements and allows the background of rows of dots to predominate. This often creates an 'optical' effect, but more significantly communicates something of the overwhelming feeling of the country, with its rows of spinifex-covered sandhills. His art can generate a sense of the power of the land.

GOREY, DADU NUNGARRAYI

A Warlpiri speaker, Dadu Nungarrayi Gorey lives at Yuendumu and has been painting for Warlukurlangu Artists since 1990, when her work was shown at the Darwin Performing Arts Centre. It has since appeared in the company's exhibitions in Perth, Melbourne, Hobart and the Gold Coast. Dadu Gorey paints her Wardapi (Goanna), Warlawurru (Eagle) and Marlu (Kangaroo) Dreamings.

GOREY, DAISY NAPANANGKA

Born at Lily Creek on 1 March 1933, Daisy is a Luritja speaker, and her country is Kulgara. She paints her mother's Snake Dreaming, her father's Seven Sisters Dreaming and her own Perentie (Lizard) Dreaming. She lives in Alice Springs, but has close family in Ernabella (two brothers), Cooper Pedy (a sister) and Wingellina (another sister). No other members of her family paint. She began painting in about 1989 with the Jukurrpa group in Alice Springs.

GOREY, VERONICA NAPURRURLA

Born in 1965 at Desert Bore, Veronica Gorey's country is Mt Allan. An Anmatyerre speaker, her Dreaming is Emu and she lives at Mt Allan.

GRANITES, JUDY NAMPIJINPA
Also cited as: Judy Nampijinpa

Born c.1934 at Warnipi, which is associated with Wayipi (*Borchiavia diffusa* — Creeper)

Dreaming. Her country is Warnipi, and Warlukurlangu, south-west of Yuendumu. Her main Dreamings — for which she is owner (Kurdu) — are Ngapa (Water), Warlu (Fire), Watiyawarnu (Wattle) and Lukarrara (Seed). She is also mananger (Kurdungurlu) for the Dogwood Dreaming, painted by Liddy Napanangka WALKER, TOPSY Napanangka and herself, which was purchased by the National Gallery of Australia from the Yuendumu artists' first Sydney exhibition in 1985. She is a Warlpiri speaker and lives at Yuendumu.

GRANITES, (LEONARD) KURT JAPANANGKA

Born c.1957 at Yurnturnu (Yuendumu) and a Warlpiri person whose country is Janyingki and his Dreamings are Mardukuja-mardukuja (Women's Dreaming), Yurrampi (Honey Ant) and Yana (Star Dreaming). He works with his wife, Peggy Napurrurla ROCKMAN, and started painting in 1985. His paintings reflect an exceptional intelligence. He worked in close association with writer/anthropologist Eric Michaels, and his bi-cultural facility has helped many other researchers to negotiate between Warlpiri and western culture. Lives at Lajamanu with his wife's family, but usually paints for Warlukurlangu Artists in Yuendumu because of the better quality materials available from the well-established Yuendumu painting company. His work has been included in numerous Warlukurlangu Artists exhibitions since 1990 and was reproduced in the catalogue of 'Australian Aboriginal Art from the Collection of Donald Kahn', which toured America in 1991–2 and has since been shown in several European cities and Israel. Collections: South Australian Museum, private collections

GRANITES, LORAINE NUNGARRAYI

A Warlpiri speaker, Loraine Granites lives at Yuendumu and began exhibiting with Warlukurlangu Artists in 1992, when her works were shown in company exhibitions in Melbourne and the Gold Coast. She paints her Karnta (Women), Witi (Ceremonial Pole), Lingka (Snake) and Yinapaka (Country) Dreamings.

GRANITES, REX DANIEL JAPANANGKA

A Warlpiri speaker, and born in Yuendumu c.1950, Rex Granites is a leading figure in the Yuendumu community: he President of the Yuendumu Council, member of the Northern Territory Committee of Road Safety Board and board member of the Alcohol Abuse Committee. He does not paint for Warlukurlangu Artists (though several members of his family do), but sells his work through private dealers and outlets in Alice Springs. He has been painting since 1988, and paints Honey Ant, Woman, Snake, Digging Stick and Dogwood Dreamings. His country is Mina Mina, 160 km west of Yuendumu towards Lake Mackay. He lives in Yuendumu, but has connections with the communities of Mt Allan and Willowra.

GREEN, ALBERT TJAMPITJIN

Born 'in the bush' at Tarkatji, south of Lake Gregory near the Stansmore Ranges, c.1925, Albert Green lives at Mulan and has been painting for Warlayirti Artists since 1989. A Kukatja tribesman, his traditional country is the Stansmore Ranges, and he paints Tingari and Two Women Dreamings for this region. The artist's work employs a complex imagery, which is probably only fully understood by other initiated men. He tends towards understatement and his works have a soft 'natural' look. They reflect the artist's quiet manner and his lifetime of knowledge of Men's Law.

GREEN, JOE JAPANANGKA/JUNGARRAYI

For reasons too complex to explain here, Joe Green has two skin names. He was born at Lajamanu, but he has moved around a lot, including to Alicurang. Born c.1960 of the Warlpiri tribe/language, his country is Jila, and he can paint Yankirrijarra (Two Emus), Warna (Snake), Watijarra (Two Men) and also Warnanarra (Rainbow Serpent) Dreamings. Joe Green and his wife, Robyn GREEN, are a formidable husband and wife team, one of several from Lajamanu. They both started painting in 1986. The two nearly always work together, helping each other with background dotting. They do also paint works separately. Joe Green is a strong individualist, whose extraordinary use of colour usually fleshes out the basic design on their paintings.

GREEN, ROBYN NAPURRURLA

Born at Gordon Downs station c.1962 of the Warlpiri language/tribe, Robyn Green's country is Yirningarra and her Dreamings Ngapa and Janmarda. Her mother, Louisa LAWSON Napaljarri, also paints. Robyn and her husband, Joe GREEN, are a formidable husband and wife team, one of several from Lajamanu. They started painting in 1986. They work together on background dotting, although both also paint works separately.

H

HAGAN, ISOBEL NUNGARRAYI
Born in 1961 of the Anmatyerre tribe, Isobel Hagan is the President of the Mt Allan Community Council. Her father was a Lutheran pastor, brought up at Hermannsburg. She paints Goanna Dreaming for her country, Mt Allan. She lives at Mt Allan.

HALL, DAVID TJANGALA
Born 'in the bush' in the area near Percival Lakes c.1930, David Hall now lives at Mulan. A Kukatja speaker, his traditional country is Kutarta, south-west of Balgo. He began painting for Warlayirti Artists in 1990 and paints Tingari and Water Dreamings. Like some other artists working out of Mulan, he uses more areas of brushwork on the canvas and does not utilise dotting as much as other artists from the Balgo Hills area. He creates unusual and subtle designs filled with his knowledge and concern for Men's Law. He works slowly and carefully, attaching great importance to his finished works. He was married to the late Ena GIMME Nungurrayai.

HARGRAVES, JENNIE NAMPIJINPA
Also cited as: Jennie Birrell Nampijinpa
Born at Yuendumu c.1962, her language and tribe is Warlpiri and she lives at Lajamanu. Pirlinyanu is her country. Her main Dreaming is Ngapa (Water). She can also paint Dreamings for the site of Kunajarrayi, for which she is kurdungurlu (manager, guardian) rather than owner, also Wanakiji (Bush Tomato), Yarla (Yam), Warna (Snake) and Laju (Witchetty Grub). She works with her mother, Lily HARGRAVES Nungarrayi, and started painting in 1987.

HARGRAVES, JOY NANGALA
Born at Yurntumu, near Yuendumu c.1967, her language/tribe is Warlpiri, her country is Pirlinyanu and her Dreamings are Ngapa and Yurrampi. She lives at Lajamanu and paints with her husband, Luke Johnson, often working on the backgrounds of his paintings. She started painting in 1987 and is a very strong young painter.

HARGRAVES, LILA NUNGARRAYI
Born at Purrpalala c.1930–5, her language/tribe is Warlpiri, her country Purrpalala and her Dreamings are Yarla (Yam), Ngalyipi (Snake Vine) and Witi (Ceremonial Pole). She lives at Lajamanu and works with her daughter, Jennie HARGRAVES Nampijinpa. Her husband is one of the old medicine men. She started painting in 1986.

HARGRAVES, MAGGIE (LILY) NUNGARRAYI

Born at Jila Well c.1930, her language/tribe is Warlpiri and her country is Kur-lurrngalinpa, starting from Granites in the north-west and through to Jila in the south-east. Her Dreamings are Mala, Ngatijirri, Witi and Ngarrka (Watijarra). She lives at Lajamanu and started painting in 1986 in the Traditional Painting course. At a time when many Western Desert painters have gone to an excess of tidiness, Lily Hargraves's approach remains intractably expressionist. 'She works like an action painter — quickly, with whatever materials are available, including house paint and poster paints — for the Dreaming, rather than the western art market. When Judith Ryan (Curator of Aboriginal Art for the National Gallery of Victoria) came to Lajamanu, she bought a set of pastels the older women had done, which were hanging in the school library, for the Gallery. The shades are pastel, muted blues and pinks. They were getting very warped in the sun and the heat, and the surface was beginning to flake off. A meeting of the artists agreed to their removal on the basis that Judith Ryan would have them all photographed life-size and framed behind glass for the Lajamanu library. When the paintings were taken down from the walls where they'd been for a couple of years, (Lily) Nungarrayi started tearing hers up — "That one's rubbish, I'm going to do you another one now." All the other ladies were trying to grab it off her. She didn't want what she regarded as her bad early work appearing in the National Gallery. She's a little person with a fiery temperament. She's called glurpunta, which means "fighting spirit"'.' (Christine Nicholls, headmistress at Lajamanu school for most of the '80s, personal communication, see *Paint Up Big*, Judith Ryan (NGV, 1990). Maggie (Lily) Hargraves has also worked at the Lajamanu school teaching dancing to the young girls. Collections: National Gallery of Victoria

HECTOR, LINDA (YINARRKI) NANGALA

Place of birth Kampu 1942, Linda Hector's language/tribe is Warlpiri and her country Kampu. Her Dreamings are Warlu, Ngapa and Yankirri (Karnanganja). She lives at Lajamanu where she works with sisters Topsy, Lucy (HECTOR) and Miyangula. She started painting in 1986 in the Traditional Painting course.

HECTOR, LUCY (YURRURNGALI) NANGALA

Born at Yarturlu-yarturlu (the Granites) c.1945. Her language/tribe is Warlpiri, her country is Jirrkarnta and her Dreamings are Ngapa, Yanjirri, Yujuku (The Shelter) and Jipilyaku. She lives at Lajamanu and works with sisters Topsy, Linda (HECTOR) and Miyungula. Started painting in 1986 as part of the Traditional Painting course run by the TAFE Unit at Lajamanu school. Collections: National Gallery of Victoria

HECTOR, MENZIES JAPALJARRI

Born on Kirkimby station c.1956, his language and tribe is Warlpiri. His country is around Lima in the Tanami. Dreamings are Ngatijirri (Budgerigar), Ngarlu (Honey), Warna (Snake) and Laju (Witchetty Grub). She lives at Lajamanu and works with his wife, Angela Hector Napanaru — who is West Australian, born near Broome. He started painting in 1986.

HERBERT, LIDDY NAKAMARRA

Born Yirninjarra c.1929 and lives at Lajamanu. Warlpiri tribe and speaker — she has only a few words of English. Her country is Yirninjarra and her Dreamings are Pirlarla (which the artist glossed as 'two women make fire' [Pirlarla are bush beans — this may be a reference to when the women burn holes in those beans for making necklaces. PG & LC]) and Manalya ('Snake' — possibly referring to a particular type or species). She started painting in 1986 in the Traditional Painting course at Lajamanu. Collections: National Gallery of Victoria

HILARY TJAPALTJARRI

Born in 1938 at Mintjilpirri, south-west of Kintore, Hilary's father instructed him in the Dreaming stories in his boyhood as the family moved around Mintjilpirri and also south-west of the Kintore Ranges. Then the family walked in to Haasts Bluff and received rations of flour and tea, remaining in the area for a time before drifting back to the Pintupi country around Illpili and Wili Rockhole. From here the family was picked up by the NT Welfare Branch patrols and taken to Haasts Bluff, where Hilary lived with Turkey TOLSON's family. Hilary was 'made a man' in the first initiation ceremonies to be carried out at Papunya in the early days of the settlement. After this Hilary worked as a stockman, and for years drove horses across the Tanami to Alice Springs. He arrived back in Papunya in the early '70s to find everyone painting and wanted to paint himself. Geoffrey Bardon gave him a few small boards to work on and gradually he learnt the use of colour, though not till after he moved to the newly established settlement of Kintore in the early '80s did he paint regularly for Papunya Tula Artists. His paintings usually depict the Snake Dreaming south-west of Kintore in his traditional country. Collections: Holmes à Court

HILDA NAPALJARRI

Hilda is Warlpiri/Anmatyerre and lives in Willowra, where she started painting in the late '80s when canvas became available through the CDEP adviser. 'I was taught to paint by my mother when I was young. That's for ceremony.' While she has no particular connections with other Western Desert artists, Hilda is aware of the context into which her work is going: 'I do send my paintings for exhibitions.' She also paints these designs on coolamons and nulla nullas. She takes a leading role in community matters, and is Chairperson of the Willowra Council.

HOLMES, MICHELLE PWERLE

An Alyawarre speaker, her country is Antarrengenye, north of the area of Irrweltye towards Ammaroo. She paints a Wild Orange Dreaming amongst others, and like most Utopia artists, had already worked in batik before the CAAMA Summer Project of

'88–9 when she first tried acrylic on canvas. She is associated with the community of Amperlatwatye and is one of a large number of Alyawarre people from this area who bear the name 'Holmes'.

HOLMES, SANDRA KEMARRE
An Alyawarre speaker, born c.1960, her country is Irrweltye Soakage, north of Utopia Aboriginal land. She has been painting since the summer of 1988–9, and before that worked in batik.

HUDSON, JEAN NAMPIJINPA
Born in 1960 and an Anmatyerre/Warlpiri, her country is Mt Wedge and Mt Allan and she paints Bush Onion Dreaming and Women Dreaming for Mt Wedge (Kerrinyarra). She lives at Mt Allan.

I

IMPANA COLLINS, see COLLINS, Impana

INKAMALA, RAY TJAMPITJINPA (c.1920–1989)

Born at Illpili, Ray grew up 'in the bush', his first contact with whitemen being the sighting of their planes overhead as a small boy. He worked as a stockman at various cattle stations across the centre, including Haasts Bluff, before taking up painting in the early '80s during Andrew Crocker's time of running Papunya Tula Artists. His 'grandfather', Johnny WARANGKULA, and close friend Dick PANTIMAS (who passed away in the early '80s) taught him how to use paint and canvas. His tribal affiliation was Pintupi/Luritja, and his traditional country lay around Illpili and the site of Winparrku in this area (there is a second Winparrku out near Kiwirrkura across the WA border). The stories he painted included Emu, Lightning and Rain Dreamings. His places of residence during the '80s included Haasts Bluff, Illpili, Papunya and Mt Leibig. After the mysterious disappearance of one of the stones at Winparrku for which Ray was custodian, the old man took sick and died in early 1989. He is survived by his three wives, several daughters and grandchildren. Collections: Flinders University Art Museum, Museums & Art Galleries of NT

J

JACK, EUNICE NAPANANGKA
Also cited as: Eunice Napanungka Jack

Born at Tjukurla c.1940, of the Pintupi/Pitjantjatjara tribe. Eunice Jack's country is Tjukurla and she paints her father TUTUMA Tjapangati's Dreaming from west of Lake McDonald, as well as a Porcupine story. She lives in the Haasts Bluff community and is married to GIDEON Tjupurrula Jack. The painter PINTA PINTA Tjapanangka is her brother (same mother). She also has connections with the Warrakuna community west of Docker River through her father Tutuma's brother. She began painting in 1992 and sells her work through the Ijuntji Women's Centre in Haasts Bluff.

JACK, TJUPURRULA
Also cited as: Jack Wayuta Jupurrurla, Jack Tangangypa Wayuta Tjupurrula

Born c.1925 at Vaughan Springs, Jack Tjupurrula is the senior custodian of Mawitji, a major Possum Dreaming site consisting of a set of hills, where Jack spent his boyhood. Possums (now locally extinct) were then plentiful. Jack worked for most of his adult life as a stockman at stations across the Centre before settling in Papunya, where he has lived for many years, though it is some distance from the areas of greatest ritual significance for him. He was one of the original group of artists, and has painted intermittently ever since. He is the uncle of Michael NELSON and his sister Violet and Michael Nelson gained early experience of the medium of paint on canvas working on the older man's paintings. After a long spell in Mt Leibig, Jack has recently moved back to Papunya. His paintings depict Possum and Flying Ant Dreamings and the Tangapurra Namanpurra story about the activities of a family group in the region of his traditional country. He is Warlpiri/Luritja. Collections: Holmes à Court

JACKIE TJAKAMARRA

Born near Kulkuta, south of Kiwirrkura, he is the brother of ANATJARI Tjakamarra. Brought into Papunya by the NT Welfare Branch patrols in the '60s, he was present when painting started in 1971 at Papunya. He painted for a few years in the early '70s before moving to Warakuna, where he lived until the early '80s. He then joined the move back to the Pintupi homelands and settled at Kintore. Since the mid '80s he has lived in Kiwirrkura, with his brother. An occasional painter for Papunya Tula Artists.

JACKO (TINGIYARI) JAKAMARRA

Born near Mongrel Downs station at a place called Rilyka known for Pirlarla (bush bean). His language group is not Warlpiri but a related group, the Katurrngarruru. His country is Wirnmawarnu. He can paint Pirlarla, Ngapa and Wintiki Dreamings. He lives at Lajamanu and works with his two wives, LIZZIE and SUSAN Napaljarri. He was one of the original group of artists at Lajamanu in 1986.

JACKSON, SHORTY TJAMPITJINPA

Born at Malka, a site in WA south-east of Kiwirrkura, he is the oldest son of UTA UTA Tjangala. He was brought in to Haasts Bluff in 1956 as a small boy five or six years old. Now in his early forties, he has been painting occasionally for Papunya Tula Artists since the late '80s. His usual place of residence is Kintore. He is custodian of the site of Ngatjaanga, a rockhole where the Snake Woman depicted in many of his father's paintings came upon the snake and killed it. Shorty's work was shown in 'Friendly Country, Friendly People' at the Araluen Arts Centre and Tandanya Cultural Institute in 1991. Collections: Holmes à Court, Australian Museum, Sydney, Art Gallery of WA

JAMES, IRENE NAPURRURLA

Born at Lajamanu c.1963 of the Warlpiri language/tribe. Her country Mungkurlurrpa and her Dreamings are Warnarri (Bush Bean), Marlujarra and Wintiki. She lives at Lajamanu. Works with her husband, Joe JAMES and started painting in 1986. She is the daughter of LIZZIE Napaljarri.

JAMES, JOE JAPANANGKA

Born Mt Doreen of the Warlpiri tribe, his country Janyinki and Dreamings are Mardukuja-mardukuja (Kana) and Warna. He lives at Lajamanu, where he works as a police aide. He and his wife Irene work together all the time. He started painting in 1986. Collections: National Gallery of Victoria, Holmes à Court

JAMES, MABEL NAPURRURLA (TILAWU)

Born at Yurntumu c.1955, Mabel James is a Warlpiri person, whose country is Yurntumu and Miya-miya and Dreaming is Ngurlu (Seed). She started painting in 1987 and lives at Lajamanu.

JANICE KNGWARREYE

The younger sister of Lucky Kngwarreye, born approximately 1958, Janice Kngwarreye is an Alyawarre speaker who began painting in the summer of 1988–9 as part of the second CAAMA project with the Utopia artists: 'The First Works on Canvas'. She has also done some batik and inventively carved wooden sculptures. Her country is Ngkawenyerre, on Alyawarre/Kaytetye Aboriginal land north of the Utopia area near Ngwarlerlaneme. Her Dreamings are Rainbow, Tjarpa Lanait (Witchetty), Edible Snake and Wild Fig. She is married to Wally Pwerle, who is known for his wood carving. The two occasionally paint together.

Friday Ararungunja, Napperby (Unmatiera)

Teddy Briscoe Jampijinpa with a portrait of his late father (taken at the artist's request)
(Photo: Grenville Turner)

Michael Tommy Tjapangati (Photo: Grenville Turner)

Susan Dixon Leo Napaltjarri and Peter Leo Tjakamarra at the Seven Sisters Dreaming depicted in their painting
(Photo: Grenville Turner)

Brenda Lynch Nungurrayi (Photo: Grenville Turner)

Kitty Pultara Napaltjarri (Photo: Grenville Turner)

Dinny Nolan Tjampitjinpa, Don Morton Japangardi and Frank Japanangka (Photo: Grenville Turner)

Linny (Frank) Nampijinpa and her daughter (Photo: Grenville Turner)

Emily Andy Napaljarri and Leslie Daniels Jampijinpa (Photo: Grenville Turner)

Denny Jampijinpa (Photo: Grenville Turner)

JESSIE NAPALTJARRI

Born c.1950 at Napperby station, where she still lives. She is married with three children. Her older sister, Kitty COCKATOO, and her husband, KENNY Tjakamarra, also paint.

JIGILI, FRED JAMPIJINPA

Born at Pirlirnyana of the Warlpiri tribe. Country is Pirlirnyana and Dreamings are Ngapa and Yamkirri. He works with his wife, Judy JIGILI Napangardi, and his daughter, Yulanti JIGILI. Started painting in 1986 and lives at Lajamanu. Collections: National Gallery of Victoria

JIGILI, JUDY NAPANGARDI

A Warlpiri person born at Janyingki, her country is Mina-mina and Janyingki, and her main Dreaming is Mardakuja-mardakuja (Women's Dreaming). She lives at Lajamanu. She started painting in 1987 and works with her husband, Fred JIGILI, and daughter, Yulanti JIGILI.

JIGILI, MARGARET NAPANGARDI

Born in the Tanami and a Warlpiri person, her country is called Kirriwarrangi and her Dreamings are Ngarrka (Men's Dreaming) and Yungkuyirrarnu. She lives at Lajamanu and started painting in 1987.

JIGILI, YULANTI NANGALA

Born at Lajamanu c.1970, Yulanti is one of the youngest people painting at Lajamanu. Of the Warlpiri tribe/language, her country is Pirlinyanu and Dreamings are Ngapa, Yankirri, Pirntina and Jarntujarra (Two Girls). She lives at Lajamanu and works with her father, Fred JIGILI, and mother, Judy JIGILI Napangardi, in their camp, but does her paintings independently of her parents. They are miniatures compared to the huge canvases many Warlpiris like to do. She started painting in 1988.

JIMIJA JUNGARRAYI (c.1908–1989)
Also cited as: Jimmy-ja Tjungarrayi, Jigija Jungarai

Born c.1908 at Yarrunkanyi (Mt Hardy), to the west of Yuendumu. Yarrunkanyi is associated with the Ngarrka (Initiated Men) Dreaming and the Mala (Western Hare Wallaby) Dreaming. He was one of the group of senior men at Yuendumu involved in the establishment of painting at the settlement. He collaborated with Paddy Japaljarri SIMS, Larry Jungarrayi SPENCER and Paddy Jupurrurla NELSON on *Munga Star Dreaming*, 1985, which was purchased by the National Gallery of Australia from the Yuendumu painters' first Sydney show. He was Warlpiri and lived at Yuendumu much of the time or on his outstation at Jila. Collections: National Gallery of Victoria

JOE, TJAKAMARRA

He is an occasional painter who lives at Mt Leibig and is a Luritja speaker. His country is Kamparrapa, west of Mt Leibig.

JOHN TJAKAMARRA
Also cited as: John Kipara Tjakamarra, John Jagamara

Born probably in the early '30s in country north of Kiwirrkura, where he grew up. His country lies in the Kulkuta area towards Sandy Blight Junction. His family were one of the first Pintupi groups to walk into Papunya in the early '60s, and were soon joined by others. When painting started at Papunya in 1971, John Tjakamarra was working with YALA YALA Gibbs and Freddy WEST, who have associations with the same country, and he continued working with this Pintupi group when the Papunya Tula painting company was formed. He usually paints Tingari stories around Kulkuta and Nimangka and resides in Kintore. Collections: Holmes à Court, Queensland Art Gallery, Art Gallery of SA, Australian Museum, Sydney, Museums & Art Galleries of NT, Burke Museum, University of Washington, Seattle

JOHN TJAPALTJARRI

Born at Patjantjanya in the Lake MacDonald region c.1941, John Tjapaltjarri is a Pintupi speaker who painted at Papunya in the early '70s, but spent long periods of time in Balgo during the later part of the '80s. He has only recently begun painting regularly for Papunya Tula Artists again and is now living at Tjukula.

JOHN JAPANGARDI

Born in 1960, John Japangardi is an Anmatyerre speaker who paints Honey Ant Dreamings for his country, Yuelamu. He is FRANK Japanangka's son and lives at Mt Allan.

JOHNNY JAPALJARRI

Born in Willowra, date of birth uncertain. A Warlpiri speaker, his country is Patirlirri (Rabbit Bore, far to the west of Willowra) and Wirliyajarrayi (Dreaming site for Willowra, meaning literally 'footprint'). He paints Ngatijirri (Budgerigar) Dreamings and Willowra Dreamings. 'I do these paintings here at Willowra with my family. I started doing my painting in the year 1982 when I was working at the school as a janitor. That's when I started teaching the children about their Dreaming. Before I started doing these paintings on canvas, I did them on boards, boomerangs and shields. I have learnt to do my ceremony dancing about my country, Patirlirri — Budgerigar Dreaming, and that's how I got to know how to do my painting.'

JOHNSON, CECIL JAPANGARDI

Born c.1940 in the Central Tanami, his language/tribe is Warlpiri and country Yinapalku. His Dreamings are Turlturlypa, Ngayaki (Bush Tomato) and Yarla (Yam). He lives at Lajamanu and sometimes works with his wife, Marlene JOHNSON. He started painting in 1986. His powerful paintings are unusual for their restricted palette — often white and brown on black.

JOHNSON, MARLENE NAMPIJINPA

Born at Mt Doreen in 1957 and lives at Lajamanu. A Warlpiri person, her traditional country is Kamira. She made a video, in conjunction with Penny McDonald, called 'We are going back to Kamira'. Her Dreamings are Ngapa (Water), Warnayarra (Rainbow Snake) and Malikijarra (Two Dogs). She sometimes works with her husband, Cecil JOHNSON, and started painting in 1987.

JOHNSON, MARTIN JAPANANGKA

Born at Lajamanu c.1955–60 of the Warlpiri tribe and language, his country is Lajamanu and he can paint Yarla, Nganja Warli, Watiya Warnu and Karntajarra (Two Women) Dreamings. One of the better known artists at Lajamanu, he works with his wife, Kay McDONALD and began painting in 1986 on canvas board. Very conscious of the economics of the painting enterprise, he is a strong and intelligent advocate of improved financial returns for artists.

JONES, FLORRIE NAPANGARDI

A Warlpiri speaker, Florrie Napangardi Jones lives at Yuendumu and exhibits with Warlukurlangu Artists. She paints her Yuparli (Bush Banana) and Pikilyi (Vaughan Springs) Dreamings.

JONES, FREDDIE KNGWARREYE

Born c.1935 at Old McDonald Downs station, Freddie is an Alyawarre speaker and second son of Jacob Jones and Dolly Kemarre. Dolly is a powerful figure in the women's business ('awelye') in the Irrweltye area. Jacob Jones is 'an extremely powerful man who speaks for enormous tracts of Alyawarre land. It is he who sanctions what can be painted on canvas' (according to Janet Holt, who runs the Delmore Downs painting company for which Freddie has painted since mid 1989). Freddie's older brother Lenny is progressively taking on this responsibility for the land as Jacob grows frail. Freddie, too, is assuming important ceremonial roles, and teaching his many nephews. He is an articulate spokesman for his family and for the Utopia community and is known for his good humour. He has a particular ritual connection with David Pwerle ROSS, such that certain Dreamings must only be transcribed by them together, in acknowledgement of joint Eastern Anmatyerre and Alyawarre custodianship of the intersection of their heritage countries. Freddie paints Meat Ant, Pink Crested Cockatoo, Sulphur Crested Cockatoo, Earthworm, Caterpillar, Snake and Spider Dreamings. His work has been exhibited in Melbourne, Sydney and Brisbane. He lives at Theleye Soakage. Collections: National Gallery of Victoria, Artbank, private collections in Australia, USA and Europe

JUDY NAMPIJINPA, see GRANITES, Judy Nampijinpa

JUGADAI, DAISY NAPALTJARRI

Born in 1956 at Haasts Bluff and a Pintupi/Luritja speaker, Daisy paints Honey Ant, Spinifex and Emu Dreamings for her country, which lies around Papunya and Haasts Bluff. Daisy comes from a family of artists which goes back to the beginning of Western Desert painting: her uncles include painters UTA UTA Tjangala and Riley MAJOR Tjangala — as well as Dapper Dapper Tjangala, one of the senior men at Haasts Bluff. Daisy's mother, Narputta Nangala JUGADAI, has recently begun painting on canvas for the Ikuntji Women's Centre in Haasts Bluff, but she learned to paint working on the backgrounds of Daisy's father Timmy JUGADAI's paintings. In 1993 a painting of Daisy's was exhibited and purchased from the Araluen Annual Art Award. Her work has also been shown in the 1993 National Aboriginal Art Award and been purchased by the National Gallery of Australia.

JUGADAI, NARPUTTA NANGALA

Born c.1933 at Karrkurutjintja, her language/tribe is Pintupi and she paints Two Women ('coming from WA'), Jangala (Two Men) and Snake for her country, Karrku-rutjintja. She is full sister to painters Riley MAJOR Tjangala and the late GEORGE Tjangala, as well as to Dapper Dapper Tjangala. She is sister-in-law to the artist Charlie TARAWA, and renowned painter UTA UTA Tjangala was her cousin. Narputta was married to Timmy JUGADAI. Their daughter, Daisy JUGADAI Napaltjarri, also paints. Narputta only began painting in her own name in 1992, but learned to paint in the 1970s, working on her late husband's canvases for Papunya Tula Artists. Narputta lives in the Haasts Bluff community, and sells her work through the Ikuntji Women's Centre.

JUGADAI, TIMMY TJUNGARRAYI (c.1930–late '80s)
Also cited as: Timmy Tjungurrayi/Jungarai

His country is Yaribilong, just north-west of Alice Springs, his language group Luritja and his Dreamings Star and Shield. Actively involved in the running of the Haasts Bluff settlement, Timmy Jugadai was a friend of LIMPI Tjapangati, one of the original group of Papunya Tula 'painting men', who also lived at Haasts Bluff. The two men occasional-ly collaborated on paintings.

JUNABEE NAPALTJARRI

Born c.1943 at Tjalitjai, to the north of Warren Creek. A Pintupi speaker, her country is Nyunmanu and Dreamings are Papa (Dog) Dreaming and Lingakurra, a site south of Kintore. Junabee has a brother, CAMERON Tjapaltjarri (who paints for Papunya Tula Artists), and a sister, Gaelene Napaltjarri, living at Kintore. She began painting in 1992 and sells her work through the Ikuntji Women's Centre in Haasts Bluff, where she currently resides.

JURRA, JOSEPH TJAPALTJARRI

Born in the desert at the site of Kiwirrkura, 200 km west of Kintore, in the early '50s. Joseph was brought into Papunya by the NT Welfare Branch patrols in the '60s while still a young boy. WILLY Tjungarrayi helped to raise him. For a time, he attended school in Papunya and later at Yuendumu when the family moved there. He worked for Yuendumu Council, then the Papunya canteen. He went to live in Balgo for a time, before settling in Kintore with his wife and three children when the new settlement was established there at the beginning of the '80s. He began painting for Papunya Tula Artists only in 1987, but his skill and inventiveness secured him one of the earliest solo exhibitions organised through Papunya Tula at the Gallery Gabrielle Pizzi in 1989. Joseph travelled to Melbourne for the show, his first time out of Central Australia. Collections: Holmes à Court, Art Gallery of WA, Supreme Court of the NT, Darwin

JURRA, PEGGY NANGALA (c.1925–1990)

A Warlpiri speaker, Peggy Nangala Jurra lived in Yuendumu and exhibited with Warlukurlangu Artists. Her work was included in the 1986 show at the Editions Gallery in Perth, which was the painting company's first major commercial and critical success. Peggy Jurra was also represented in 'Mythscapes' at the National Gallery of Victoria in 1989, and many commercial shows of Warlukurlangu Artists through the late '80s. She usually painted her Ngapa (Water) Dreaming. Collections: National Gallery of Victoria, South Australian Museum

JURRA, RACHEL NAPALJARRI

Born in 1960 at Yuendumu and a Warlpiri speaker, she began painting in 1985. Her country is Jila Well, west of Yuendumu, and she paints Kangaroo, Pirki (Cave), Prickle and Green Parrot Dreamings. She was married to the late Isaac Yama. She lives sometimes at Yuendumu and sometimes at Hidden Valley, a town camp on the edge of Alice Springs, where she works with other painters like Rosie FLEMING Nangala and Polly Napangardi WATSON. Her cousin, EUNICE Napangardi, taught her to paint her Dreamings. She usually works with the Jukurrpa group. She has sold her work to the Centre for Aboriginal Artists, but is primarily associated with the Jukurrpa group. 'Living at my little sister's camp and watching Eunice Napangardi; my aunty told me my Dreamings.'

JURRA, SAMANTHA NAPURRURLA

Born at Yuendumu in 1978, Samantha came to Alice Springs with her aunt, Rachel Napaljarri JURRA, in 1980. Samantha's relatives live at Yuendumu, Willowra, Lajamanu, Jila and Nyirrpi. She is a Warlpiri speaker and her country is Jila Well, west of Yuendumu. In 1991 Rachel Jurra started to teach her young niece to paint her Dreamings, Warna (Snake), Yuparli (Bush Banana) and (Mulju) Soakage.

JURRA, TILO NANGALA

Born in 1944, Tilo Jurra is a Warlpiri speaker who lives at Yuendumu and has been painting for Warlukurlangu Artists since the mid '80s. She paints her Ngapa (Water) and Yankirri (Emu) Dreamings. Her work has been exhibited with that of other Yuendumu painters in exhibitions in Perth, Alice Springs, Adelaide, Melbourne, Canberra, Sydney and Darwin and was included in the 'Dreamings — Art of Aboriginal Australia' exhibition which toured the USA in 1988–9, and 'Mythscapes' at the National Gallery of Victoria in 1989. Tilo was one of 42 Yuendumu painters who worked on the 7 x 3 m canvas which toured Europe with the 1993 'Aratjara — Australian Aboriginal and Torres Strait Islander Art' exhibition. Collections: National Gallery of Australia, Canberra, National Gallery of Victoria, Christensen Fund, private collections

K

KAAPA TJAMPITJINPA (c.1920–1989)
Also cited as: Kaapa Mbitjana Tjampitjinpa, Kaapa Djanbidjimba

Kaapa was born on Napperby station (Lurumbu) c.1920. He was initiated at Napperby, then did stockwork at Mt Riddock station. While still in his younger days, he moved to Haasts Bluff, where he worked at the government cattle station. He recalled stockwork as hard and dangerous, especially branding bullocks. Kaapa was amongst those (like Johnny WARANGKULA, TWO BOB Tjungarrayi and a number of the other artists) brought across to Papunya at the start of the '60s when Papunya settlement was established to replace Haasts Bluff as the main population centre because of lack of drinkable water there. An elder of the region, Kaapa's tribal affiliation is Anmatyerre/Arrente (the name 'Mbitjana' is an Arrente skin name corresponding to Tjampitjinpa in the Western Desert system of skin names). His father, born at Warlukurlangu west of Yuendumu, was of mixed Anmatyerre/Warlpiri descent, as was his mother, who was born at Napperby. Kaapa's sites included Mikanji, a rainmaking place near Mt Denison. The Dreamings which he regularly painted included Owl, Shield, Witchetty Grub, Pelican, Snake (connected with rainmaking rituals), Black Goanna, Emu and Yam. Kaapa had been involved with the painting movement since its inception, and was the artist chosen by the other men to paint the mural on the Papunya school wall because of his mastery of the brush method. As Geoffrey Bardon notes in his account of these events, 'Kaapa Tjampitjinpa had been a most enterprising and independent artist in the traditional manner before my arrival at Papunya. A separate group quite close to Kaapa were the pensioners who were in fact the old men of the community, and they were interested in having ceremonial objects painted or carved in the ancient manner.' (Bardon, *Aboriginal Art of the Western Desert* [Rigby, 1981]). In August 1971 Kaapa shared first prize in the Alice Springs Caltex Golden Jubilee Art Award, the first public recognition the Papunya artists had received for their work, and when Papunya Tula Artists was established as a company, Kaapa was chosen as its first Chairman. The Victorian Tapestry Workshop made a tapestry of his *Winparrku Serpents* 1974, which now hangs in the foyer of the Playhouse Theatre, Victorian Art Centre. In the last years of his life he divided his time between Papunya and Alice Springs. A forceful and highly intelligent man, Kaapa's influence among the Papunya-based artists remained strong until his death in October 1989. Collections: National Gallery of Australia, Canberra, Australian Museum, Sydney, Holmes à Court, Queensland Art Gallery, Art Gallery of WA, Art Gallery of SA, University of WA Anthropology Museum, National Museum of Australia, Canberra, Museums & Art Galleries of NT etc.

KAME, EMILY KNGWARREYE, see EMILY Kame Kngwarreye

KANYA TJAPANGATI

Born near Kiwirrkura in the early '50s, Kanya grew up 'in the bush' and was brought in to Papunya by one of the NT Welfare Branch patrols in the late '60s quite late in his youth. In Papunya, he received instruction from the older Pintupi men at the settlement, in particular Timmy PAYUNGKA, one of the original group of 'painting men' at Papunya. In Peter Fannin's time of running the artists' company, a few years after painting began at Papunya, Kanya moved to Balgo in WA, to Docker River, Warakuna, and then to the Pintupi camp at Yai Yai, where he assisted some of the older artists with their paintings. But it was not till he moved to Kintore with the majority of his Pintupi tribesmen and women at the start of the '80s that he began to paint, as he put it, 'properly'. He now lives at Kiwirrkura, and paints Tingari stories in the region of his country, which includes the sites of Mukula, Yardinga, Nungami and Likilinga, west from Kiwirrkura. Collections: Holmes à Court, Art Gallery of WA, Art Gallery of SA

KATHLEEN PETYARRE

An Anmatyerre speaker, born c.1930, Kathleen Petyarre's traditional country is Atnangkere, an important soakage on the western boundary of Utopia station which, on account of the abundance of food it provided, was keenly sought by neighbouring Eastern Arrente groups. Her father had three wives, and several daughters, who in recent times have managed to hold onto the area as a group, establishing camp at Atneltyeye Boundary Bore. Kathleen's Dreamings include Women Hunting Emu with Dingo, and Mountain Devil Lizard, and like most of the Utopia artists, she took up painting in 1988–9 as part of CAAMA's Summer Project after previously working in batik. A talented batik artist, Kathleen is enjoying exploring the technical possibilities of acrylic on canvas. A 6 x 3 m silk batik in the collection of Museums & Art Galleries of NT shows reciprocally the influence of working with paint on both the scale and the technique of her batiks.

KATHY NANGALA

Born at Willowra, Kathy remembers the onset of World War II as part of her early childhood at Willowra settlement. A Warlpiri speaker, her traditional country is the site of Wirliyajarrayi, the Dreaming site for Willowra. She paints Ngapa (Water) and Ngurlu (Damper Seed) Dreamings on her canvases. For the women's ceremonies, in which she takes an active part, Kathy has her own Rain Dreaming body paint design which she usually paints, and sometimes Ngurlu. She is the classificatory granddaughter of artists MAY and MOLLY Napurrurla and niece of PEGGY and LUCY Nampijinpa. She began painting in the late '80s together with May, Lucy and others at Willowra.

KELLY, ALICE NAPALJARRI

Place of birth Yinapaku c.1920, her language and tribe is Warlpiri and she lives at Lajamanu. Her country is Yinapaku and her Dreaming is Watijarra (Two Men). She sometimes does paintings with Gladys KELLY Napangardi, who is a co-wife of Jimmy

KELLY, himself a fine painter. All three are about seventy years of age and senior figures in the ritual life of the community. Alice is known at Lajamanu as an excellent dancer, and is one of the leaders of the women's business.

KELLY, GLADYS NAPANGARDI (KUNGARIYA)

Place of birth Mamingirri c.1940, Gladys's language/tribe is Warlpiri and she lives at Lajamanu. Her country is Jarrardajarrayi and her Dreamings are Yarla, Ngayaki and Wardapi (Goanna). She is renowned in Lajamanu as an extraordinary dancer of the goanna ceremony. She started painting in 1986. Collections: National Gallery of Victoria

KELLY, JIMMY JAMPIJINPA

Born at Mikanji (Mt Doreen), c.1924, of the Warlpiri tribe, his country is War-lukurlangu (Wayilinpa), quite close to Yuendumu. He lives at Lajamanu and his Dreamings are Warlukurlangu, Watiyawarnu (Ngapa, Yakirri) and Watijarra. He started painting in 1986 and shares some Dreamings with ABIE Jangala. Both are senior men in the Lajamanu community. Collections: National Gallery of Victoria

KELLY, LILY NAPANGATI

Born at Haasts Bluff in 1948, Lily has country in the Haasts Bluff area, also the Women Dreaming story associated with Kunajarrayi. She came to the newly established settlement of Papunya in the early '60s as a young girl and remained in the settlement for many years before moving to Mt Leibig, where she now resides with her husband, Norman KELLY, also a painter. They have three children and five grandchildren. A Luritja speaker, she has been painting for Papunya Tula Artists since the mid '80s and is included in the Araluen Trust's collection of Western Desert paintings. In 1986 she won the Northern Territory Art Award.

KELLY, NORMAN TJAMPITJINPA

Born 'in the bush' c.1938 to the north of Mt Leibig and about five miles (8 km) south of present day Yuendumu, Norman Kelly is one of the senior men of the Mt Leibig community, where he and his wife, Lily KELLY, live with their family. After years working as a stockman, mustering cattle all across the Centre, Norman began painting occasionally for Papunya Tula Artists in the mid '80s when the company began to service the artists at Mt Leibig. A Warlpiri speaker, Norman's country lies around Mt Leibig (Yamanturngu), 80 km west of Papunya and further north. His father's country lies in Warlpiri territory around Waylilimpa and he paints Bush Potato, Watanuma (Flying Ant), Mulga Tree and other Bush Tucker stories, Watia Wanu (Women with Digging Stick and Coolamon at Mt Leibig) Dreamings. Norman's paintings are now usually sold through the Centre for Aboriginal Artists or freelance art dealers. He is the stepson of Paddy Tjangala, and step brother of SANDRA Nampitjinpa, Sonder TURNER and PETRA Nampitjinpa. Of late, his output has slowed, possibly related to problems of distribution experienced in the Mt Leibig community over the past few years. His sister, Diana Marshall Nampitjinpa, also about the same age as Norman, has also painted occasionally — mainly Bushfire and 'Lover Boy' Dreamings, which she sold through the Centre for Aboriginal Artists in Alice Springs. Norman's work was shown at the Gauguin Museum, Tahiti in 1988. Collections: Flinders University Art Museum, Holmes à Court, Australian Museum, Sydney

KENNEDY, LUCY NAPALJARRI
Also cited as: Lucy Napaljarri

Born c.1926 of the Warlpiri/Anmatyerre tribe/language, she lives at Yuendumu and is one of the senior women of the Yuendumu community whose interest in rendering traditional women's designs in western materials was one of the driving forces behind early experiments with canvas at the settlement. Her work was included in the first exhibition of Yuendumu paintings at the Araluen Arts Centre in Alice Springs in October 1985 and in many exhibitions of Warlukurlangu Artists since in Perth, Alice Springs, Adelaide, Sydney, Melbourne and Darwin, also in England as part of the 1987 Portsmouth Festival. She participated in the SA Museum's 'Yuendumu: Paintings out of the Desert' in 1987–8, and the 'Dreamings' exhibition which toured the USA in 1988–9 included *Sugarleaf Dreaming at Ngarlu*, 1986, on which Lucy colloborated with her countrywomen Ruth and Hilda MARTIN Napaljarri. Lucy's heritage country is in the Coniston station and Mt Allan area and she paints Miinypa (Native Fuschia), Marlu (Kangaroo) and Janganpa (Possum) Dreamings for this country. Lucy, Dolly DANIELS and Bessie SIMS are the only three women on the Yuendumu Council. Collections: Museum of Mankind, British Museum, UK, SA Museum, Australian Museum, Sydney, Flinders University Art Museum

KENNEDY, TIM JUPURRURLA

Born at Mt Singleton c.1947 of the Warlpiri tribe and language. His country is Mt Singleton and he lives at Lajamanu. His Dreamings are Kurrkurrpa, Waringarri and Jurntu. He works with his wife, Iris DIXON, and also with ABIE Jangala, and has been painting since 1986. Collections: National Gallery of Victoria

KENNY TJAKAMARRA

Born in the early '50s in his mother's country north of Haasts Bluff, Kenny grew up in his father's country around Coniston and is an Amnatyerre speaker. He worked as a stockman at Coniston and stations all over the Centre before coming to live at Napperby with his wife JESSIE Napaltjarri's family. His country lies around the site of Winparrku. He paints Snake Dreaming and Two Women Dreaming stories from this area around Haasts Bluff and the Perentie Dreaming story which runs from Kintore through Haasts Bluff.

KINALUJA NUNGARRAYI

Born at Jila Well c.1945, and a Warlpiri person, he lives at Lajamanu. His country is Kurlurrngalinypa and his main Dreaming Mala (Wallaby). Started painting in 1986.

KITSON, JIMMY JUNGARRAYI

Born in 1961 at Ali Curang, Jimmy is Warlpiri/Anmatyerre. His country is Rabbit Bore, north-west of Willowra. His Dreamings are Budgerigar and Kangaroo. He lives in the Mutitjulu community at Ayers Rock. He has been painting since 1983, and usually sells his work through Marukus and Crafts. He has family ties with the Willowra community. 'We paint to keep our country strong. When I pass away, my son Japaljarri will take it on.'

KITTY PULTARA NAPALTJARRI

Born in 1938 (perhaps as early as 1925) at Napperby, where she has lived all her life, Kitty Pultara is the sister of Clifford POSSUM and his late brother, Tim LEURA Tjapaltjarri, and the wife of Malcolm Tjampitjinpa, one of the tribal leaders in the Napperby community. Kitty is an Anmatyerre speaker with Northern Arrente affiliations (Pultara is an Arrente skin name) and a senior and respected head woman in the Napperby community. She took up painting in 1986 after having worked as a domestic servant at the station for much of her earlier life. Kitty paints her Storm and Lightning, Plum and Butterfly Dreamings, her father's Yalka (Bush Onion) Dreaming, Possum Dreaming, Rain Dreaming from around Mt Wedge, and Kungka Berry, a mulberry-like fruit which is plentiful at a soakage north of the Napperby homestead, which is situated in Kitty's grandfather's traditional country. Kitty's daughter, Beatrix DIXON Nangala, also paints. Kitty's work has been exhibited in several national capitals and the USA and was featured in an issue of *Belle* magazine.

KUNBRY, PEIPEI, see PEIPEI, Kunbry

KUNINTJI, RITA NAMPITJINPA

Born 'in the bush', probably near the Stansmore Range, in approximately 1932, Rita Kunintjji is a Kukatja speaker now living at Balgo. Her country is Mangkai in the Stansmore Range, and her main Dreamings are Tingari stories. She also paints women's stories for the site of Muntjuku, south of Lake Gregory. She has been painting for Warlayirti Artists since 1988. A senior leader of Women's Law at Balgo, she enjoys working with other artists, including her husband, Albert NAGOMARA. Her enjoyment of painting is evident in the diversity of styles Kunintji uses — and yet all exhibit qualities of strength and Law. Her works often create an almost 'mandala'-like effect, with the painting radiating out from a central motif.

KUNTI KUNTI, JACK TJAMPIJINPA (c.1930–6/1990)

Born west of Kintore and a Pintupi speaker he had an outstation west of Kintore, though in the late '80s spent much time in Alice Springs, where he painted for the Centre for Aboriginal Artists. He began painting for Papunya Tula Artists in the early '80s while living for a time in Papunya. Collections: Museums & Art Galleries of NT, National Gallery of Australia, Canberra

KUYATA, YIPATI (1946–1992)

Born 18 November 1946 'in the bush' at Ernabella. Her mother came into the mission from Angatja. Her father's country is Pukara. Yipati grew up on the mission and attended Ernabella school. She had two daughters, Tjimpuna and Carol. Yipati's chosen subjects for paintings included principally scenes from the Piltati Dreaming line and depictions of food gathering on Pitjantjatjara lands. She was previous Chairperson of Ernabella Arts, the organisation which she joined in 1965 as a young girl, training in weaving and developing her painting skills. Her death in 1992 ended a long and distinguished artistic career, which is not elaborated here at the express wish of her immediate family. Collections: Art Gallery of SA (batiks), SA Museum (1977 watercolour, 1983 screenprint), Kelton Collection (acrylic, batik 1991)

L

LADY NAPALJARRI

Lady Napaljarri was born at Coniston, date of birth uncertain. Her country is Wirliya-jarrayi (Willowra). She paints the Dreamings for this country and also Jiri (Prickle Dreaming). She has no particular connections with communities other than Willowra, or with other artists at Willowra. Her tribal identification is Warlpiri/Anmatyerre. 'I started painting when I was six years old. I've learnt ceremony dancing from my mother and grandma. I've learnt singing my song for the dancing about my country that went with the designs.'

LANGDON, CHARLOTTE NABANANGKA

Born in Yuendumu in 1967, Charlotte Langdon is a Warlpiri speaker. Her country is Yuendumu and she paints Bush Tomato, Goanna and Snake Dreamings. She began painting in 1985, probably in the early years of the painting enterprise at the settlement, and still lives in Yuendumu. However, she sells her work through private dealers and outlets in town rather than through Warlukurlangu Artists — hence the outdated orthographical conventions for the usual spelling of her skin name.

LANGDON, MOLLY NAMPIJINPA

Molly Langdon is a Warlpiri speaker from Yuendumu whose main Dreaming is Warlukurlangu (Fire). One of the early group of senior women painters at Yuendumu, she has been exhibiting around Australia with Warlukurlangu Artists since the show at the Editions Gallery in Perth 1986. Her 1984 *Fire Dreaming at Ngarna* painting from this exhibition is reproduced in the *Dreamings* catalogue, where she is also shown teaching young children to dance. She was included in the 'Yuendumu: Paintings out of the Desert' show at the SA Museum in 1988. Collections: SA Museum, Australian Museum, Sydney and many private collections

LANKIN, EMILY

A Luritja speaker, born near the Finke mission in the 1930s, Emily now lives in Alice Springs and is a student of the Institute of Aboriginal Development literacy course. She began painting in 1991/2 while at IAD, painting her mother's (Emu) and father's (Snake) Dreamings. She has sold her work through Jukurrpa artists' co-operative, based at IAD.

LAWSON, LOUISA (PUPIYA) NAPALJARRI

Born at Kunajarrayi c.1931, Louisa lived as a child around Ngarrupalya. Her language/tribe is Warlpiri and her country Kunajarrayi. A senior woman in the ceremonial life of the Lajamanu community, she is custodian of many Dreamings, including Warna,

Ngalyipi (Medicine Vine), Mala (Wallaby), Laju (Witchetty Grub), Yurrampi (Honey Ant), Jutiya (King Brown Snake), Walu (Bushfire), Ngarlkirdi (Witchetty Tree), Yiwara (Milky Way) and Yatulu Yartulu (Granites). Her first contact with Europeans was while on holidays in Alice Springs. In her younger days she worked as a cook at the Granites goldmine. She is a fluent speaker of the old Aboriginal English spoken on the minefields. Her daughter by one of the miners, Robyn Napurrurla GREEN, now paints with her husband, Joe GREEN. Louisa is the sister (same mother) of Yuendumu artist Paddy Japaljarri SIMS and of Alec Holmes Japaljarri. Two of her paintings are reproduced in the catalogue for the 'Mythscapes' exhibition at the National Gallery of Victoria in 1989, and five in the catalogue of 'Paint Up Big', also at the National Gallery of Victoria, 1991. One of the best known painters in Lajamanu.

LAWSON, RONNIE JAKAMARRA

Place of birth Rilyi-rilyi, 1930 or earlier. A very old man, Ronnie Lawson is Pintupi/Warlpiri and is well-known and liked by everyone in Lajamanu for the sweetness of his disposition. His country is Rilyi-rilyi and his Dreamings Karnta (Women), Janmarda (Bush Onion) and Wintiki. A Ronnie Lawson painting of Pituri Dreaming features on the cover of an award winning thesis on adult education at Lajamanu by David MacLeay and another of Bush Bean on the cover of the catalogue of the Donald Kahn Collection, which has been touring the USA and Europe since 1991. Ronnie often works with his wife, Louisa LAWSON Napaljarri. They are both highly regarded painters. Ronnie Lawson started painting in 1986 in the Traditional Painting course organised by the TAFE Unit at Lajamanu school. Collections: National Gallery of Victoria etc.

LECHLEITNER, DICK TJAPANANGKA

Born at Coniston in 1944 of the Anmatyerre language group, Dick grew up 'walking the bush'. His boyhood companions included Clifford POSSUM and his older brother, Tim LEURA. He recalled how he and Clifford used to paint dots on the boomerangs they made to sell while living at Narwietooma station — long before painting began at Papunya. They also did watercolours off and on, selling them to the Centre for Aboriginal Artists in Alice Springs. Dick moved into Alice Springs, establishing himself at Morris Soak. At the beginning of the '80s he began painting on canvas in the Western Desert style independently of Papunya Tula Artists — one of the first to do so — selling his work through the Centre for Aboriginal Artists. In 1980 he applied for a grant from the Aboriginal Arts Board to support his work and received $500. Dick served for nine years on the Aboriginal Congress and was co-author of *Settle Down Country* and *Health Business* with Pam Nathan. His country lies around Mt Allen, and his work usually portrays Sugar Ant and Women Dreamings from this region. He is married with nine children, two from a previous marriage. His daughter, Wendy LECHLEITNER has recently begun painting. Nowadays he lives at Town Bore, an outstation of Papunya, and paints mostly for Papunya Tula Artists. Collections: Holmes à Court, Art Gallery of SA, Flinders University Art Museum

LECHLEITNER, WENDY NAPANGATI

Born in the early '60s, Wendy is married with two children. The eldest child of Dick LECHLEITNER, she lives in Alice Springs and began painting in about 1987, her father showing her the use of paint and canvas. Her works are usually Bush Tucker stories. Collections: Holmes à Court

LEE, DONKEYMAN TJUPURRULA

Born 'in the bush' near the present site of the Kiwirrkura community c.1925, Donkeyman Lee is a Kukatja speaker. His principal site is Walla Walla, just out of Kiwirrkura, and his paintings, which he began producing in 1985 at Balgo, are mainly Tingari stories for this area. Donkeyman usually works on large-scale canvases and with these he manages to convey a sense of his desert country. His works, which are included in the National Gallery of Australia and the National Gallery of Victoria, are always bold and strong and full of his personal experiences of Men's Law. They are also surprisingly innovative for an older man, and convey something of the easy-going good humour of the artist. He lives in Balgo and sells his paintings through Warlayirti Artists.

LEE, PATRICIA NAPANGATI

Although one of the younger Balgo artists — she was born near Gordon Downs station c.1961 — Patricia Lee is more active than most in the activities of the older women in the Balgo community, including painting and ceremonial life. A Warlpiri speaker, she works closely with her mother, Margaret Anjule, and grandmother, Dora Napaltjarri, both good artists in their own right. Her traditional country is in the Tanami Desert at Mongrel Downs, and her paintings often depict Wanayarra (Rainbow Snake) and Bush Tomato Dreamings from this area. Her work has a strong narrative element and she may be credited with 'introducing' the technique of paint flicking into Balgo art. She began painting in 1984, and her work is included in the National Gallery of Australia collection. She usually sells her work through Warlayirti Artists. It was also featured on the cover of the *Balance* exhibition catalogue (Queensland Art Gallery, 1990) and included in 'Flash Pictures' at the National Gallery of Australia in 1991–2.

LENA PWERLE

An Eastern Anmatyerre speaker, born c.1920, like most of the Utopia painters, she began to work in acrylic on canvas in the summer of 1988–9. She paints Bush Tomato, Intjingya Tree, Flower, Seed, Leaf and Yam, Kilkarra Medicine, Yam, and Wild Banana, and also Wild Plum and Bush Turkey. Her country is Ahalpere and she is associated with the Ngkwarlerlaneme community.

LEO, BARBARA NAKAMARRA

An Anmatyerre speaker, she was born in Alice Springs and lives at Ti-Tree with her husband and six children. Began painting on canvas in early 1988 with the Jukurrpa group based at IAD in Alice Springs.

LEO, (DIXON) SUSAN NAPALTJARRI

Born on Napperby station in July 1956, Susan Leo is an Anmatyerre speaker. She usually paints Fish and Sugar Ant Dreamings from her country, which lies around Tilmouth Well, Napperby and Central Mt Wedge. The daughter-in-law of Ronnie McNAMARA, she started painting in 1986 and lives at Napperby.

LEO, PETER TJAKAMARRA

Born on Coniston station c.1950, Peter Leo Tjakamarra is an Anmatyerre speaker. His traditional country is Coniston (Aruka) and the area around Tilmouth Well on Napperby station. He paints Witchetty Grub, Hunting, Yam and Snake Dreamings and often works with his wife, Susan LEO. They live at Napperby and have been painting since 1986. Peter Leo's work has been exhibited in major Australian cities and the USA.

LEURA, DAISY NAKAMARRA

Born at Umbungurru Creek c.1938 of the Anmatyerre language group, Daisy was living at Narwietooma station with her husband, Tim LEURA Tjapaltjarri, then a stockman, when the building program at Papunya was commenced. Later they moved to Papunya, where Daisy still lives. The couple had six children, and Daisy now has many grandchildren. Daisy's husband, who was one of the first and finest artists of the movement, taught her to paint. She was one of the first women to paint for Papunya Tula Artists in her own right. Her first canvases were done at the beginning of the '80s with her husband's assistance. Before that, though some women assisted their fathers and husbands with infilling of backgrounds, women were not actively involved with the paintings, which were seen as the men's sphere. Daisy feels very strongly that women should paint only secular themes from the women's sphere and is worried to see some of the younger women painting stories of which traditionally it was not proper for women to know. She lives in Papunya, where she is one of the senior women of the community. Collections: Art Gallery of SA, Flinders University Art Museum, National Gallery of Australia, Canberra

LEURA, TIM TJAPALTJARRI (c.1939–84)
Also cited as: Timmy Leurah Tjapaltjarri, Tjapaltjarri, Djabaldjari

Though the paintings of Tim Leura remain through reproduction a telling influence on the work of many Western Desert artists, little has been documented of the artist's life. He was born in Napperby Creek, probably in the late '30s, and grew up around Napperby station, on his traditional Anmatyerre/Arrente country. Like his younger brother, Clifford POSSUM Tjapaltjarri, he had such skill at wood carving that his name was already known in Central Australia as a brilliant craftsman before the painting movement began in Papunya. From Narwietooma station, where he had worked as a stockman, he moved to Papunya with his wife, Daisy LEURA, and their young family when the construction program for the new settlement began. When painting started up in 1971, he presented himself to Geoffrey Bardon and asked to do a painting. The two men became friends, and from this position Tim Leura played a leading role in the emerging painting enterprise, including his enlistment of his brother Clifford to the group of artists. Geoff Bardon described Tim Leura in his first book about Papunya painting, *Aboriginal Art of the Western Desert* (Rigby, Australia, 1979) as 'the most suitable man for a position of "leader" or "spokesman" for the painting group'. Geoffrey Bardon's latest book, *Papunya Tula: Art of the Western Desert*, contains a detailed map drawn by the artist showing his Dreaming area and the sites of the Possum, Yam, Fire, Blue Tongue Lizard, Sun, Moon and Morning Star and other Dreamings which were the subject of his paintings. His paintings were often sombre, reflecting (some have said) his profound sadness at the loss of the old ways of living. His 27' (8.2 m) *Napperby Death Spirit (Possum) Dreaming* (painted in 1980 with assistance from Clifford Possum) was the centrepiece of the 'Dreamings: Art of Aboriginal Australia' exhibition which toured the USA in 1988–9, and is increasingly cited as one of the greatest paintings of the movement. The painting of *Warlugalong*, 1976 (Art Gallery of NSW) with his brother Clifford is documented in the BBC documentary *Desert Dreamers* of that year. He died in 1984 after a long illness. Collections: National Gallery of Australia, Canberra, National Gallery of Victoria, Holmes à Court, Art Gallery of WA, Art Gallery of SA, University of WA Anthropology Museum, Flinders University Art Museum, SA Museum etc.

LEWIS, JOHN TJAPANGATI

Born at Yuendumu c.1955, he is a Warlpiri speaker, and now lives in Billiluna. A quiet man, he began painting in 1985 and is one of the younger men of the Balgo group of artists associated with Warlayirti Artists. His work often depicts Emu and Crow Dreamings from his traditional country, on the east side of Lake White and Lake Wills. His paintings show a strong sense of design and employ a lot of figurative elements, which are crafted with meticulous technique. His wife, Jane Gordon, is also a talented artist. Collections: Art Gallery of WA, Holmes à Court

LEWIS, MARGARET NAPANGARDI

Born at Yuendumu in 1956, Margaret Lewis has family at Yuendumu and Nyirrpi, where she often stays, but currently lives in Alice Springs, where she sells her work to several local galleries. She began painting for Warlukurlangu Artists in the late '80s and still paints for them when visiting the settlement. She paints Karnta (Women's) Dreaming for her country Janyinki. Dorothy Napangardi ROBINSON is one of her sisters.

LEWIS, WANATJURA

Born at Ernabella and a Pitjantjatjara speaker, she paints Ngintaka Wanampi (Snake) Dreaming. She was included in the *Anangu Way* (HALT project published by Nganampa Health Council, 1991) which encouraged many from communities in the north of South Australia to work with paint and canvas for the first time. She has connections with Ernabella and Mimili and is the daughter of Ernabella artist Tjulkiwa ATIRA-ATIRA. She lives at Amata.

LIDDLE, BESSIE

Born at Middleton Ponds, south-west of Alice Springs. Her mother was a Luritja woman from Tempe Downs. Her father was a Pertame man whose country was around Henbury station: Watarka, Lilla and Wanmara. Bessie Liddle gives her tribal affiliation as Luritja/Pertame and her country as Angus Downs station — Kings Creek. She has family at Angus Downs, and connections with the communities at Enbery station and Hermannsburg, also Wallace Rockhole, Maryvale and Uluru/Ayers Rock. She paints the Gecko Dreaming from Middleton Ponds, Seven Sisters Dreaming, and Kungka Kutjara (Two Sisters) Dreaming that passes through Kings Canyon. She remembers as a child her grandmothers and grandfathers telling stories and drawing them in the sand. They all passed away before 'dot painting' started, but this is how she learnt the stories she paints. She began painting in early 1987, after looking at the paintings in galleries in Alice Springs and deciding to try it herself. She began on art boards and experimented with colour and style, but always staying true to the Dreaming story and designs. Initially she sold through the CAAMA shop, but after eighteen months came to join the group at Jukurrpa, of which she is now the President. She has had work in exhibitions in Brisbane, Canberra, Melbourne, Adelaide, Darwin and WA (through CAAMA), London, New York and Geneva (where a postcard was made of one of her paintings).

LIKIRRIYA NAPALJARRI (MAISIE)

Place of birth Yinapaka (Lake Surprise) c.1925. A senior member of the Lajamanu community, her language/tribe is Warlpiri and she has two countries — Yinapaka, and Kurlurrnglinpa — from both parents. Her Dreamings are Witi (witi poles are associated with the male initiates Dreaming, but are not secret) and Ngatijirri (Budgerigar). She started painting in 1986 with the Traditional Painting course put on by the TAFE Unit at Lajamanu school.

LILLIAN NAKAMARRA

Born at Coniston of the Warlpiri/Anmatyerre tribe, her country is Yurrkuru (Brooks Soakage). She paints Bandicoot and Karnta (Women's) Dreamings and began doing paintings when canvas and board became available in Willowra at the end of the '80s. She states that she does her paintings with her own Dreaming, not wanting others to get involved, and emphasises the connection of these designs with land rights claims in which she has been actively involved: 'I do all the Dreaming about my country. When we had a Land Claim meeting, I got painted up with my design and showed how the Bandicoot Dreaming is. I did the dancing at Brooks when we had a Land Claim meeting when the judge came over to have a look.'

LILY (SANDOVER) KNGWARREYE

Born c.1937 at McDonald Downs station, Lily Kngwarreye is an Alyawarre speaker. Her country is Entibera, and she is the senior woman for this site, referred to by all Petyarre skin-group nieces on Entibera women's business. She is the eldest daughter of a very senior and important Alyawarre elder, Jacob Jones. Her main Dreaming is Two Sisters. She also paints various bush food stories, including Honey Grevillea, and like most of the Utopia artists, began painting in summer 1988–9 for CAAMA, after years of previous experience making batik. She is currently part of the Arawerre community in the north of Utopia Aboriginal Land. EMILY Kngwarreye is her adopted sister. She exhibited at the Gallery Gabrielle Pizzi in Melbourne in 1989 and Hogarth and Coo-ee Galleries in 1991. Collections: National Gallery of Australia, Canberra

LIMPI TJAPANGATI (c.1930–85)
Also cited as: Limpi Puntungka Tjapangati, Djabangardi

Born at Mereenie near Haasts Bluff c.1930, Limpi Tjapangati was one of the original painting group at Papunya who developed a distinctive style, which remained constant over a long period of time, and influenced other artists, especially those also working out of Haasts Bluff. One feature of this style was the use of alternating double bands of brown and yellow in the background dotting. Warlpiri artists like Paddy CARROLL and TWO BOB Tjungarrayi adopted the striped style for a period, and Turkey TOLSON also experimented with it. Until his dramatic death in 1985 — he collapsed and died while addressing a Land Council meeting — Limpi lived with his family at Haasts Bluff, a stunning outcrop of rock about 50 km east of Papunya. Hearts and diamond shapes, explained by the artist as traditional symbols, made a startling appearance in his work in the early '80s. His traditional country at Mereenie Bore, west of Hermannsburg, was the site of a rich find of natural gas. His tribal affiliation was Luritja/Arrente and he painted Wild Tomato, Magpie, Bush Onion and Crow Dreamings.

LINNY (FRANK) NAMPIJINPA

An Anmatyerre speaker, Linny was born in 1959 and paints Water, Women's Corroboree, Honey Ant and Watiya (Trees) for the country around Mt Allan. She is married to JOHN Japangardi and they both live at Mt Allan.

LIONEL KANTAWARRA (d. 1988)

An associate of LIMPI Tjapangati, with whom he lived at Haasts Bluff during the mid '80s, painting intermittently for Papunya Tula Artists, his Dreamings included Bush Onion.

LISA PULTARA

Born in Alice Springs c.1961, Lisa Pultara is an Anmatyerre speaker with Northern Arrente affiliations. Lisa's traditional country lies around Napperby station. She paints Water, Fish and Sugar Ant Dreamings for this region, and has been painting since 1986. She Lives at Napperby.

LIZZIE NAPALJARRI

Born east of the Granites at Wiingali, Lizzie Napaljarri is a Warlpiri person whose country is Wiingali and main Dreaming Ngatijirri (Budgerigar). She works with her husband Tingiyari (otherwise known as JACKO Jagamarra) and his co-wife SUSAN and lives at Lajamanu. She started painting in 1986 with the Traditional Painting course.

LOCKYER, MAY NANGALA

Born in Hermannsburg in 1948, May Lockyer now lives in Hidden Valley town camp in Alice Springs. Her father was Arrente, her mother Luritja/Pintupi. Since the early '90s May has been painting the Dreamings she inherited from her father's family (Green Caterpillar) and from her mother's family (Honey Ant, Witchetty Grub and Bush Potato). Her paintings have been sold through various galleries in Alice Springs.

LONG, JANET NAKAMARRA

Born at Anningie in 1960, Janet Long is a Warlpiri speaker whose traditional country is Wantapari. Her aunts, MAY and MOLLY Napurrurla, showed her the body paint designs for Wantapari Dreaming. She began painting on small boards in 1989 when the Willowra store first began stocking paint and canvas to supply local artists. Her half brother, MALCOLM Jagamara, showed her how to paint in the new medium. On canvas, she paints Frog, Snake, Orphan Child and Witchetty Grub Dreamings. Janet Long is the literacy worker at Willowra school, producing bi-lingual literature for use in the teaching program. She has lived all her life in Willowra, but her bi-lingualism and skill in dealing with western systems are increasingly drawing her into wider contacts, including research assistance in the gathering of biographical data on the Willowra artists for this dictionary. All statements in this dictionary from Willowra artists were gathered and translated into English by Janet.

LONG, JOE (TJANGARA) JANGALA

Born at Puyurru, his language and tribe is Warlpiri and he lives at Lajamanu. His country is Puyurru and his Dreamings are Ngapa (Water) and Yankirri (Emu). Started painting in 1986 with the Traditional Painting course.

LONG, NORAH NAPANANGKA

Born at Willowra c.1945, Norah is of the Warlpiri tribe. Her country is Willowra, and she paints Goanna, Bush Potato, Bush Beans and Bush Onion Dreamings for this country. She lives at Willowra, but has connections with the Aboriginal communities at Ti-Tree and Yuendumu. She started painting in 1985, learning from other members of her family who also paint.

LOOMOO, LUCY NUNGURRAYAI
Also cited as: Lucy Loomoo Nungarrayi

Born c.1935 'in the bush' near Jupiter Well, Lucy Loomoo is a Wangkatjunka tribeswoman and one of the senior women at Balgo from the far Western Desert area. Her country is Jupiter Well and west to the Canning Stock Route. She began painting for Warlayirti Artists in 1988. Her powerful paintings, which usually depict Tingari Dreamings, exhibit a strongly 'traditional' look and portray the food and water sources in her country and the associated Women's Law.

LORNA NAPURRURLA

Lorna Napurrurla lives at Lajamanu and her language/tribe is Warlpiri and country Yumurrpa. Her Dreamings are Yarla, Wapirti and Marlujarra and she started painting in 1986. Details of her place and date of birth are not avalaible. She is over sixty years of age and has been described by Christine Nicholls, former headmistress of Lajamanu school as 'the toughest old lady I've ever met in my life'. She appears on one of a series of screen-printed posters holding a fighting stick, with the caption 'You are on Aboriginal Land'. Collections: National Gallery of Victoria

LORRAINE NAMPIJINPA (d.)

One of Mt Allan's younger artists, Lorraine Nampijinpa was born in 1970. She was Anmatyerre. Her country was Coniston, and she painted Witchetty Dreaming. She died in the early '90s.

LOUIS PWERLE

Born c.1938 at the old sheep camp, Dneiper station, Central Australia, Louis Pwerle is an Eastern Anmatyerre speaker whose country lies on the central-western area of Utopia station, with significant areas also on neighbouring Mt Skinner station. As the eldest of his brothers (who include COWBOY Louie Pwerle), he is 'boss' of the stories for this area and an important ceremonial leader of the Eastern Anmatyerre, held in high esteem by the community. Known as a good stockman, Louis has worked over the years for several stations across the north-east. Though he has been painting only since the end of the '80s, his distinctive personal style with its bold designs and optical intensity, has won Louis considerable recognition in Australia and overseas. In 1990 he had a solo exhibition at Utopia Art, Sydney and was, with EMILY Kngwarreye, CAAMA/Utopia artist-in-residence at the Perth Institute of Contemporary Art (Reference: Batty, P. and Sheridan, N., *Utopia Artist in Residence Project* [Holmes à Court Foundation, Perth, 1990]). He has a family outstation at Mosquito Bore (Lyentye) in the north-west of Utopia Aboriginal Land. He is married to Angelina Kngwarreye and Sarah Kngwarreye. Collections: Holmes à Court, National Gallery of Victoria

LOWRY, TOMMY TJAPALTJARRI (c.1935–1987)
Also cited as: Tommy Larry Japaljarri

At the time of his death in 1987, Tommy Lowry was living at Kiwirrkura. His traditional country was Patja, in the Clutterbuck Hills, far to the south-west of Kintore and across the WA border towards Warburton. He spoke Pintupi/Ngardajarra and painted

Tingari Dreamings, specifically the Snake Men stories for this area, with increasing condensation of the complex narratives of his first paintings for Papunya Tula Artists in the mid '70s. His last works were like enlargements of sections of the earlier works, with distinctive creamy pulsating surfaces in the dotting. Before painting, Tommy Lowry was on the books of Papunya Tula Artists as a carver of wooden implements. Collections: Holmes à Court, SA Museum

LUCKY KNGWARREYE

An Alyawarre speaker, born c.1952 on Utopia station, she is the oldest daughter of Billy Morton Petyarre and his wife, Mary Morton. The family formerly lived at Ngkwarler-laneme, but have recently established an outstation on their country at Ngkawenyerre, near Lucky's Dreaming place, on the northern area of Utopia in the heart of Alyawarre lands. Like most of the Utopia artists, she did her first works on canvas with acrylics as part of CAAMA's 1988–9 Summer Project. Her principal Dreaming is Rainbow, which she often depicts in her paintings with dominant multi-coloured striped arcs. Lucky's other Dreamings include Tjarpa Lanait (Witchetty Grub) and various other bush tucker species. She is also a skilled wood carver. Her younger sister is painter JANICE Kngwarreye.

LUCY NAMPIJINPA

Born at Willowra in the 1930s, Lucy Nampijinpa has camped in this region all her life. Her heritage country is Mt Barkly, to the south of Willowra, and she is a Warlpiri speaker. She paints the same Ngurlu (Damper Seed) story as MAY and MOLLY Napurrurla, a Dreaming that was her great great grandfather's; also Sugar Bag Dreaming, and her mother's Budgerigar Dreaming. She is kurdungurlu ('mother boss') for the Sugar Bag and Budgerigar Dreamings in the dancing, and states that before she learnt to work on canvas she painted these designs on bodies. Grandmother of Janet LONG Nakamarra and MALCOLM Jagamara, she started painting at the same time as May and Molly Napurrurla, when many men and women were supplied with materials through the CDEP adviser in Willowra.

LUCY, NAPALJARRI, see KENNEDY, Lucy Napaljarri

LUNGKARDA, SHORTY TJUNGARRAYI (c.1920–1987)
Also cited as: Shorty Lungkata Tjungurrayi, Jungarai

One of the last men to join the original painting group in Papunya, some little time after the other Pintupi men had begun painting full time. From the beginning, his work was bold, simple, and singularly intense. Geoffrey Bardon recalls that he spoke almost no English, drawing on the translating services of other Pintupi in the group or his friend Johnny WARANGKULA Tjupurrula, when he needed to communicate his needs to the young art teacher. Within the Pintupi community at Papunya he was one of the leading senior men, renowned for his hunting and dancing skill and an authority on ritual matters. He moved to Kintore in the early '80s, closer to his heritage country in the Gibson Desert south of Lake McDonald. He painted Blue-Tongue Lizard, Goanna, Bush Banana, Snake and Bandicoot Dreamings for this area. After her father's death, he raised Musty Syddick's daughter, Linda SYDDICK, and later taught her to paint. Collections: Queensland Art Gallery, National Gallery of Victoria, Museums & Art Galleries of NT, SA Museum etc.

LYNCH, BRENDA NUNGURRAYI

Born at Coniston station in 1958, Brenda is the wife of Michael ROSS. Her father-in-law, Teddy BRISCOE Jampijinpa, is one of the senior men at Mt Allan. An Anmatyerre speaker, Brenda's country is around Coniston station and Supplejack on Napperby station. She began painting in 1986, and paints Rain Water, Water Snake, Witchetty Grub, Corkwood and Yam Dreamings from this region. Her work has been exhibited in national capitals and the UK. She has also sold her work through the Centre for Aboriginal Artists in Alice Springs. She currently resides at Pulardi (Desert Bore) outstation. At one time the most accomplished of Napperby's 'school of Clifford Possum' painters, she has now absorbed this and other influences in the development of her own personal style.

LYNCH, JOHNNY TJAPANGATI (c.1922 — c.1981)

One of the original group of painters at Papunya — the last, according to Geoff Bardon, to come forward wanting to paint. At the time, Johnny Lynch was a leading stockman at nearby Narwietooma station. His tribal affiliation was Anmatyerre/Arrente, and his paintings often depicted events along the Honey Ant Dreaming trail which ends 'across the bitumen' at Woodgreen station, his traditional country. He continued painting intermittently until his death in the early '80s.

LYNCH, NORBETT KNGWARREYE

Born c.1950 at Yambah station, where Norbett grew up. Over the years, he has worked as a labourer and a bus driver for Yipirinya school in Alice Springs. He speaks Arrente (Aranda), specifically Eastern Arrente, and lives most of the year at the Wenton Rubuntja camp in Alice Springs. He also spends several months a year on the family's traditional land. Norbett started painting in 1986 and does the five Corkwood Dreaming stories his father, Don 'Popsie' Lynch, has given him to do. Norbett's sisters Pamela and Margaret have also been given one Corkwood story each, but they rarely paint. Some of his five children have also begun to paint the Corkwood Dreaming stories. Norbett's work is represented in many private collections overseas, one of which, the Donald Kahn Collection, has been touring the USA and Europe since 1991, with Norbett's the largest piece in the show. Like other artists living in Alice Springs who began working in the Western Desert style in the late '80s, Norbett's work exhibits a conscious dialogue with the expectations of the western art market. It includes T-shirt designs as well as paintings.

M

McCORMACK, COLIN TJAKAMARRA

Born in the mid '50s in Alice Springs, Colin's father was a Pintupi speaker and his mother Pitjantjatjara/Arrente. As a boy, Colin attended boarding school in Alice Springs. He works at the Institute of Aboriginal Development in Alice Springs in the 'cross culture' section of the IAD Language Department. Colin started painting in 1991, selling his paintings through the Gondawana Gallery and other shops and galleries in Alice Springs. He works alone. The National Gallery of Australia in Canberra has expressed interest in acquiring one of his large *Honey Ant Dreaming* paintings. His style is distinctive, with bright colours — he would like to change to traditional colours later, but 'It's easier to work with bright colours and get good effects.' Colin paints landscapes and bush food, but does not use traditional Dreaming designs in his work.

McCORMACK, LOLA NAMPIJINPA

Born in 1952, Lola McCormack is an Anmatyerre speaker. Her country is Mt Allan and she paints Honey Ant, Bush Potato and Yiparli Dreamings. She is married to artist Tim McCORMACK and lives at Mt Allan.

McCORMACK, TIM JAPANGARDI

Born in 1937 at Coniston, Tim McCormack is a member of the Anmatyerre tribe and one of the main custodians of Mt Allan, which was his grandfather's country. He paints Bush Potato, Bush Banana, Yuelamu (Honey Ant), Woman, Emu and Witchetty (from his uncle) Dreamings. He has also painted for Warlukurlangu Artists in Yuendumu, but lives at Mt Allan.

McDONALD, KAY NUNGARRAYI

Place of birth Ali Curang c.1955–60. Of the Warlpiri language and tribe, she lives at Lajamanu. No details of country or Dreamings. She started painting in 1987, a bit later than many others in Lajamanu, and works with her husband, Martin JOHNSON.

McNAMARA, RONNIE TJAPANANGKA

Born Nyirrpi, west of Yuendumu c.1942, Ronnie McNamara is an Anmatyerre speaker. He paints Kangaroo, Snake and Bushfire Dreamings from his country west of Yuendumu, and has been painting intermittently since 1975. He lives at Napperby.

MAISIE NAPANGARDI (KAJINGARRA)
Also cited as: Maisie Napangardi (Kajingarra) Kelly

Born at Janyinki c.1930, Maisie Napangardi's language/tribe is Warlpiri and she lives at Lajamanu. Her country is Janyinki and her Dreamings are Mardukuja-mardukuja, Kanakurlangu and Yunkaranyi (Pirrkanji). She started painting in 1986, and is the younger sister of Yadaya Napangardi — RUBY ROSE. Collections: National Gallery of Victoria

MAJOR, RILEY TJANGALA

Born at Putjarra (Brown's Bore) south of Mt Leibig in the late 1940s. His father passed away when he was a small boy, and his mother took him into Haasts Bluff, where he grew up. For a time, he attended school at Hermannsburg and later worked with donkeys at Jay Creek before going through ceremonies near Haasts Bluff to make him a man. He lived in Papunya for a time in the late '60s prior to the start of the painting movement, working as a cleaner supervising housing, then spent two years at Haasts Bluff as a stockman. Back in Papunya, he served for a time as Secretary of the Papunya Council. During this time he tried his hand at painting on two small canvases. But it was not until after the Pintupi move back to Kintore in 1981 (Riley was among the first group to do so) that his older brother, GEORGE Tjangala, taught him how on paint on canvas in about 1982. He has since painted regularly for Papunya Tula Artists. Riley's country lies around Piltarta and Muruntji, south-west of Mt Leibig. He often paints the Snake Dreaming story associated with the site Kakarra. He has served as Chairman of Kintore Council. He has two wives and several children, and is one of a new generation of Pintupi artists who began working for Papunya Tula Artists after the establishment of the Pintupi homeland settlement at Kintore. Collections: Holmes à Court, Queensland Art Gallery, Museums & Art Galleries of NT

MALBUNKA, MARY ANNE

Mary Anne Malbunka is of Purrula skin, was born in 1971 of the Western Aranda (Arrente) tribe and speaks the Western Aranda (Arrente) language. The Western Aranda (Arrente) land of Ipolera is the community at which she lives and works. Ipolera is 180 km west of Alice Springs. Mary Anne lived at Hermannsburg till 1980, when the people of Ipolera moved back to the land that belonged to them. Mary Anne started painting in 1989 when artist Stephanie Radke came to live at Ipolera. Mary Anne paints one story of Gosse Bluff, now called Thourala again. This is a story that belongs to her family, but she only paints about that which is allowed to be told. Mary Anne is the cousin of the leader of Ipolera, Herman Malbunka. She not only works as an artist, but also helps the Ipolera community to run the Art and Craft Centre, and also helps to show around those tourists who come to do a cultural tour run by Herman and Mavis Malbunka. Mary Anne and other Ipolera artists mainly paint of everyday life, of food gathering, the various forms of food — wild bananas, coconut, berries, witchetty grubs, honey ants etc. Very rarely are stories told in paintings. They are kept closely guarded. (Reference: Mary Anne Malbunka)

MALCOLM JAGAMARA
Also cited as: Malcolm Maloney Jakamarra

Born in the Willowra area at Aningie station near Central Mt Stuart in 1955, Malcolm Jagamara describes himself as a Lander River Warlpiri. He is the son of MINNIE Napanangka. His traditional country is Wantapari, some 60 km west of Willowra in the Tanami Desert. He attended Adelaide Boys High School, launching a ten year career as a footballer, which earned him a place in a publication *200 Unsung Heroes and Heroines of Australian History*. In 1976 he returned from Adelaide to Willowra and began his Aboriginal education, sincluding instruction in how to paint for ceremony. His principal Dreamings are Wana (Snake), Walu (Fire) and Ngapa (Water). He has also painted Budgerigar, Seven Sisters and Goanna stories with which he has family connections. He began painting in 1985, after observing the development of the art movement for a decade. His first two boards were done in Darwin in what he described as a moment of 'desperation'. Later his uncle, Willie REILLY Japanangka, one of the first people to start painting in Willowra, helped to get him started properly. Malcolm also has family ties with the communities of Yuendumu and Mt Allan. A very articulate man with a strong consciousness of cultural and political issues, the artist was the first of his people to become actively involved in commerce in Western Desert art: 'OK, they had their role model for an artist — and that was Namatjira, but up to this stage they had no role model for the dealer of their own art. I'm talking about Yapa here — an Aboriginal person. There's been none of that. To be able to sit down and deal with Yapa levels.' This sensibility and intelligence appears also in the variety of influences and the exploration of new directions in his art (e.g. use of oils). One of his works features on a Telecom phonecard, and in 1992 he was artist-in-residence at the Art Gallery of New South Wales and in 1993 at Macquarie University, where he painted a large mural with the assistance of student helpers. He has also recently travelled to North America. Collections: Kelton Foundation

MARINGKA NANGALA

The wife of Charlie MARSHALL, she is one of the first women in Papunya to begin painting in her own right. She lives at Mt Leibig.

MARSHALL, CHARLIE TJUNGARRAYI

Born in the late '40s at Kunatjarrayi and a member of the Warlpiri language group, he began painting in the early '80s after Daphne Williams took over the running of the Papunya Tula Artists company. Residing at Mt Leibig, he paints Witchetty Grub, Wallaby, Man and Woman and Centipede Dreamings around the area of Kunajarrayi. He earned the nickname 'Whitlam' for his imposing figure after being photographed with the then Australian Prime Minister. Collections: National Gallery of Australia, Canberra, Holmes à Court, University of WA Anthropology Museum

MARSHALL, JOE JAPANGARDI

Born at Yuendumu and belonging to the Warlpiri language/tribe, he lives at Lajamanu and his country is Yurntumu and Yinjirrimarda. His Dreamings are Yuparli (Bush Banana), Pikilyi (Old Man), Yurrampi and Mala. He sometimes works with his wife, Janie PETERS. The couple are among the most highly regarded painters in the Lajamanu community. He started painting in 1986, being the first man in Lajamanu to do so. From having lived previously in Yuendumu, he knew how to stretch canvases, and was a leading figure in the early days of the painting enterprise at Lajamanu.

MARSHALL, MARIKA NANGALA, see MARINGKA Nangala

MARSHALL, SUSAN NAKAMARRA

Born c.1955, Susan Marshall is a Warlpiri speaker. She paints Snake and Warlukurlangu (Fire) Dreamings for her country west of Nyirrpi. She lives at Nyirrpi.

MARTIN, ANDREA NUNGARRAYI

Born 1965, Andrea Nungarrayi Martin is a Warlpiri speaker who lives at Yuendumu and paints for Warlukurlangu Artists. She paints Wardapi (Goanna), Warlawurru (Eagle) and Marlu (Kangaroo) Dreamings. Her work has been included in exhibitions of Warlukurlangu Artists in Perth, Alice Springs, Darwin, Canberra, Hobart, Melbourne and Sydney since 1990. She is represented in the collection of the Musée National des Arts Africains at Oceaniens, Paris.

MARTIN, DOMINIC TJUPURRULA

Born 'in the bush', probably just north of present day Kiwirrkura, c.1938, Dominic Martin has not spoken since a boyhood accident. He lives in Balgo and sells his work through Warlayirti Artists. The artist's traditional country lies in Kukatja lands west of Lake Mackay. He usually depicts Bandicoot and Emu Dreamings and has been painting since 1985. He continues to paint in a fairly 'traditional style' which is simple and direct. However, his work also shows awareness of developments in other artists' work and a willingness to try new approaches. A prolific painter, he usually prefers to work on smaller sized canvases. Collections: Holmes à Court

MARTIN, GEORGINA NAPANGARDI

Born at Alicurang (Warrabri) in 1962, Georgina Martin is Warlpiri/Katitji. Her country is Mt Theo and she paints Goanna, Bush Bean and Bush Onion Dreamings. She lives at Willowra and started painting in 1988 through the CDEP program. 'We always go bush, hunting you know, bush tomato, kangaroo, everything, take the kids, everybody.'

MARTIN, HILDA NAPALJARRI

Born c.1941, she is Warlpiri/Anmatyerre and her is country is Coniston station and Mt Allan area. She is one of the senior Yuendumu women whose powerful collaborative works in the mid '80s first drew attention to Warlukurlangu Artists, for whom she now paints occasionally. Her work was first exhibited in Warlukurlangu Artists' exhibition at the Sydney Opera House in 1987. Her Dreamings include Ngatijirri (Budgerigar), Marlu (Kangaroo), Owl, Ngarlajiyi (Bush Yam), Yanyinlingi (Sugar leaf) and Native Fuschia. Collections: South Australian Museum, private collections

MARTIN, PEGGY NAPANGATI

Born c.1950 and a Warlpiri person, based in Ti-Tree. She was a carver who started painting for the Centre for Aboriginal Artists in Alice Springs in 1990.

MARTIN, POMPEY JAPANANGKA (c.1932–1989)
Also cited as: Pompei Martin Japanangka

Born c.1932 at Janyinki, west of Yuendumu, the custodians of this area being Napanangka/Japanangka and Napangardi/ Japangardi. He was Warlpiri and had lived in Yuendumu for many years. He was involved with the group of senior men who began painting at Yuendumu in the mid '80s. His 1986 *Janyinki Jukurrpa*, purchased by the National Gallery of Australia, depicted the site of Janyinki, which is associated with Ngarrka (Initiated Men) and Ngalyipi (Vine) and Ruutju (Women) Dreamings.

MARTIN, UNI NAMPITJINPA

Born c.1932 of the Warlpiri tribe, lives at Yuendumu. Her country is Warlukurlangu, south-west of Yuendumu and her Dreamings are Warlukurlangu (Fire) and Yankirri (Emu). She began painting in the late '80s, first exhibiting with Warlukurlangu Artists in August 1987. Since then, her work has been included in many Warlukurlangu group exhibitions in capital cities around Australia, in 'Mythscapes', at the National Gallery of Victoria in September 1989 and in 'l'été Australien', Musée Fabre, Montpellier, France in June 1990. Uni Martin was one of 42 Yuendumu painters who worked on the 7 x 3 m canvas which toured Europe in 1993 as part of 'Aratjara: Australian Aboriginal and Torres Strait Islander Art'. Collections: National Gallery of Victoria, South Australian Museum, Australian Museum, Sydney, Musée National des Arts Africain et Oceaniens, Paris, private collections. (References: Ryan J., *Mythscapes*; Crossman S. & Bardou J-P., *L'été Australien*)

MAVIS NAKAMARRA

Born in 1938 of the Anmatyerre tribe, Mavis Nakamarra's traditional country is Mt Allan. She paints Caterpillar, Bush Potato and Bush Onion Dreamings. One of her *Yala Dreamings* was sold to Hazel Hawke, the wife of the then Prime Minister, when she came to Mt Allan in 1988 to open the Yuelamu Museum and Art Gallery. Mavis lived for a time with her mother at Hermannsburg, but is now back in Mt Allan.

MAXIE TJAMPITJINPA

Born in Haasts Bluff c.1945, he is part of the Warlpiri language group, his father's traditional country of Watunuma lying in Warlpiri territory west of Yuendumu around Waite Creek. His mother was of mixed Warlpiri/Luritja descent from Kunajarrayi, also near Waite Creek. The family moved across from Haasts Bluff in the early '60s so that the children could attend the school opened in Papunya. Maxie also attended high school at Nightcliff, Darwin and worked various jobs in Darwin, Maningrida and Port Keats before settling in Papunya. He worked on the settlement as a tractor driver, bus driver and police tracker before taking up painting in 1980 under the expert instruction of OLD MICK Tjakamarra, one of the senior artists of the movement, who instilled his own love of painting in his pupil. Maxie's usual subjects are Flying Ant Dreaming and Women Dreaming, though he has recently based an entire show around Bushfire Dreaming. In 1984 Maxie won the NT Art Award. He was artist-in-residence with Dinny NOLAN at Wagga Wagga City Art Gallery in 1988. In 1992 he exhibited at the Aboriginal Arts Australia gallery in Sydney with EUNICE Napangardi and had a solo exhibition at Utopia Arts, Sydney. Since the mid '80s, he has lived mostly in Alice Springs, selling his work mainly through Papunya Tula Artists and the Centre for Aboriginal Artists. Over the past eight years, he has developed and refined the flicked style of background infilling, which now has many imitators, especially in Alice Springs, though few have achieved Maxie's mastery of it. His Papunya based wife, Mavis Napangati, also paints occasionally. Collections: National Gallery of Australia, Canberra, Parliament House, Canberra, National Gallery of Victoria, Flinders University Art Museum, Museum & Art Galleries of NT, Wollongong City Art Gallery, Federal Airports Corporation, Holmes à Court, University of WA, Auckland City Art Gallery, Sydney University Union, Moree Plains Art Gallery, Queensland Art Gallery, Araluen Arts Centre, Alice Springs, Art Gallery of SA

MAY NAPURRURLA

Born at Coniston in the early '40s. She grew up in the region of Yurrnkuru and shares with her older sister MOLLY Napurrurla the country round Yurrnkuru, as well as Coniston and Kanakurlangu. She is a Warlpiri speaker and came to live in Willowra at the same time as her sister MOLLY. For the women's dancing, May paints up with Wardiji and Lukarrara (Mulga Seed) designs. Her canvases depict Frog, Snake, Orphan Child and Witchetty Grub Dreamings. She began painting in 1989 at the same time as her sister Molly, with encouragement from the Willowra CDEP adviser.

MELODY NAPALJARRI

Born in 1967, Melody is a Luritja speaker whose heritage country is Mt Wedge. She paints Kerrinyarra (Mt Wedge) Dreaming, also Bush Potato, Bush Onion, Corroboree and Honey Ant Dreamings. She lives at Mt Allan.

MICHAEL, YILPI see ATIRA-ATIRA, Yilpi

MICK, JOSEPHINE

Born at Ernabella in 1955, Josephine moved to Alice Springs in 1983. A Pitjantjatjara speaker, she started painting her father's Dreamings, Kungka Kutjara (Two Women) and Water Snake, in 1986. She has sold her work to Alice Springs galleries and, with the help of her husband, Ushma Sales, to galleries overseas too. Josephine's sister, Tjulkiwa ATIRA-ATIRA, is also a painter.

MICK, WALLANKARRI TJAKAMARRA
Also cited as: Old Mick Tjakamarra/Tjagamara/Jagamara/Djagamara

Born c.1900 at Watikipinrri, close to Watulpunya, west of Central Mt Wedge, Old Mick is the senior custodian ('Boss') of Kerrinyarra (Mt Wedge). When interviewed for this dictionary, Mick gave his tribal affiliation as Aranda/Luritja (however, he and old Bert Nganangana have also been named as the last surviving Kukatja tribesmen from this area). Mick worked as a stockman at Glen Helen and Narwietooma stations in his younger days. Despite being a pensioner when the painting movement started in 1971, Old Mick became one of the most important artists painting for Papunya Tula because of his high ceremonial status and his knowledge of stories and designs. Old Mick shared with Old Tom Onion the custodianship of the Honey Ant design of the original mural painted on the Papunya school wall. In recent years, failing eyesight and physical frailty have stopped his once prolific output, but his love of painting and elements of his style can be found in the work of younger artists whom he influenced. These include MAXIE Tjampijinpa, whom he taught to paint at Papunya in 1981, and DON Tjungarrayi, whom Mick brought up after his father passed away. Old Mick's country stretches across the Papunya, Mt Wedge, Mt Leibig region covering the Warumpi (Sugar Ant), Water, Yarla (Yam), Yarripirri (Snake) (who was carried to the sea at Darwin, and then came back to Winparrku), and Woman Dreamings which the artist usually paints. His usual place of residence is Papunya, though he has recently spent time in Alice Springs for medical treatment. His work was exhibited in the Asia Society's 'Dreamings' show which toured the USA in 1988–9. He was the first Western Desert artist to be purchased by the National Gallery of Australia. Collections: National Gallery of Australia, Canberra, Asia Pacific Museum, Los Angeles, Australian Museum, Sydney, Holmes à Court, National Gallery of Victoria, Art Gallery of WA, Museums & Art Galleries of NT, Flinders University Art Museum, SA Museum

MICKININIE, OLD (c.1920–mid '80s)
Also cited as: Old Mekinini

An associate of Limpi Tjapangati, with whom he lived at Haasts Bluff, and painted intermittently. A very gentle old man.

MILLER, KITTY

A Pitjanjatjara speaker from Ernabella originally, her traditional country lies across the WA border around Pukhara. She has been painting since 1986 and her work often depicts Seven Sisters, Pitjiri Water and Sugarbag Honeysuckle Dreamings in a loose and spontaneous style. She works with the Jukurrpa group in Alice Springs.

MILLER, LIDDY NAMPIJINPA
Place of birth Jila c.1940, her tribe/language is Warlpiri and she lives at Lajamanu. Her country is Parrulyu/Puyurru and her Dreamings are Ngapa, Yujuku and Watiyawarnu. She started painting in 1986 in the Traditional Painting course. Collections: National Gallery of Victoria

MILLIGA NAPALTJARRI
Born near Kiwirrkura c.1920, Milliga is a Kukatja speaker. Her country is Purrungu and Mulyurtju. She lives at Balgo and started painting for Warlayirti Artists in 1989. Despite being very elderly, the artist loves painting and seems to enjoy conveying something of her feelings for her country. All of her works tell of the food and wood sources in the area where she lived for many years. Recently, she has produced a series of totally abstract works marked by layers of hazy dotting.

MILNER, BOXER TJAMPITJIN
Born at Milnga-Milnga, south-west of Billiluna near Sturt Creek c.1934, Boxer Milner belongs to the Tjaru people from the area north of Balgo and now lives at Billiluna. He began painting for Warlayirti Artists in 1989. He usually paints Water Dreaming stories of his traditional country of Sturt Creek. Whereas desert peoples paint mostly rockholes and claypans, Tjaru country is an area of creekbeds and flood plains, and this is reflected in the art of Tjaru artists like Boxer. The area of Milnga-Milnga is a major flood plain for Sturt Creek and is inundated every summer after the rains. This is important for all nature, including people, and the artist's family, who have always lived here, 'look after' the area by keeping its associated Law and ceremonies. Boxer Milner is one of the more consistent and successful painters currently working out of Billiluna. He creates simple linear designs that speak of his care for, and knowledge of his country. Collections: National Gallery of Victoria

MINNIE NAPANANGKA
Born at Willowra in the period when birthdates were not recorded, but is a senior women in the Willowra community. A Warlpiri speaker, her country is Ngarnallkurru (little Sandy River) and Mt Theo. She paints a Cave story and Bush Onion, Bush Tomato, and Bush Bean Dreamings. She learnt to paint through relatives who are painters. 'I haven't started painting when I was young. I started doing painting when we got canvas boards. I did the designs very carefully because I had to remember the designs. Yes, we also do our painting on our bodies with these Dreamings. It also represents our country when we do these designs for ceremonies. Some of these Dreaming designs are very important to us.'

MINOR, RICHARD TJANGALA

Born at Haasts Bluff in 1950, Richard attended school in Papunya in the '60s and moved to Kintore in 1986, where he began painting for Papunya Tula Artists in about 1987. His country is from his grandfather's side around Kintore. His work often depicts the Snake Dreaming which travels from the west towards the east through Murunti, given to him to paint by his stepbrother, Riley MAJOR. He also paints an Emu Dreaming story that passes through Kintore going west. Collections: Wollongong City Art Gallery

MOLLY NAPURRURLA

Born near Brooks Soakage in the 1930s, Molly Napurrurla grew up in the Coniston area before marrying a Willowra man and coming to live at Willowra. A Warlpiri speaker, her traditional country is Coniston, Kanakurlangu and Yurrnkuru. She is one of the senior women at Willowra for the dancing, where she always paints up with the Damper Seed designs — or sometimes Snake Dreaming. On her paintings, she depicts this Snake story, as well as Frog, Orphan Child and Witchetty Grub Dreamings. She states that her grandmother taught her to paint, and her mother, and that she began working in acrylics on board in 1989 when the Willowra CDEP coordinator made some paint and canvas available. She had seen paintings before in Alice Springs, where she took her work to sell when it was finished.

MOORE, ELSIE NAMPIJINPA

Born in 1950 of the Anmatyerre tribe, Elsie's traditional country is Desert Bore, and she paints Dingo, Witchetty, Women's Corroboree and Kangaroo Dreamings. She is married to WALKER Japangardi and lives at Pine Hill.

MORRIS, HARPER TJUNGARRAYI

A well respected artist who has been painting since the early '70s, he often paints the Emu mythology associated with the locality of Anangra Waterhole, close to Utopia station, north of Alice Springs. His language group is Alyawarre (Aliaywara), and after having resided for periods in Papunya and Haasts Bluff, during which he painted for Papunya Tula Artists, he now lives on an outstation near Utopia. He is the brother of EMILY Kngwarreye. Collections: Art Gallery of SA, Flinders University Art Museum, National Gallery of Victoria, Holmes à Court, SA Museum

MORRIS, TIGER JAPALJARRI

Born at Kunajarrayi, north-west of Nyirrpi, in the 1920s, Tiger Morris is a Warlpiri speaker. He paints Warna (Snake), Rock Wallaby, Honey Ant and Witchetty Grub Dreamings for his country, Kunajarrayi. He also executed three paintings on the school buildings at Nyirrpi. He has close links with Yuendumu, but lives mostly at Nyirrpi, and has been painting since the late '80s.

MORRIS TJAPANANGKA

Born near Mt Denison in 1944, Morris began painting at Napperby in the late '80s. He previously worked as a stockman and drover at Coniston station and paints the stories of his country around Mt Denison — Kangaroo, Wild Potato and Men and Women's Dreamings associated with a place called Chadabunya (Tjatapunja) on Mt Denison. Morris is of the Anmatyerre language group and lives at Napperby.

MORRIS, VALERIE NAPURRURLA

Born at Mt Doreen in the early '50s, Valerie is a Warlpiri speaker. She lives at Nyirrpi, but has family connections to Yuendumu, Papunya and Alice Springs. She has painted the Possum Dreaming for her country Mt Davis since 1987. She has participated in exhibitions in Canberra and Adelaide, but sells most of her work through the local store and church.

MORRISON, TEDDY JUPURRURLA

Born at Miya-miya in the mid '40s, Teddy is a Warlpiri speaker who lives at Lajamanu. His country is Miya-miya and Malungurru and his Dreamings are Ngurlu (Seed), Jungunypa (Bush Louse), Kalajirri (Hawk). An older man and brother of the late Maurice Luther Tjupurrurla, who led the Lajamanu Council until his death in 1985, Teddy commands a lot of respect in the Lajamanu community, where he lives.

MORTON, DON JAPANGARDI

Born in the late '30s at Mt Allan, Don Morton and his brother, Tim McCORMACK, are senior custodians of the Yuelamu site. In his youth, Don Morton worked as a stockman on Mt Allan station. An Anmatyerre tribesman, he is married to Evelyn Nampijinpa and lives at Mt Allan. He can paint Honey Ant, Yulka (Bush Onion) and the Women Dreaming for Mt Wedge. The Yuelamu Museum was Don's brainchild, and it was his authority that sanctioned the installation — within a section of the building sealed off to women and children — of a ground painting for the Yuelamu Honey Ant Dreaming. He began painting in about 1987.

MORTON, SARAH NAPANANGKA

Born in 1970 of the Anmatyerre tribe, Sarah is the daughter of Don MORTON and Evelyn Nampijinpa. Her country is Mt Allan, where she lives, and her Dreamings are Honey Ant, Men and Women.

MOSQUITO, JOHN TJAPANGATI

Born 'in the bush' c.1920, probably in the area of the Southern Tablelands, John Mosquito is a member of the Kukatja/Walmatjari language group whose country lies around Walkali and Kurtal (Helena Springs). He is custodian of the site of Puntukutjara, south-west of Balgo. The artist is acknowledged as the senior Rainmaker in the Balgo community, a theme which appears frequently in his paintings, with often powerful and dramatic effects. He has painted since 1986 for Warlayirti Artists. His works usually depict Tingari and Water Dreaming stories, and reflect the artist's years of involvement in Men's Law, suggesting forces barely comprehended by outsiders. Collections: National Gallery of Victoria

MOTNA, ERNA NAKAMARRA

Born at Hermannsburg on 18 October 1938, Erna speaks both Northern and Western Arrente. She spent her early years in Hermannsburg and at Glen Helen, which is part of her family's heritage country. Her father, Cyril Motna, was a pastor at Hermannsburg. Most of her relatives at the time, including Albert Namatjira, Benjamin Landara and Noel Raggett (all now deceased), were painting watercolours. Erna was educated at the mission school, and as a young girl was taught the dancing and body painting for a number of women's ceremonies. She now teaches young girls ready for 'girls' time' the body paint designs and the dancing for these ceremonies. In about 1986 Erna began painting these Dreamings on canvas for the Corkwood Gallery in Alice Springs. She also paints Bush Tucker Dreamings passed on to her by her mother, a Warlpiri woman from Napperby. Her work has been shown in exhibitions in Perth, Adelaide and Sydney, Italy, Canada and Florida, USA and has appeared in the *New York Times*.

MUDJIDELL, BRIDGET NAPANANGKA

Born 'in the bush' in 1935, probably in the area of Lake Dennis, Bridget Mudjidell is a member of the Ngarti language group. Her country is Tulku, on the west side of Lake White near Yagga Yagga. She mainly paints about food and water sources in this region. The artist spent the first part of her life in the area and knows it intimately. A gregarious, friendly woman, Bridget Mudjidell is a leader in women's activities at Balgo. Her works all reflect a great knowledge and love of the land. An energetic painter, her work is always deeply personal, telling of her recent visits to places and of her ancestors' activities there. She began painting for Warlayirti Artists in 1988.

MUNTI, YIPATI RILEY
Also cited as: Yipati Munti

Born at Ernabella on 22 December 1966, Yipati is a Pitjantjatjara speaker and paints Snake, Lizard and Wild Fig Dreamings. She started painting in 1985 and has close ties with both Ernabella and Fregon communities. Her sister Isobel and aunt Nyurpaya also paint occasionally. She lives in Amata.

MUNTJA NUNGURRAYAI
Also cited as: Muntja Nungarrayi

Born 'in the bush' around the Tobin Lake area c.1930, the artist is a Kukatja/ Wangkatjunka speaker whose traditional country is in the area surrounding the northern Canning Stock Route. Muntja is the 'boss' woman for the Wangkatjunta mob at Balgo — both by the force of her personality and her knowledge of Women's Law. She has worked closely with anthropologists in the past and is a recognised authority at many gatherings. She has been painting her Tingari and Dingo Dreamings since 1986 in works which display her authority in matters of the Law. Her husband, John MOSQUITO, is also an artist of note. She sells her work through Warlayirti Artists. Collections: National Gallery of Australia, Canberra, etc.

MUTJI, MICHAEL TJANGALA

Born near Well 33 on the Canning Stock Route c.1940, Michael Mutji is a Kukatja speaker with country at Kinyu and Tjunpartja. He now resides at Balgo, where he began painting for Warlayirti Artists in 1988. He usually paints Dingo/Wati Kutjarra (Two Men) Dreaming. A quiet man who does a lot of painting and has tried many different approaches to his art, yet always imparts the look of tradition. The head of a household which contains a number of artists, he paints with great diligence and seriousness.

N

NAGOMARA, ALBERT TJAKAMARRA

Born 'in the bush' around Lake Wills c.1925, Nagomara is one of several Tjakamarra men in the Balgo community whose works primarily concern Water Dreaming and rituals associated with rainmaking. His country is in the Stansmore Ranges around Mangkai. He is custodian of various Tingari and Water Dreaming stories for this area. He has also painted the area around Nguntalpi, a very sacred place of many rocks and caves, where his father is buried. A Kukatja speaker, Albert Nagomara began painting for Warlayirti Artists in 1988. His works generally use strong, simple motifs, such as roundels and watercourses, but beneath their simplicity lies a great reservoir of Law matters.

NALA, ANGELINA PWERLE, see ANGELINA Na(nga)la Pwerle

NAMARARI, OLD MICK TJAPALTJARRI
Also cited as: Mick Numerari Japaltjari, Mick Numieri Tjapaltjari, Old Mick Namari

Born c.1926 at Marnpi in the sandhill country south-west of Mt Rennie. According to Tindale's records, the family group was camped near Putarti Spring, south-west of Mt Leibig, when encountered in 1932. Mick remembers as a little boy walking east to Haasts Bluff with his family to collect rations of flour, brown sugar, honey, jam and square tins of tobacco. For the next decade, the family stayed around the Haasts Bluff /Hermannsburg area. Mick was initiated at Areyonga and worked as a stockman on various stations, including Tempe Downs and Areyonga, in this period. He also married his first wife at Haasts Bluff. He was serving on the Papunya Council when Geoffrey Bardon arrived in Papunya and with fellow councillor Johnny WARANGKULA soon made his interest in painting known to the obliging art teacher. He remembered painting on anything — any piece of prepared timber in the settlement was used. During these early years, Mick travelled to Sydney with Geoffrey Bardon for the making of Geoffrey's film, *Mick and the Moon*, about the artist and his work. Old Mick was one of a few Pintupi who stayed on in Papunya for some years after the majority of their people had made the move back to Kintore and their homelands. Painting prolifically in this period of the early '80s, he travelled to Sydney with NOSEPEG and Old TUTUMA in 1981 for what was probably the first 'renegade' exhibition of Western Desert painting, mounted at Sid's, Darlinghurst, in support of an Aboriginal controlled health service at Papunya. Later Mick joined his countrymen and women at Kintore, and set up an outstation at Nyunmanu to the south-east of the settlement towards Marnpi. More recently he has lived at Njutulnya outstation with his second wife Elizabeth and their two young children. A senior man, Mick's paintings cover many Dreamings, principally

Kangaroo, Dingo, Water, Mingajurra (Wild Bandicoot). In recent years his work has increasingly explored new directions and remains fresh and exciting after twenty years of continuous output. In 1989 he travelled to Melbourne for an exhibition of Papunya Tula Artists at the National Gallery of Victoria. His painting *Bandicoot Dreaming* won the 1991 National Aboriginal Art Award. In 1991 and 1992 he had solo exhibitions of his work at Gallery Gabrielle Pizzi, Melbourne. Collections: Art Gallery of SA, National Gallery of Victoria, Australian Museum, Sydney, Holmes à Court, Queensland Art Gallery, Art Gallery of WA, Museums & Art Galleries of NT, Flinders University Art Museum, National Gallery of Australia, Canberra

NANYUMA, ROSIE NAPURRULA
Born north of the Stansmore Ranges c.1940, Rosie Nanyuma is a Kukatja speaker who paints Tingari stories for her country, Parkar, Larkar and Yunpu. All her paintings concern places where she lived when she was younger, and are filled with her knowledge of the country and its Law. She now lives at Balgo and is married to Bob Dingle, and started painting for Warlayirti Artists in 1989. A productive and very consistent artist whose works all show great visual strength.

NEIL, DOROTHY PETYARRE
Born at Bond Spring c.1950, and an Arrente speaker, Dorothy lives with her family on a block of land outside Alice Springs. She works for the Tangentyere Council, and has painted Women's Dreaming, Bush Berry and Euro Dreamings since the early '90s and sold them through the Jukurrpa artists' co-operative, based at IAD. One of her paintings was given by the Arrente Council to the Royal Australian Navy on the occasion of the naming of their ship *Arunta* in October 1992. Dorothy's country is Sandy Bore.

NELSON, FRANK 'BRONSON' JAKAMARRA
Also cited as: Frank Jakamarra Nelson
Born on 5 May 1948 at Yuendumu, and a Warlpiri, Bronson Nelson was one of the younger men who joined the painting group as the art enterprise started to take off in Yuendumu in 1986. His early paintings revealed an original and sophisticated mind. One of Haley's Comet used a design based on a technical drawing in a magazine showing the comet's trajectory, but incorporated the important Milky Way and Seven Sisters Dreamings. Another entitled *Living Together*, blended images of the Aboriginal and Northern Territory flag with traditional Dreaming designs and won first prize in the National Aboriginal Art Award in 1986. In addition to numerous exhibitions since mid '86 with Warlukurlangu Artists (of which he is co-Chairperson), Bronson has also branched out in successful two person exhibitions, the first at Chandler Coventry Gallery in Sydney in 1987 and then in February 1990 at the Dreamtime Gallery as part of the Perth Festival a group show with his wife, Norah NELSON. Such individual 'career' initiatives are unusual amongst Yuendumu artists, but may be seen as a further dimension of the 'bi-cultural' facility evident in his paintings. That it is not at the cost

of his connections to Warlpiri society is shown by his selection to travel to Paris with five other Warlpiri men, amongst them several of the leaders in the 'men's business' at Yuendumu, to create a ground painting installation at the exhibition 'Magiciens de la Terre' at the Centre Georges Pompidou. The trip took place in May 1989 and the painting met with worldwide acclaim. His Dreamings are Wapirti (Small Yam), Yarla (Big Yam), Ngapa (Water), Marlu (Kangaroo) and Pamapardu (Flying Ant). Collections: National Gallery of Victoria, Art Galleries & Museums of NT, Christensen Fund, International Olympic Committee President Juan Antonio Samaranch, private collections. Reference: Diggins, L., *Myriad of Dreamings* (Malakoff Fine Art Press, Melbourne, 1989), West, M., *The Inspired Dream* (Queensland Art Gallery, Brisbane, 1988)

NELSON, DAISY NAPANANGKA

Born c.1924 at Yinjirrimardi, a site near two soakages where Two Dreamtime Women emerged from underground. Daisy Nelson is Warlpiri and lives at Yuendumu with her husband, Paddy Jupurrurla NELSON. She paints Warnayarra/Pikilyi (Rainbow Serpent/ Vaughan Springs), Watakiyi (Bush Orange) and Yuparli (Bush Banana) Dreamings, the last inherited from her father. Some of these Dreamings she gave permission for her son, Michael Jagamara NELSON, to paint in his work for the 1986 Sydney Biennale. Daisy Nelson has been part of the group of senior women artists at Yuendumu since the beginnings of the painting enterprise at Yuendumu, showing in the first exhibition of their work at the Araluen Arts Centre in Alice Springs in October 1985. Since then, her work has been included in exhibitions of Warlukurlangu Artists in Perth, Melbourne, Adelaide, Canberra, Sydney and Brisbane, and in shows in Portsmouth, UK, Seattle, USA, and Madrid, Spain. In 1988 she won an award for Best Painting at the Victor Harbor Art Show. She was represented in 'Yuendumu — Paintings out of the Desert' at the SA Museum in 1988, 'Windows on the Dreaming' at the National Gallery of Australia in 1989 and 'Tigari Lai': Contemporary Aboriginal Art from Australia at the Third Eye Centre, Glasgow, Scotland in 1990. In 1993 her work was shown in 'Aratjara Australian Aboriginal Art', Kunstsammlung, Nordrhein, Dusseldorf, Germany, and other European cities. Collections: National Gallery of Australia, Canberra, South Australian Museum, Australian Museum, Sydney, many private collections. Reference: Johnson, V., *The Painted Dream* (Auckland City Art Gallery, New Zealand, 1991)

NELSON, GERALDINE NAKAMARRA

Born in 1972 at Alice Springs. Geraldine's father is a Warlpiri speaker and her mother, Maudie Napanangka NELSON, is an Anmatyerre speaker. Her country is Boarrinji and she paints Ngurlu (Bush Seed) and Honey Ant Dreamings. She has connections with Ali Curung, Willowra and Napperby communities. Her mother showed her how to paint in 1989. She now lives in Hidden Valley town camp and works with the Jukurrpa group in Alice Springs.

NELSON, HELEN NAPALJARRI

A Warlpiri speaker, Helen Napaljarri Nelson lives at Yuendumu and has been exhibiting with Warlukurlangu Artists since the late '80s. She paints her Ngarlkirdi (Witchetty Grub) and Wardapi (Goanna) Dreamings. In 1991 her work was shown in the USA as part of the 'Dreamscapes' exhibition in Pittsburgh and Tucson, Arizona. Collections: South Australian Museum, Art Gallery of South Australia

NELSON, IRMA NAPANANGKA

Born at Janyingki and a Warlpiri person, Irma lives at Lajamanu. Her country is Janyingki and her Dreamings are Yunkaranyi and Mardukiya-Mardukiya (Women's Dreaming). She moves between Millingimbi and Lajamanu, where she has two children, and began painting in 1986.

NELSON, JORNA NAPURRURLA

A Warlpiri speaker, Jorna Nelson lives at Yuendumu and has been exhibiting with Warlukurlangu Artists since the beginning of the '90s. She paints Yarla (Yam) and Janganpa (Possum) Dreamings. Collections: Australian Museum, Sydney, South Australian Museum

NELSON, LIDDY NAKAMARRA

Place of birth Yumurrpa/Wapurtarli c.1929, and tribe and language Warlpiri. The artist lives at Lajamanu, her country being Wapurtali, Yumurrpa, Nyurripatu and her Dreamings Ngarlajiyi, Mamikiji (Bush Grapes), Purranyu (Small Snake) Pilkardi and Marlujarra. Started painting in 1986. Changed her name from Herbert because of the death of her husband, and was married to Junti Japaljarri. She is a sister of Michael Jagamara NELSON. Collections: National Gallery of Victoria

NELSON, MAUDIE NAPANANGKA

An Anmatyerre speaker, born at Ailerron station at the beginning of the '60s, she grew up in Alice Springs, then lived at Mt Allan. Pauline WOODS and Rene ROBINSON taught her the Dreamings she could paint: Honey Ant (from her great great grandfather), Emu with Baby, Bush Tucker, Bush Bean, Wild Fig and Women, and she had just started to paint them when interviewed in 1989. She has worked with the Jukurrpa group in Alice Springs.

NELSON, MICHAEL JAGAMARA
Also cited as: Michael Nelson Tjakamarra, Jakamarra

Born at Pikilyi (Vaughan Springs), west of Yuendumu, c.1949, he grew up 'in the bush' 'without clothes', first seeing white men at Mt Doreen station. He remembers hiding in the bush in fear. Michael lived at Haasts Bluff for a time with the same family group as Long Jack PHILLIPUS. Later his parents took him to Yuendumu for European education at the mission school. He left school at thirteen, after initiation, and worked buffalo shooting (1962, on the East and South Alligator Rivers), driving trucks, droving cattle, and in the army, before coming back to Yuendumu and then to Papunya to settle and marry his current wife, Marjorie. He came to Papunya in 1976, working for a time in the government store and for the Council, observing the work of the older artists for years before beginning to paint regularly for himself in 1983. His parents were both Warlpiri, and his father was an important 'medicine man' in the Yuendumu community. After his father's death in 1976, Michael worked under the instruction of his uncle, JACK Tjupurrula. Michael paints Possum, Snake, Two Kangaroos, Flying Ant and Yam Dreamings for the area around Pikilyi. In 1984 he won the National Aboriginal Art Award; in 1986 he exhibited in the Biennale of Sydney and was included in 'The State of the Art', a British art documentary. In 1987 a 27' (8.2 m) painting by Michael Nelson was installed in the foyer of the Sydney Opera House. In 1988 he was introduced to the Queen at the opening of the new national Parliament as the designer of the 196 sq metre mosaic in the forecourt of the building. His 1985 painting *Five Stories* was one of the most reproduced works of Australian art of the '80s. It appears on the cover of the catalogue of the Asia Society's 'Dreamings' exhibition which toured the USA in 1988–90. The artist travelled to New York with Billy STOCKMAN for the opening of the show. In 1989 he had his first solo exhibition in Melbourne at the Gallery Gabrielle Pizzi and participated in the BMW Art Car Project by hand-painting an M3 race car. His wife, Marjorie Nelson Napaltjarri, and sister, Violet Nelson Nakamarra, also paint, in Marjorie's case mainly on the backgrounds of her husband's large commissions — e.g. the Opera House and BMW projects. Solo Exhibitions: 1989, 1990 Gallery Gabrielle Pizzi, Melbourne, and 1993 Utopia Art, Sydney. In 1993 he received the Australia Medal for services to Aboriginal Art and an Artist's Fellowship, Visual Art Board, Australia Council. Collections: Parliament House, National Gallery of Australia, Canberra, Holmes à Court, Australian Museum, Sydney, Queensland Art Gallery, Art Gallery of WA, Museums & Art Galleries of NT, SA Museum, Art Gallery of South Australia, Broken Hill Art Gallery etc.

NELSON, NORAH NAPALJARRI

Born on 26 October 1956 at Haasts Bluff, NT, Norah Nelson is a Warlpiri speaker who lives at Yuendumu. Her main country is the Ngarlkirdu Dreaming at Naru. She began assisting her husband, Bronson (Frank) Jakamarra NELSON, on his paintings in about 1986, emerging within a year as an artist in her own right. She first exhibited in September 1987 at the 'Karnta' (Women) exhibition at the Esplanade Gallery in Darwin, and has since shown her work widely, in exhibitions of Warlukurlangu Artists in Melbourne, Perth, Adelaide and Alice Springs. She has also shown at Galeria Alfredo Melgar in Madrid and, independently of Warlukurlangu Artists, at the Dreamtime Gallery in Perth, where her first two person show with Bronson Nelson in February 1990 was a featured event at the Perth Festival. She paints Ngaru (Bush Plum), Ngarlkirdi (Witchetty Grubs), Ngarlikirdi/Warna (Witchetty Grub/Snake), Karntajarra (Two Women) and Pangkurlangu (Giant) Dreamings and recently her very successful series of Yiwarra (Milky Way) Dreamings, which are painted with the permission of Paddy SIMS, a senior custodian of that Dreaming in the Yuendumu community. All of this series of works have gone into major public and private collections including the National Gallery of Victoria, the Holmes à Court Collection and the Darwin Supreme Court, which also selected the painting to be made into a mosaic for the central courtyard of the new court complex.

NELSON, PADDY JUPURRURLA

Born c.1919 at Napanangkajarra near Yuendumu, Paddy Nelson's country runs from Yumurrpa to Watikinpirri area, south-west of Yuendumu through New Haven station. A Warlpiri speaker, Paddy is a senior ceremonial and religious leader in the Yuendumu community. He was one of the first Yuendumu men to paint with acrylics, and one of the senior men who painted the doors of the school in 1983. With Paddy SIMS, Larry SPENCER Jungarrayi and JIMIJA Jungarrayi, he worked on the 1985 *Star Dreaming* painting, the purchase of which by the National Gallery of Australia from the Yuendumu artists' first show in the eastern states helped to launch the new painting enterprise in the local art world. His main site is Ngama, a Snake Dreaming place. He paints Yarla (Big Yam) and Ngarlajiyi (Small Yam), Warna (Snake), Ngapa (Water), Karrku (Mt Stanley Ochre Mines), Janganpa (Possum), Mukaki (Bush Plum), Karnta (Women's) and Watijarra (Two Men) Dreamings. A prolific painter, distinctive for his fluid impulsive brushwork and subtly different renderings of his classic iconography, his work has been shown in almost every exhibition of Warlukurlangu Artists since the mid '80s and in major touring exhibitions of Aboriginal art, including 'Art and Aboriginality' at the Portsmouth Festival, 1987 and Sydney Opera House, 1988 (Paddy Nelson's painting appears on the cover of the catalogue) and 'Dreamings: The Art of Aboriginal Australia' in New York, Chicago, Los Angeles etc. 1989–90. In 1988 Paddy Nelson was one of five Warlpiri men from Yuendumu selected by the Power Gallery, Sydney University, to travel to Paris to create a ground painting installation at the exhibition 'Magiciens de la Terre' at the Centre Georges Pompidou in Paris in May 1989. Several of Paddy's relatives, including his wife, Daisy NELSON, and her sons, Michael Jagamara NELSON and Bronson Jakamarra NELSON, are also artists of renown. Collections: National Gallery of Australia, South Australian Museum, National Gallery of Victoria, the Christensen Fund and other private collections. Reference: *Yuendumu Kuruwarri: Doors*, Warlukurlangu Artists (AIAS, 1987); *Art and Aboriginality*, Exhibition catalogue (Aspex Gallery, Portsmouth, UK, 1987); *Dreamings: The Art of Aboriginal Australia*, (ed.) P. Sutton; *Windows on the Dreaming*, (ed.) W. Caruana (Ellsyd Press, Sydney, 1989); *Aboriginal Art and Spirituality*, (ed.) R. Crumlin; *Australian Aboriginal Art from the Collection of Donald Kahn*, Lowe Art Museum, University of Miami, 1991

NJAMME NAPANGATI

Born 'in the bush' near the Stansmore Range c.1940, Njamme is a leading woman in the Balgo community with a large extended family, many of whom are also practising

artists, including her husband, Jimmy Njamme. A Kukatja speaker, her country lies
near Mangkai in the Stansmore Range, and her principal stories are Tingari and Water
Dreamings. She began painting for Warlayirti Artists in 1988, and often works with
one or two of her daughters — thus her work can exhibit several different styles. The
artist's great knowledge of her country and its associated mythology is, however, always
evident in her paintings.

NOLAN, BILLY TJAPANGATI

Born c.1945 at Nyinna Nyinna, south of Kintore towards Docker River, Billy grew up
'in the bush', traversing the vast reaches of Pintupi territory across the WA border to
Kiwirrkura and beyond. He came in to Papunya by donkey in one of the early Pintupi
migrations to the new settlement. He had observed the painting group at West Camp
for many years before taking up painting himself at the end of the '70s. He lives at
Kintore and usually paints Tingari stories for his country. Collections: Holmes à Court,
University of WA Anthroplogy Museum

NOLAN, DINNY TJAMPITJINPA

Dinny's date of birth has been put as far back as 1922 or even earlier (and as far forward
as 1944). The artist says he survived the Coniston massacre of 1928, which lends cre-
dence to the earlier date. His place of birth is west of Mt Allan, close to present-day
Yuendumu. Dinny spent many years working as a stockman across the Territory before
arriving in Papunya in the mid '70s. As a senior custodian for the Warlpiri people, he is
officially recognised as leader of rainmaking and Water Dreaming ceremonies. He
'polices' other corroborees and paints the bodies of those taking part in the ceremonies
and is well known for his powerful singing voice. Being a cousin to Clifford POSSUM
and Billy STOCKMAN, and elder brother to KAAPA, it was logical for Dinny to join
the painting group. He travelled to Melbourne in 1977 for a show of Papunya Tula
Artists at the Realities Gallery and one of his designs was used for a stained glass
window in the National Gallery of Victoria. He stayed with artist Trevor Nickolls, on
whom his visit had a powerful influence. In 1981 Dinny visited Sydney with Paddy
CARROLL to construct the first sand painting ever seen outside of Central Australia,
and afterwards travelled to Melbourne to execute a print at the Victorian Print Work-
shop. In May 1988 he and MAXIE Tjampitjinpa were artists-in-residence at the
Wagga City Art Gallery. When in Alice Springs, he also paints for the Centre for
Aboriginal Artists. The Dreamings he paints include Water, Willy Willy, Pelican,
Bush Turkey, Emu, Goanna and Bushfire. In 1991 he travelled with Paddy Carroll to
US colleges and Native American communities on a tour organised by poets Billy
Marshall-Stoneking and Nigel Roberts. Collections: National Gallery of Australia,
Canberra, Artbank, Holmes à Court, University of WA Anthropology Museum,
National Gallery of Victoria, Art Gallery of WA, National Museum of Australia,
Canberra, Victorian Museum, Victorian Arts Centre. Reference: Tjampitjinpa, Dinny
Nolan, *Tjalkupla Kuwarritja* (Papunya Literature Production Centre — in press)

NORA NAPALJARRI, see ANDY, Nora Napaltjarri

NORAH NAPANANGKA

Born at Willowra in the late '40s, Norah has lived in the Willowra area all her life. She is Warlpiri/Anmatyerre and her country is Ngarnalkurru (little Sandy River) and Mt Theo. The Dreamings she paints are Goanna, Wanakiji (Bush Tomato), Yakajirri (Bush Raisin) and Malpa (Bush Beans). Norah began painting in the late '80s on boards purchased from the community store. She learnt to paint from other members of her family. She is an active participant in the women's dancing, and in this context paints a Cave story and a Yalka (Bush Onion) story as well as the Malpa story. Amanda Nakamarra, one of the artist's four children has also taken up painting. 'Before I have started doing my paintings, I have to learn more about my Dreaming designs. When I was used to it, then I finally started doing paintings on canvas. These designs belong to my father and my great great grandfather. I also use these designs for ceremonies or initiation business. Some of these designs are very special to me, and I still remember when I was taught them when I was young. But I still carry on forever.'

NORMAN, ALLAN JAMPIJINPA

Born at Yuendumu in 1950, Allan Norman is the husband of Lilly NORMAN Napaljarri. The couple often visit Lilly's uncle, Paddy CARROLL, in Papunya and paint there when not at Mt Allan. Allan Norman's country is around Yuendumu and he paints Pelican, Rain, Bushfire and Blue Tongue Lizard Dreamings. He is a Warlpiri speaker.

NORMAN, LILLY NAPALJARRI

Born in 1958, Lilly Norman is the niece of Papunya artist Paddy CARROLL, who raised her as his daughter and taught her to paint. Her tribal affiliation is Luritja. She paints the Witchetty Dreaming for her country, Kunajarrayi. She also paints Bush Plum, Bush Onion and the Mt Wedge Women's Corroboree. She has been painting since 1988. She is married to Allan NORMAN, and lives mostly in Mt Allan, though spends time visiting her uncle at Papunya or his outstation.

NOSEPEG TJUPURRULA d. 1993
Also cited as: Nosepeg Tjunkata Tjupurrula, Jungkata Nosepeg Tjupurrula j156

Born c.1920 in Pintupi/Wenampa country around Lake Mackay, west of the Rollinson Ranges close to present day Kintore. An account of Nosepeg's early contacts with European culture, including the episode in which he and Charlie Tarawa enlisted in the Army during World War II, is included in *Wildbird Dreaming*, by Amadio & Kimber. Nosepeg began painting at the beginning of the art movement in Papunya — including depictions of his Bush Tobacco and Grass Seed Dreaming stories, but his role in the community has always taken precedence over painting. His remarkable life is the subject of a documentary 'Nosepeg, A Man For All Times' directed by Billy Marshall-Stoneking (1989). He has reputedly appeared in more screen roles than any other Australian, including *Jedda, Journey Out Of Darkness* and the television series 'Whiplash' and 'Boney'. At seventy, he is still a leading identity and one of the most important elders in Aboriginal Central Australia — a man at ease in all cultures, who is a friend of politicians as diverse as Gough Whitlam and Malcolm Fraser. Among his other notable achievements, Nosepeg was a co-discoverer of the grave of the legendary explorer Lasseter and a driving force in the outstation movement of the 1960s, '70s and '80s. He usually lives in Papunya. Collections: Art Gallery of WA, Museums & Art Galleries of NT, Kelton Foundation Reference: *Wildbird Dreaming*, Amadio, N. & Kimber R.

NYUKANA BAKER, see BAKER, Nyukana

NYUMI, ELIZABETH NUNGURRAYAI
Also cited as: Elizabeth Nyumi Nungarrayi

Born 'in the bush' near Jupiter Well c.1945, Elizabeth Nyumi is a Pintupi speaker. She began painting for Warlayirti Artists in 1988. The artist is unusual in that all her works are variations on one theme associated with her traditional country, Tapinna/Nyunkun, near Jupiter Well, which lies several hundred kilometres to the south-west of where she currently lives, in Billiluna. The reasons why she sticks to this one subject are unclear, but it is interesting to follow the various ways that she paints it. All her works, however, deal with women's concerns and Women's Law (Tingari cycle) in the desert area. She is married to painter Palmer GORDON.

O

OLD MICK WALLANKARRI TJAKAMARRA, see MICK, Wallankarri Tjakamarra

OLD WALTER TJAMPITJINPA, see WALTER, Tjampitjinpa

OLDFIELD, DAVID JUPURRURLA
Also cited as: Big Dave Oldfield Jupurrurla
Born in the early 1940s, Big Dave's country is near Yuendumu and he is custodian for a number of different stories in this region, including Snake, Bush Potato, Black Kite, Emu, Dingo, Bush Yams, Spear, Possum and Witchetty Grubs. He has painted for Warlukurlangu Artists since the mid '80s and his work was included in many of their exhibitions in the late '80s in Perth, Alice Springs, Melbourne, Adelaide, the Gold Coast, Canberra and Sydney, Portsmouth England, Seattle, USA and in the 'Dreamscapes' exhibition in Pittsburgh, USA in 1991. For a time, medical treatment required him to remain in Alice Springs, where he works as an independent, selling his work through the Centre for Aboriginal Artists. Collections: Museum of Mankind, British Museum, private collections

OLDFIELD, EVA NUNGARRAYI
A Warlpiri speaker, Eva Nungarrayi Oldfield lives sometimes at Mt Allan, sometimes in Alice Springs, but usually paints for Warlukurlangu Artists. Her work has been included in exhibitions of the Yuendumu company's artists since 1987 in Melbourne, Canberra, Seattle, USA, Adelaide, Brisbane, Darwin and Perth. It was reproduced in the catalogue of 'A Myriad of Dreamings', Melbourne and Sydney, 1989. Collections: Art Gallery of South Australia, National Gallery of Victoria, private collections

OLDFIELD, RUTH NAPALJARRI
A Warlpiri speaker, Ruth Napaljarri Oldfield lives in Yuendumu and has been exhibiting with Warlukurlangu Artists since the 1986 show at the Editions Gallery in Perth which marked the first major critical and commercial success of the Yuendumu painters. Her work was reproduced in the catalogue of the 'Dreamings — Art of Aboriginal Australia' exhibition which toured the USA in 1988–9 and shown in Portsmouth, England in 1987, and Seattle and Los Angeles, USA in 1988. In Australia she has shown with Warlukurlangu Artists in Perth, Alice Springs, Adelaide, the Gold Coast, Canberra, Melbourne and Sydney. She was one of 42 Yuendumu artists who worked on a 7 x 3 m canvas which toured European cities in 1993 as part of 'Aratjara — Australian Aboriginal Art'. Collections: Museum of Mankind, British Museum, South Australian Museum, Australian Museum, Sydney, Musée des Arts Africain et Oceaniens, Paris, private collections

OLODOODI, PATRICK TJUNGURRAYAI
Also cited as: Patrick Olodoodi Tjungarrayi

Born 'in the bush' near Jupiter Well c.1935, Patrick Olodoodi is a Pintupi speaker who divides his time between Balgo and the Pintupi homeland community of Kiwirrkura to the south. He paints Tingari and Wanayarra (Rainbow Snake) Dreamings around the Jupiter Well area and began painting in 1986. The artist comes from the heart of the Gibson Desert and his art displays the profound degree of abstraction typical of painters from that area. The designs are invariably powerfully direct and resonate with the artist's great understanding of the Law. He sells his work through Warlayirti Artists. Collections: Art Gallery of Western Australia

P

PADDY TJANGALA, see SANDRA Nampitjinpa, Sonder Nampitjinpa TURNER, PETRA Nampitjinpa

PANSY NAPANGATI

Born at Haasts Bluff in the late 1940s in the early years of the mission settlement. Of Luritja/Warlpiri descent, her father, a Warlpiri tribesman, was born at Pikilyi (Vaughan Springs), west of Papunya, and her grandfather before that. From the artist Rene ROBINSON, Pansy learnt the Dreamings for her father's country: Bush Banana, Water Snake, Marlu (Kangaroo), Cockatoo, Bush Mangoes and Willy Wagtail. Her mother, who was Luritja, was born at the site of Illpili. Her mother's cousin taught Pansy the Dreamings from her mother's side: Seven Sisters, Hail, Desert Raisin and Kungkakutjara (Two Women). From 1960 onwards Pansy lived in Papunya, where she observed older artists like Johnny WARANGKULA and KAAPA Tjampitjinpa and began developing her own style. She recalls her grandmother and grandfather telling her stories about her Dreamings and showing her in the sand how to depict them. She practised on paper and later used her designs to do collages made up of glue and the ininti seeds from which women usually make necklaces. Unlike other women artists now associated with Papunya Tula Artists, she did not serve an apprenticeship by working up until the '80s on the paintings of her male relatives, but began working for herself from the early '70s. The resources of Papunya Tula Artists were at this time exclusively the province of the senior initiated men who had started the painting enterprise, and Pansy sold her works independently in Alice Springs. She worked in this manner for about five years, followed by a long gap until 1983, when she resumed painting, working for Papunya Tula Artists. During the late '80s she emerged as Papunya Tula's foremost woman artist. Her work was included in the company's display at the 1988 Brisbane Expo, and featured on the cover of *The Inspired Dream* catalogue of a major survey of Aboriginal Art shown at the same time at the Queensland Art Gallery. She has had two solo exhibitions, the first at the Sydney Opera House in September 1988, through the Centre for Aboriginal Artists (for whom she still paints occasionally), followed by the Gallery Gabrielle Pizzi in Melbourne in May 1989, through Papunya Tula Artists. In 1989 she won the sixth National Aboriginal Art Award. She showed again at the Gallery Gabrielle Pizzi in late 1991 and in Brisbane with EUNICE Napangati in early 1992. Her work has appeared in several recent major surveys of Aboriginal art, including 'Mythscapes' at the National Gallery of Victoria in 1989 and 'Karnta' a show of Aboriginal women's work at the Art Gallery of NSW in 1991. She has a son and four other adopted children, with the youngest of whom she now lives in Alice Springs, attending literacy classes at the IAD with many of the women from the Jukurrpa painting group based at the Institute. Her sister, Alice Napangati, is married to artist Dinny NOLAN and lives in Papunya. Her younger brother, BROGAS Tjapangati, also paints for Papunya Tula Artists. Collections: Holmes à Court, Artbank, National Gallery of Victoria, Queensland Art Gallery, Museums & Art Galleries of NT

PANTIMAS, DICK TJUPURRULA (c.1940–1983)
Also cited as: Dick Pantimus/Pantimatu Tjupurrula

Dick Pantimas's country was Yippa, north of Sandy Blight Junction, near NT/WA border, and his language was Luritja. His Dreaming was Kalipimpa (Water) and he began painting for Papunya Tula Artists in the late '70s. He was a close friend of Ray INKAMALA. Until his untimely death in 1983, the artist was one of the most promising of the second generation of painters which began to emerge in Papunya in the early '80s. Dick Pantimas's house was next door to the painting company premises in Papunya, and he was a close observer of the older artists for many years before beginning to paint himself. He was survived by his wife Wendy and several young children. In 1990 the central Water Dreaming iconograph from one of his paintings was used as the design for a mosaic in the new Alice Springs Airport. Collections: Holmes à Court, National Gallery of Victoria, Flinders University Art Museum, Federal Airports Corporation

PATRICK, BETH NUNGARRAYI

Place of birth Yuendumu c.1950. Beth is of the Warlpiri tribe and lives at Lajamanu. Pirrpirrpakarnu is her country and Warlu (Nagalyipi) is her main Dreaming. She works with her sister, Maggie WATSON Nungarrayi, and started painting in 1987. The ex-wife of Paddy PATRICK Jangala, she is an important figure in the Lajamanu community, with whom she sometimes painted.

PATRICK, FREDDY JANGALA

Born west of Willowra near Mungurlarri c.1930, Freddy Patrick came to Lajamanu as a 'single fellow'. He is a Warlpiri speaker and his country is Mungurlarri and Lult-ja (Lajamanu). An excellent carver, he was one of the first to start painting in Lajamanu. He paints Ngapa (Water), Emu, Yawakyi (Bush Plum), Wirlki (Boomerang), Watiya Warnu (seed of tree) and Warna Pawu (Snake from Willowra) Dreamings, for which Jampijinpa/Jangala are custodians. He often works together with his wife, artist Myra Nungarrayi PATRICK. They live just outside of Lajamanu settlement. Collections: National Gallery of Victoria

PATRICK, MYRA NUNGARRAYI

Born at Willowra c.1946. Her country is Wirliyajarrayi (Two Feet), which is the Warlpiri name for Willowra. She paints Mala, Juwurrpa, Ngatijirri (Bush Budgerigar), Witi/kurlarda (Spear/Pole) — from Kurlangalimpa (Duck Pond), Jurdiya (Snake), Ngalyipi (Snake Vine), Jurlpa (Butcher Bird), Watiya and Karrkarrdu (Cockatoo) Dreamings, some of these in conjunction with her husband, Freddy PATRICK Jangala — they often paint sitting down together, though mostly they do separate paintings.

Pansy Napangati (Photo: Hank Ebes)

Gabriella Possum Nungurrayi (Photo: Grenville Turner)

Entalura Nangala (Photo: Jennifer Isaacs)

Ada Andy Napaljarri (Photo: Grenville Turner)

Gladys Napanangka (Photo: Grenville Turner)

Coral Napangardi Gallagher (Photo: Anne Mosey)

Louisa Lawson Napaljarri (Photo: Vivien Johnson)

Sister Gibson Nakamarra (Photo: Christine Nicholls)

Lucy Hector Nangala (Photo: Lee Cataldi)

Petra Nampitjinpa (Photo: John Corker)

Mary Dixon Nungarrayi (Photo: John Corker)

Nora Andy Napaljarri (Photo: Grenville Turner)

They live just outside of Lajamanu settlement. Myra started painting in 1986. Her work was immediately identifiable by her absolutely miniscule dots, which were part of Myra's conscious development of her own individualistic style. Minute dots are now a familiar technique, but few have used them with such subtle refinement. She collects tiny twigs and sharpens them to do the dots. She estimates that she takes about five weeks to complete a canvas. By the early '90s Myra had developed RSI from painting, and was told to quit, but refused to. Her work is like pointillism, but with assymmetrical qualities that distinguish it from pop art. She has worked these effects on pottery for an exhibition at the National Gallery of Victoria in 1990. A Botany glass factory has also signed a contract with Myra Patrick and Marjorie WATSON to blow their designs into glass. Collections: National Gallery of Victoria (pottery and painting)

PATRICK, PADDY JANGALA
Born at Thompson Rockhole (Pirti-pirti) at a place called Wardilyka in 1944. In *Stories From Lajamanu* (NT Department of Education, 1985), he talks about how his father died a week later and his mother, Margaret Nungarrayi, took him out into the desert south of Lajamanu in her traditional Warlpiri country. He describes his early life 'out bush', and then at various settlements and cattle stations across the north-west and his experiences with a pastoralist called John Patrick, who whipped the youth in his employ until they ran away, spearing his cattle as they went. His traditional country is Pirti-pirti and his Dreamings are Ngapa (Water), Watiyawarnu, Yawakiyi and Wirnpa. He started painting in 1986 with the original group. The motto for the Lajamanu school T-shirt, 'Past and the present and the future all brought together at Lajamanu School' — loosely translated as Lajamanu School Forever — was written by Paddy Patrick, whose painting is printed on the shirt front.

PATTERSON, BANJO JAMPIJINPA
Born at Coniston in 1940, Banjo is an Anmatyerre speaker. His country is Coniston and he paints Men and Women Talking, Honey Ant and Women's Dreamings for Coniston. He is married to painter Rosie Napangardi, sister of FRANK Japangardi, and lives at Mt Allan.

PATTERSON, GLENDA NUNGARRAYI
Born in 1970, Glenda is the daughter of Banjo PATTERSON Jampijinpa and Rosie PATTERSON Napangardi. An Anmatyerre speaker, her traditional country is Mt Allan and she can paint Bush Onion, Lightning and Kangaroo Dreamings. She has spent time at Ti-Tree in recent years as well as Mt Allan.

PATTERSON, NELLIE NUNGARRAYI
Born 1 July 1943 at Pipalyatjare, and a Pitjanjatjara speaker. Her country is Pipalyatjare and she paints Malu and Welljajeme (Seven Sisters) Dreamings. She lives in the Mutitjulu community at Uluru. She is married to Tommy Wengi and has a daughter,

Patricia Donegan. Her sister is Merlejere Wilson. Nellie has been painting since 1986 and sells her work through Maruku Arts and Crafts at Uluru.

PATTERSON, REX JUPURRURLA

Born near Tennant Creek close to the country of his mother. His father came from Yarturlu-yarturlu, which is the Granites. His Dreamings are Jangangpa and Laju. He is Warlpiri and often works with his wife, Valerie PATTERSON, a common pattern at Lajamanu. They started painting in 1986. They are both devout Christians. Rex Patterson Jupurrurla is going to study for the ministry.

PATTERSON, ROSIE NAPANGARDI

Born c.1950, Rosie Patterson is an Anmatyerre speaker. Her country is Yuelamu and she paints Honey Ant, Women and Kangaroo Dreamings for this country, as well as Witchetty Dreaming (her uncle's Dreaming) and Men and Women Talking. She is married to Banjo PATTERSON and lives at Mt Allan.

PATTERSON, SERGEANT JUPURRURLA

Place of birth Murnunyu c.1916, his language/tribe is Warlpiri and he lives at Lajamanu. His country is Murnunyu and his Dreamings are Wampana (Wallaby), Karlajirdi, Yawakiyi and Lukarrara. Father of Rex PATTERSON (though for reasons too intricate to explain, they have the same skin name), he started painting in 1986.

PATTERSON, VALERIE NAPANANGKA

Born in Lajamanu in c.1955 of the Warlpiri language/tribe. Valerie lives at Lajamanu, her country is Janyinki and her Dreamings are Mardukuja-mardukuja (Karna) — Women Dreaming, Ngalyipi and Warna. Valerie gathered most of the material for the *Stories from Lajamanu* publication. Though she did not go to school until she was twelve and has no formal training as a linguist, she recently translated *Stormboy* into Warlpiri so the teachers could have a novel for the children to study in Warlpiri — one of the longest vernacular English novel translations ever.

PAYUNGKA, TIMMY TJAPANGATI
Also cited as: Tim Payunka, Timmy Payungu, Timmy Pyungu Japangardi

Born c.1942 just west of Central Lake Mackay. The family came eastwards to the Haasts Bluff area in search of rations of flour and tea when Timmy was a child. Later, the family travelled back into Pintupi territory. Contacted in 1962 whilst camped at Yarrana Rockhole due west of Kintore with his wife and young child, Timmy was among the first group of Pintupi to be brought in to the newly established settlement of Papunya in the '60s. He travelled into Alice Springs before returning west to bring his wife and child to Papunya. Part of the original group of painters at Papunya in 1971, he moved to Kintore when it was established in 1981 and further west to Kiwirrkura — where he now resides — in the mid '80s. He is a key figure for the important claypan site of Parrayingi, where in pre-contact times many people gathered in the large depressions formed by the claypan hollows for ceremonies after good rains. Also the Lake Hazlett area further to the north. He paints Dancing Women, Dingo, Snake and Water Dreaming stories from this region. A key ritual figure since the late '70s, he was in the forefront of moves to establish the settlement at Kiwirrkura. His work featured in the 'Dreamings' exhibition which toured the USA in 1988–9. Collections: Holmes à Court, Australian Museum, National Gallery of Victoria, Museums & Art Galleries of NT, SA Museum

PEGGY NAMPIJINPA

Born at Willowra during World War II, Peggy Nampijinpa has lived all her life in the Willowra community and is closely related to several other artists there, including her younger sister, LUCY Nampijinpa. Her tribe is Warlpiri and her heritage country lies around Mt Barkly. She paints her uncle's Budgerigar Dreaming and the same Damper Seed and Sugarbag Dreamings as her sister. She began painting on canvas in the late '80s at the same time as Lucy and most of the others now painting at Willowra, but she learnt to paint originally for ceremonial purposes, body paintings and dancing boards (nulla nullas).

PEIPEI, KUNBRY

Born at Areyonga, NT, Kunbry Peipei came to live at Ayers Rock (Uluru) as a child. She went to school in Areyonga, coming back home for the holidays. In those days, she and her family made these journeys by camel. As a child, Kunbry used to take the tourists on camel rides around the Rock for money. Her mother worked in one of the Ayers Rock motels, cooking and cleaning for the tourists. Kunbry also used to make music sticks for the tourists when she was little. Her parents, who made spears, boomerangs, perenties (lizards) etc to sell to the tourists, taught her to carve and decorate artefacts with pokerwork. She still uses the pokerwork technique to create beautiful designs on the backs of her carved wooden bowls, including water designs and various bush tucker ones. She has done batik, having trained in batik techniques in Indonesia. Kunbry has been painting for a few years. She taught herself to paint and her paintings are about the women's places at the Rock. Common themes are Kuniya and Liru (Snakes), Women's Inma (Song and Dance), and the Seven Sisters story. She enjoys painting and says the 'money is OK' but would still paint even if she worked full-time. When she has canvas, she paints 'day and night'. She prefers big paintings because they 'look better', and says that everyone at Uluru paints well: 'They paint a true story; tourists buy to get true story — really right; it's good to buy paintings because one gets a true story.' A Pitjanjatjara speaker, Kunbry has five children and has been a member of the Mutitjulu Community Council for several years. She is also an active member of the local Lutheran Church. Collections: Museum of Victoria

163

PETERS, JANIE NAKAMARRA

Place of birth Yuendumu c.1955, her language/tribe is Warlpiri and her country is Yarturlu-yarturlu and her Dreamings are Yawakiyi, Ngurlu, Janganjpa (Possum), Lakijirri (Ssticky Grass) and Wampana. She started painting in 1987 and sometimes paints with her husband, Joe MARSHALL. She lives at Lajamanu, where she has worked as an assistant teacher at Lajamanu school.

PETERSEN, FABRIANNE NAMPITJINPA

Born at Papunya on 22 July 1965, attended school in Papunya and later for four years at Yirara College, where she reached Year 10. After leaving Yirara, she started painting at Mt Leibig, where she was living with her mother, Maudie PETERSEN. She learned by watching SANDRA Nampitjinpa and her sisters. In 1982 she worked in the school as a teachers aide. Later she moved to Kintore with her husband, the son of Johnny and Narpula SCOBIE, and is one of the few young women painting at Kintore, Narrpula being the only older woman artist. A Luritja speaker, her country is north-west of Mt Leibig. She paints Bush Potato, Witchetty Grub, Honey Ant and Kunatjarrayi Dreamings. In 1986 she entered the Moet & Chandon Touring Exhibition. Collections: Holmes à Court

PETERSEN, MAUDIE NUNGARRAYI

Born at Napperby station in 1937, Maudie grew up at Haasts Bluff, where she had the first of her two daughters. Her husband passed away in 1980. She has been painting — coolamons and boomerangs — since she was first married, but only in the last five years or so on canvas. A Luritja speaker, she paints Kunajarrayi (Witchetty Grub) Dreaming, Napaltjarris Dreaming (from her grandfather) and Grandmother story. She lives at Mt Leibig. Collections: Holmes à Court

PETRA NAMPITJINPA
Also cited as: Petra Turner Nampitjinpa

Born at Papunya on 8 November 1966, Petra is the youngest daughter of Paddy Tjangala, an important figure in the Mt Leibig community. Her mother, Betty Nungarrayi, was from Haasts Bluff. The family lived at Yuendumu, Papunya, and then Mt Leibig, where they settled 'to follow their Dreaming' — the Bushfire Dreaming which begins at Warlukurlangu west of Yuendumu, old Paddy's birthplace, and swept down through Mt Leibig to Amata in SA. Taught to paint on canvas in the early '80s by her sister SANDRA, who was in turn taught by their father, Petra paints Bushfire and Two Women Dancing Dreaming stories. She lives at Mt Leibig with her young child. In 1986 her work was included in the Moet & Chandon Touring Exhibition. Collections: Holmes à Court, Museums & Art Galleries of NT

PHILLIPUS, LONG JACK TJAKAMARRA
Also cited as: Longjack Phillipus, Jack Phillipus

Born c.1932 at Kalimpinpa, an important Rain Dreaming site north-east of Kintore. His father, who was Warlpiri, came from Parikurlangu to the north of Kalimpinpa and his mother, who was of mixed Warlpiri/Luritja descent, also came from Kalimpinpa. Long Jack grew up in the bush west of Mt Farewell and came into Haasts Bluff settlement with his whole family as a teenager. He worked at Haasts Bluff as a timber contractor and stockman and married Georgette Napaltjarri. They have two sons, three daughters and many grandchildren. Long Jack has been part of the Papunya painting movement since the beginning of the '70s when he was a Councillor at Papunya. It was Long Jack, together with Billy STOCKMAN, who was also a school yardman at the time, who offered their help with painting the smaller murals around the Papunya school, which preceded the large Honey Ant mural. Long Jack has painted intermittently since those times, taking out the NT Golden Jubilee Art Award in 1983 and the Alice Springs Art Prize in 1984. In 1984 he was ordained as a Lutheran pastor. Of the Warlpiri/Luritja language group, Long Jack's paintings depict Hare, Wallaby, Kingfisher, Dingo and other Dreamings in the Mt Singleton area. He lives in Papunya and remains close to his 'brother', Michael NELSON, with whom his family camped at Haasts Bluff in the early years before the Papunya settlement. His younger sister, Pauline WOODS, is a well-known Western Desert artist currently working out of Alice Springs. Collections: Holmes à Court, National Gallery of Victoria, Art Gallery of WA, Art Gallery of SA, Art Gallery of NSW, University of WA Anthropology Museum, Museums & Art Galleries of NT

PINTA PINTA TJAPANANGKA

Born at Yumari in the late 1930s, Pinta Pinta and his family were amongst the Pintupi who walked in to Haasts Bluff in the early '50s to receive rations of flour and tea. In his youth Pinta Pinta also worked as a stockman. He started painting in the early '70s, joining the group of artists at Papunya when Peter Fannin, who took over from Geoffrey Bardon in 1972, was running the painting company. He moved to Kintore in 1981 at the start of the re-settlement of Pintupi lands and now paints only intermittently. He appeared as the black tracker in the film *Evil Angels*. Pinta Pinta paints Tingari stories, stories associated Yumari and his father's Dreamings around the western site of Winparrku. Collections: Holmes à Court, National Gallery of Victoria, Australian Museum, Sydney

POLLY NAPANGATI
Also cited as: Polly Watson Napangardi

Polly Watson was born in the early 1930s at Mt Doreen station: she remembers the start of World War II when she was a young girl. Her country is Mt Doreen/Yuendumu and she is a Warlpiri speaker. She paints Mouse Dreaming and Maliki, a black bush berry. She previously lived at Mt Doreen, but has been in Alice Springs for the past twenty years, and now resides with the Hidden Valley community. She began painting in about

1984, at the same time as the other Hidden Valley artists, with whom she still works, including April Spencer Napaltjarri and Rosie FLEMING Nangala. Her cousin, Rene ROBINSON, taught her how to paint. Her daughter, Susie Nangala, is just learning to paint too. Polly's work was included in the Centre for Aboriginal Artists shows at Blaxland Gallery and the Tin Sheds. In 1990 she won the Centralian Advocate Art Award, and in 1991 a major commission for an exhibition at the Australian Embassy in Paris.

POSSUM, CLIFFORD TJAPALTJARRI

Born c.1932 at Napperby station of the Anmatyerre language/tribe. His father was born at the site of Ngarlu (Ngwerritye Alatiye) west of Mt Allan. His mother came from Warlugulong, south-west of Yuendumu. The name 'Possum' was given to Clifford by his paternal grandfather. Clifford received no formal education, growing up 'in the bush' and then at Jay Creek during the late '40s. He did stockwork at various stations across the Centre, including Hamilton Downs, Glen Helen, Mt Wedge, Mt Allan and Napperby. One of last men to join Geoffrey Bardon's group of 'painting men' at the beginning of the '70s — with the encouragement of his brother, Tim LEURA — Clifford Possum was already a woodcarver of renown, and had been employed at Papunya school teaching wood carving to the children; he was Chairman of Papunya Tula Artists during the late '70s and early '80s. He and his family lived at Papunya, Napperby station, Umbungurru outstation near Glen Helen, and then Alice Springs from the mid '80s. More recently, Clifford has divided his time between Alice Springs and the homes of his daughters, Gabriella POSSUM and Michelle POSSUM, in Melbourne and Adelaide. Clifford Possum has country around Mt Wedge (Kerrinyarra), Napperby station (Tjuirri) and Mt Allan and a vast repertoire of Dreamings which he paints, including Possum, Fire, Water, Kangaroo, Fish, Snake, Man's Love Story, Lightning, Mala, Goanna etc. Exhibitions, Prizes and Commissions include: 'The Past and Present of the Australian Aborigine', Pacific Asia Museum, Los Angeles, 1980–1; Perspecta, Art Gallery of NSW, Sydney, 1981; Sao Paulo Bienal, 1983; 'Three Papunya Painters', Adelaide Arts Festival, 1984; Mural design, Araluen Arts Centre, Alice Springs, 1985; Alice Springs Art Prize, 1983; Community Arts Centre, Brisbane 1987; 'Clifford Possum Tjapaltjarri Paintings 1973–86', Institute of Contemporary Arts, London, 1988; 'Dreamings': The Art of Aboriginal Australia, New York, Chicago, Los Angeles, Melbourne, Adelaide, 1988–9; Austral Gallery, St Louis, 1988; 'Songlines', Rebecca Hossack Gallery, London, 1990. Visited USA (St Louis, New York) 1989; Solo exhibition Rebecca Hossack Gallery, London, 1990. In 1991, he completed two large commissions, for the new Strehlow Research Foundation, Alice Springs and the new Alice Springs Airport. Collections: National Gallery of Australia, Canberra, National Gallery of Victoria, Flinders University Art Museum, Victorian Centre for the Performing Arts, Parliament House, Canberra, Pacific Asia Museum, Los Angeles, University of WA Anthropology Museum, Art Gallery of NSW, SA Museum, Broken Hill Art Gallery, Araluen Arts Centre, Alice Springs etc. Reference: *The Art of Clifford Possum Tjapaltjarri*, V. Johnson

POSSUM, GABRIELLA NUNGURRAYI

An Anmatyerre speaker born in Mt Allan in 1967, Gabriella Possum is the older daughter of Clifford POSSUM Tjapaltjarri, one of the most renowned of the founding group of Papunya painters. Taught by her father, Gabriella began painting at an early age and gained an award in the 1983 Alice Springs Art Prize while still a student at Yirara College. She now lives in Melbourne with her husband and three small children. Her Dreamings include Bush Coconut, Black Seed (for making damper), Exploding Seed Pod and Women's stories from the Mt Allan area. She exhibited with her father, sister Michelle POSSUM, and brother-in-law Heath in Brisbane in 1987 and again at Coo-ee Gallery in Sydney in 1992. Gabriella has designed several record covers, including one for Coloured Stone, and several T-shirts for CAAMA.

POSSUM, MICHELLE NUNGURRAYI

Born in the Mt Allan area in 1970, Michelle Possum is the younger daughter of Clifford POSSUM Tjapaltjarri. She began painting in 1984 under her father's instruction while the family was living at Umbungurru, near Glen Helen station. Of the Anmatyerre language group, she paints women's stories from the Mt Allan area. Michelle is married to Heath Ramjan Tjangala. They now live in Adelaide with their young son and two daughters.

POSSUM TJAPANGATI (d.)

Born 'in the bush' near Godfrey's Tank on the Canning Stock Route c.1940. His death in 1989 robbed the community of Billiluna, where he had lived, of a gentle, quiet man who was a good artist. Possum was a Walmatjari speaker, whose country was around Kaningarra (Godfrey's Tank). His principal Dreaming was Water. He began painting for Warlayirti Artists in 1988. His style was less typical of Balgo and more similar to other Kimberley art (especially Turkey Creek and Fitzroy Crossing). It was simple, obviously deeply felt, sometimes with human figures and usually surrounded by a pattern of hills.

POULSON, CLARISE NAMPIJINPA

Born in 1957 in Yuendumu and a Warlpiri speaker, her country is Wantungurru and her Dreamings are Yankirri (Emu), Ngapa (Water), Pamapardu (Flying Ant). She lives at Yuendumu, and though she began painting only at the end of the '80s, and is one of the youngest artists with Warlukurlangu Artists, Clarise quickly emerged as one of the leading painters at Yuendumu. She has developed to a high degree the strong design sense discernible in her earlier work and perfected a distinctive style of highly ornate and detailed background dotting. She sometimes paints with her husband, Michael Japangardi POULSON. She colloborated with others in the SA Museum's 'Yuendumu — Paintings out of the Desert' and her first solo work was shown in the ANCAA exhibition in Darwin in September 1988. Since then, she has been represented in many exhibitions of Warlukurlangu Artists. In 1989 her work was seen in 'Mythscapes' at the

National Gallery of Victoria in 1990, in 'Balance 1990' at the Queensland Art Gallery, the National Aboriginal Art Award at the Darwin Performing Arts Centre, and 'L'été Australien' at the Musée Fabre, Montpellier, France, and in 1991 in the 'Crossroads' exhibition at the Araluen Arts Centre in Alice Springs. In 1992 she had her first solo exhibition at Hogarth Gallery in Sydney. She exhibited in 'Australian Perspecta 1993' at the Art Gallery of NSW. Collections: many public and private collections, including Museums and Art Galleries of the NT, National Gallery of Victoria, Queensland Art Gallery and the Kohane Family collection. References: Ryan J., *Mythscapes*; *Australian Aboriginal Art from the Collection of Donald Kahn*

POULSON, IVY NAPANGARDI

Born in 1959, Ivy Napangardi Poulson lives in Yuendumu and has been exhibiting paintings of her Yuparli (Bush Banana) and Pikilyi (Vaughan Springs) Dreamings with Warlukurlangu Artists since 1990, when she was included in the 'Women's Exhibition' at the Women's Gallery in Melbourne.

POULSON, MAGGIE NAPURRURLA

Born c.1935, she lives at Yuendumu and is a Warlpiri speaker. Now in her mid fifties, Maggie Poulson was one of the senior women whose interest in rendering traditional women's designs in western materials inspired the first experiments with acrylic on canvas at Yuendumu. She has been exhibiting her work with Warlukurlangu Artists since the Yuendumu painters' first exhibition in Alice Springs in 1985. She has also been represented in shows of Aboriginal women's art in Adelaide and Darwin. In 1987 Artforms produced a poster of a painting by Maggie Poulson and her sister, Peggy Napurrurla POULSON. With her sister and Bessie Nakamarra SIMS, Maggie also featured in the 'Dreamings: Art of Aboriginal Australia' video, painting an elaborately detailed Janganpa (Possum) Dreaming. She also paints Ngarlajiyi (Small Yam) Dreaming. Collections: South Australian Museum, many private collections. Reference: Diggins, L., *Myriad of Dreamings*; Johnson, V., *The Painted Dream*; *Australian Aboriginal Art from the Collection of Donald Kahn*

POULSON, MICHAEL JAPANGARDI

A Warlpiri speaker, Michael Japangardi Poulson lives in Yuendumu. He and his wife, Clarise Nampijinpa POULSON, began painting for Warlukurlangu Artists at the end of the '80s, often working together on ornate canvases with small meticulous white dotting. Michael Poulson's main Dreamings are Yurrampi (Honey Ant) and Warnayarra/Pikilyi (Rainbow Serpent/Vaughan Springs). He has exhibited with Warlukurlangu Artists in Adelaide, Melbourne, Sydney, Darwin and Alice Springs. Collections: many private collections

POULSON, MONA NAPURRURLA

A Warlpiri speaker, Mona Poulson lives in Yuendumu and has been exhibiting with Warlukurlangu Artists since late 1990 in the 'Women's Exhibition' at the Women's Gallery in Melbourne. She paints Janganpa (Possum) and Yarla (Yam) Dreamings and has shown in Sydney and the Gold Coast in Warlukurlangu exhibitions.

POULSON, NEVILLE JAPANGARDI

Born in the late 1940s, Neville Poulson has painted intermittently for Warlukurlangu Artists since the mid '80s. His traditional country is Pikilyi. He is an important figure in both Aboriginal ceremonial life and the Christian community at Yuendumu. Strongly committed to Aboriginal cultural survival in changed historical circumstances, Neville occupies several responsible positions in the community, and paints only occasionally for the painting company. He painted a mural for the local Yuendumu Baptist Church as a Bicentennial project. His mother, Maggie Napurrurla POULSON, and his sister-in-law Clarise Nampijinpa POULSON, are also painters.

POULSON, PEGGY NAPURRURLA

Born c.1935 near Wapurtali in Warlpiri country, she is a senior custodian of the Janganpa (Possum), Patanjarnngi, Ngalajiyi (Bush Carrot) and Mantala Dreamings. She has lived in Alice Springs since about 1989, but previously lived at Yuendumu and still does at different times. Peggy Poulson was one of the early women painters whose powerful paintings about women's ceremonial life in traditional Warlpiri society helped to put the new Warlukurlangu Artists company on the artistic map in the mid '80s. Before that she was a craftswoman, carving coolamons for the tourist trade. She has many relatives at Yuendumu who also paint, including her sister, Maggie and Clarise POULSON. She was one of six Warlpiri women artists commissioned by the South Australian Museum in 1988 to paint an external mural at the Museum. She is a close friend of Rosie FLEMING, another senior woman artist, and the two often paint together and influence one another's styles. Collections: Australian Museum, Sydney, South Australian Museum

PRICE, RONNIE MPETYANE, see under GLORIA Petyarre

PULTARA, KITTY NAPALTJARRI, see KITTY Pultara Napaltjarri

PULTARA, LISA, see LISA Pultara

PURVIS, JULIE MPETYANE

Born c.1950 at Alcoota. The artist is an Anmatyerre speaker and her country is Woolla Downs and Wood Green. She and her sister, Wendy Purvis Mpetyane, who also paints, were both doing batik before they took up painting on canvas, though in Julie's case only since 1985, some eight years after the establishment of the Utopia group. Julie's involvement dated from Cathy Barnes' time as art coordinator for the Utopia batik makers. She and Wendy did their first paintings as part of CAAMA's Summer Project 1988. Julie shares with her sister Kangaroo and Engedkina (Potato Pumpkin) Dreamings for this country. Their mother, Lorna Panunga, who began working in batik at the same time as Julie, has country at Bushy Park and sometimes paints her Katchera Dreaming. The family resides at Mulga Bore. All of Julie's other sisters, Annie, Angela, Susan and Peggy, now paint occasionally, and most have been involved with the Utopia batik enterprise from the beginning.

Q

QUEENIE KEMARRE

Born approximately 1920, Queenie is a senior woman of the Alyawarre tribe, who paints her Red Mallee, Bush Tomato, Night Bird and Intjingya (tree, flower, seed and leaf) Dreamings. Like most of the Utopia painters, she did her first works with canvas and acrylics in the summer of 1988–9. Her country is Irrweltye, and she is associated with the Ngkwarlerlaneme community on Alyawarre/Kaytetye Aboriginal land to the north of Utopia.

R

RAYMOND, DICK JAPALJARRI

Place of birth Yartula-yartula (the Granites) c.1936 of the Warlpiri language and tribe. He lives at Lajamanu, his country being Jila and his main Dreamings are Mala (Wallaby) and Janganpa (Possum). He also paints a Ngatijirri (Budgerigar) story for the site of Wirliyajarrayi where the budgerigar ancestors emerged, travelling on through Jila. A version of this Dreaming was purchased for the National Gallery of Victoria's collection and shown in 'Mythscapes', Melbourne 1989. He started painting in 1986.

REGGIE TJUPURRULA (d.)

Born on 10 November 1949, he lived at Papunya and spoke Pintubi/Arrente. Warumpi (Honey Ant) — Papunya was his country and his Dreamings included the Papunya Honey Ant story. Painted for Papunya Tula Artists occasionally from the early '80s. He died in August 1993.

RICE, THOMAS JANGALA

Thomas Jangala Rice has been exhibiting with Warlukurlangu Artists since late 1987, when he took part in the SA Museum's 'Yuendumu: Paintings out of the Desert' project, which opened in March 1988. A Warlpiri speaker, he lives in Yuendumu. He usually paints Ngapa (Water) Dreamings. His work is included in the Akademie Der Kunst in Berlin.

ROBERTSON, BERYL NAPANGARDI

A Warlpiri speaker, Beryl Napangardi Robertson lives in Yuendumu and has been painting for Warlukurlangu Artists since the mid '80s. She was one of the senior Warlpiri women of the Yuendumu community whose interest in painting helped spark off the art enterprise at the settlement. Her Dreamings include Karnta (Woman). Her work has been exhibited in New Zealand in 'The Painted Dream' at Auckland City Art Gallery and Te Whare Taonga o Aetearoa National Art Gallery and Museum, Wellington in 1991, and was included in the 'Women's Exhibition' at the Women's Gallery, Melbourne in 1990, consisting predominantly of paintings by Warlukurlangu Artists.

ROBERTSON, JIMMY JAMPIJINPA (JANGYANYKA)

Born at Yinjirri c.1944–6, he lives at Lajamanu. His country is Waparlingki, north-east of Mt Doreen station and Jila Well, Yunga (a site closely connected to Warlukurlangu — 'after the Warlukurlangu mob sing'), Warntapari (where the Water Dreaming 'finishes up'), Makarrangu (Dog Dreaming, which only Jimmy's family may paint), Jurntuwarriji (from his grandfather) and Ngurlurlirrinya. The Dreamings he paints are

Pamapardu (Flying Ant), Malikijarra (Two Dogs Dreaming), Watiyawarnu, Ngapa and Purruparnta (occasionally). He works with his wife, Denise TASMAN Napangardi, and started painting in 1986 with the original group at Lajamanu. One of the best known painters in Lajamanu, he has taken dances, songs and paintings to Sydney, Perth and Adelaide, the USA and Paris. He is remembered by some in Paris for taking a trunk full of boomerangs and setting up a roadside stall on one of the main boulevardes — an amazing and colourful individual, who attended the very first exhibition of the Lajamanu artists at the Gallery Gabrielle Pizzi in Melbourne in 1987. He has plans to return to the States. He lives in Lajamanu with his two wives and nine children, and teaches dancing to young boys at Lajamanu school. Collections: National Gallery of Victoria

ROBERTSON, LADY NUNGARRAYI
Born c.1930 in the region of Jila Well, Lady Robertson is a senior woman in the Aboriginal community at Yuendumu. She shares the country of Yanjilypiri (Star) with other senior Warlpiri women, including artists Sheila Napaljarri BROWN and Mabel Napaljarri JURRA, and Paddy Japaljarri SIMS. It was this Dreaming that created Yiwarra, the Milky Way.

ROBERTSON, YVONNE NAMPIJINPA
Born at Yuendumu in 1962, Yvonne is a Warlpiri speaker whose country is Watiyawanu, to the east of Yuendumu. In 1984 she started painting wooden artefacts and later her Ngurlu (Seed) and Rain Dreamings on canvas. While living in Yuendumu, she sold her works through Warlukurlangu Artists, and later to shops and galleries in Alice Springs. She now lives in Alice Springs, where she is attending the Bridging Course at the IAD, through which she became involved with the Jukurrpa artists' co-operative, based at the Institute.

ROBINSON, DOROTHY NAPANGARDI
Born at Yuendumu of the Warlpiri tribe, Dorothy Robinson paints Karnta (Women's) Dreaming like her older sister Margaret Napangardi LEWIS, as well as Bush Banana Dreaming. She is an Alice Springs resident, living northside near the Warlpiri town camp.

ROBINSON, RENE NAPANGARDI
A Warlpiri speaker born in the early 1960s, Rene Robinson lives in Alice Springs and was one of those instrumental in establishing and consolidating Jukurrpa artists' co-operative as a serious painting enterprise. From Yuendumu originally, where she started painting in about 1987, in the early years of the Warlukurlangu painting enterprise, Rene has connections in the Willowra community, where she has been spending more time recently. Her paintings depict Yuparli (Bush Banana), Honey Ant, Ngalyipi (Climbing Vine) and Water Snake and Bush Mango Dreamings in a simple bold style.

Her entry in the 1987 Alice Springs Art Prize was highly commended. She is EUNICE Napangati's sister-in-law, and the two painters worked together on the Bicentennial Authority exhibition painting their designs on furniture for a commission organised by the Centre for Aboriginal Artists, for whom Rene also paints occasionally. Rene was included in the 'Tjukurrpa' exhibition of the Centre's artists at the Blaxland Gallery in Sydney in 1988. Collections: public and private collections

ROCKMAN, BIDDY NAPALJARRI
Place of birth Mongrel Downs area, WA, her language/tribe is Warlpiri and she lives at Lajamanu. Her country is Jarluwangu and her Dreamings are Ngatijirri and Warna. She started painting in 1986. Collections: National Gallery of Victoria

ROCKMAN, MONA NAPALJARRI
Place of birth Mongrel Downs area, WA c.1924 of the Warlpiri language/tribe, and lives at Lajamanu. Her country is Jarluwangu and her Dreamings are Ngatijirri (Budgerigar) and Warna (Snake). She started painting in 1986. She is one of five sisters who are all co-wives of an old man known as Jampo (which means left-handed) and who all, except one, paint. Mona and her sister, Peggy ROCKMAN, have received recognition for their work, mainly through exposure at the National Gallery of Victoria, which includes Mona's painting and pottery.

ROCKMAN, PEGGY (YALURRNGALI) NAPALJARRI
Born 'in the bush' at Lima, NT c.1935, of the Warlpiri language/tribe, her country is Jaluwangu and she lives at Lajamanu. Her Dreamings are Ngatijirri, Warna, Laju and Ngarlu. Started painting in 1986. Though an older woman who 'never saw white people when she was little', Peggy Rockman learnt English while working as the school cleaner, an occupation she had for many years. Visiting anthropologists and others now make use of her skill to translate for them (see Acknowledgments). Collections: National Gallery of Victoria

ROCKMAN, PEGGY NAPURRURLA
Born at Ringer's Soak, c.1960 of the Warlpiri tribe, she lives at Lajamanu. Mungkururrpa — west of Yuendumu, out towards Balgo — is her country, and her Dreamings are Warnarri (Bush Beans) and Ngurlu (Seed). She started painting in 1986 and is the daughter of Peggy ROCKMAN Napaljarri.

RONNIE TJAMPITJINPA
Born c.1943 around Muyinnga, about 100 km west of the Kintore Ranges across the WA border. Ronnie's family travelled extensively across Pintupi territory, moving throughout this region and also in the area around Lake Mackay in the NT. He was initiated into Aboriginal Law at Yumari, near his birthplace. Ronnie and his younger brother, Smithy ZIMARRON, originally came in from the bush at Yuendumu, and

later joined relatives living in Papunya, where Ronnie worked as a labourer, assisting with the fencing of the aerodrome. Ronnie began to paint in the early years of the painting movement. Over the years, moving between Papunya, Yuendumu and Mt Doreen station, Ronnie talked to many people about returning to traditional lands, a move which was made possible with the establishment of Kintore in 1981. Ronnie moved there with his family in the early '80s, and has since emerged as one of Papunya Tula Artists' major painters. In 1988 he won the Alice Springs Art Prize. In 1989 he had his first solo exhibition at the Gallery Gabrielle Pizzi, travelling to Melbourne for the exhibition and was included in 'Australian Perspecta 1993' at the Art Gallery of NSW. Chairman of the Kintore Outstation Council, Ronnie currently resides on his outstation at Redbank (Ininti) with his younger brother, Kenny WILLIAMS. Collections: National Gallery of Australia, Canberra, Araluen Arts Centre, Alice Springs, Art Gallery of SA, Holmes à Court, Art Gallery of WA, Museums & Art Galleries of NT, Darwin Supreme Court, Musée National des Africans et Oceaniens, Paris etc.

ROSIE NAPURRURLA (sometimes TASMAN)
Born at Yarturlu-yarturlu c.1935 of the Warlpiri language/tribe Warlpiri and lives at Lajamanu. Her country is Miya-miya and Malungurra and her Dreamings are Ngurlu, Kaljirri and Karangu (name of country). Started painting in 1986. Collections: National Gallery of Victoria

ROSS, DARBY JAMPIJINPA
A senior and respected figure both in Warlpiri ceremonial life and in the art movement at Yuendumu. He was born at Ngarilyikirlangu, north of the present day site of Yuendumu, in about 1910. His main totems are Emu and Bandicoot, and he usually paints Ngapa (Water), Yankirri (Emu) and Wardilyka (Bush Turkey) Dreamings, though he has also painted the Pamapardu (Flying Ant) Dreaming which passes close to Yuendumu travelling west. Darby's family has responsibility for the Dreaming as it crosses Warlpiri country. Darby has been an active member of the painting group at Yuendumu since the early years as one of the group of senior men of the Yuendumu community who painted the 27 doors of the Yuendumu school with their Dreamings. Since the Yuendumu painting company's first Araluen Arts Centre exhibition in October 1985, his works have been included in numerous exhibitions of Warlukurlangu Artists in Perth, Adelaide, Melbourne, Sydney, Darwin, Alice Springs and the Gold Coast. Like most artists of the Western Desert — or anywhere else — Darby Ross has progressively refined his approach to and execution of his subject matter, yet his paintings have retained their distinctive early style of loose, exuberant paintwork and complex, richly textured surfaces, sometimes strongly reminiscent of cave paintings from the Western Desert area. Darby's work has been included in the 'Dreamings: Art of Aboriginal Australia' exhibition which toured the USA in 1988–9, the 'Mythscapes' exhibition at the National Gallery of Victoria in 1989 and many other important national and international exhibitions since then. Collections: National Gallery of

Victoria, Art Gallery of WA, South Australian Museum, Australian Museum, Sydney, major private collections including the Kohane family. References: *Dreamings: The Art of Aboriginal Australia*, (ed.) Sutton, P.; Diggins, L., *Myriad of Dreamings*; Ryan, J., *Mythscapes*; Johnson, V., *The Painted Dream*; *Australian Aboriginal Art from the Collection of Donald Kahn*

ROSS, DAVID PWERLE

Born c.1935 at Mt Riddock station, where he lived until his father's death. He then worked in the woolsheds at McDonald Downs and Delmore Downs stations before marrying and moving to Utopia station. He is the most senior lawman amongst the Eastern Anmatyerre people from the area north-east of Alice Springs, whose ritual responsibilities extend beyond his own group into the neighbouring Alyawarre and Eastern Aranda (Arrente) ceremonial life. According to Janet Holt, who runs the painting company at Delmore Downs station, David Ross 'is involved in every major ceremony between the Sandover River and the Queensland border as the ultimate Aboriginal legal authority'. In painting, too, David Ross is a strong traditionalist, allowing no elements of decorativeness to detract from the correctness of the design. He took up painting as a response to the changed historical circumstances of his people and the need 'to put down' his knowledge in a permanent medium for his children and posterity. Though he has been painting for only a short time, his work has been included in group exhibitions in Australia, the former USSR and the USA and in 1990 he had a solo exhibition at Coventry Gallery in Sydney. Collections: National Gallery of Victoria, Art Gallery of WA, Queensland Art Gallery etc., private collections in Australia and overseas

ROSS, ELIZABETH NUNGARRAYI

Born at Yurntumu c.1950, her language/tribe is Warlpiri and lives at Lajamanu. Her country is Kunajarrayi and her Dreamings are Warna, Ngarlkirdi (name of the tree that the witchetty grub comes from as opposed to the actual witchetty grub, Laju). She works with her husband, Peter ROSS, and started painting in 1986.

ROSS, JACK JAKAMARRA

Born c.1925, he is a Warlpiri speaker whose country is Warlputarli, home of the Bush Carrot ancestor which spread out from here to Ngamirliri in one direction and Yintara-murru in the other. Jack also paints the Yarla (Bush Potato) Dreaming for Yamaparnta, belonging to Jakamarra/Jupurrurla. Other Dreamings he paints include Wapirti (Small Yam), Liwirringki (Burrowing Skink), Pamapardu (Flying Ant), Marlu (Kangaroo), Walpajirri (Rabbit-eared Bandicoot or Bilby), Yurduwaruwaru (Bearded Dragon), Karlanjirri (Dragon) and Patanjarngi (Parrakelia). He lives at Yuendumu and has been painting for Warlukurlangu Artists since the mid '80s. His work was included in 'Yuendumu: Paintings out of the Desert' at the South Australian Museum in 1988, 'The Painted Dream' in Auckland and Wellington 1991 and many Warlukurlangu exhibitions in Sydney, Melbourne, Canberra, Perth, Darwin, Adelaide and Alice

Springs. He was one of 42 artists from Yuendumu who worked on a 7 x 3 m canvas which toured European cities in 1993 as part of 'Aratjara — Australian Aboriginal Art'. Collections: South Australian Museum, Christensen Fund, private collections

ROSS, JIMMY TJAMPITJINPA
Born 'in the bush' in the late 1940s out Yinmi way — south of Kiwirrkura midway to Jupiter Well, deep in Pintupi country. He began painting in Balgo, possibly influenced by the visits there of ANATJARI Tjampitjinpa, and has painted for Papunya Tula Artists since coming to live in Kiwirrkura.

ROSS, MICHAEL JANGALA
Born in 1960, Michael Ross is of the Anmatyerre tribe. He has country in the region of both Mt Allan and Napperby, and divides his time between Mt Allan and Desert Bore, an outstation of Napperby where several other artists, including his father, Teddy *Briscoe*, also live. He paints Dingo and Kangaroo Dreamings. He is married to Brenda LYNCH, one of Napperby's most well-known painters.

ROSS, PETER JANGALA
Born at Lurnpakurlangu (Mt Doreen) c.1937. He lives at Lajamanu. A Warlpiri, his country is Puyurru and his Dreamings are Ngapa (Water) and Yankirri. He works with his wife, Elizabeth ROSS Nungarrayi, and started painting in 1986. Collections: National Gallery of Victoria

ROSS, THERESA NAPURRURLA
A Warlpiri speaker, Theresa Napurrurla Ross lives in Yuendumu and paints her Pamapardu (Flying Ant) and Janganpa (Possum) Dreamings for Warlukurlangu Artists. She was included in group exhibitions of Yuendumu painters between 1990 and 1992 in Darwin, Perth, Melbourne and Canberra.

ROWENA NUNGARRAYI
Born in 1965, she is an Anmatyerre speaker whose country is Mt Allan and Dreamings are Bush Potato and Kangaroo. She lives at Six Mile, outside of Ti-Tree.

RUBUNTJA, WENTON
An Arrernte person, living in Alice Springs, Wenton Rubuntja grew up at Telegraph Station, Alice Springs and has worked as a timber cutter and drover at stations across Central Australia, including Hamilton Downs in his grandfather's country Ntyerlpe, Undoolya station, Maryvale and Napperby. Albert Namatjira was his father's cousin and their fathers had shared the country around Palm Valley known as Ilyape, a Honey Ant Dreaming site. Namatjira called himself Wenton's uncle, and taught him to paint in response to the boy's interest. Wenton remembers selling his first painting for five pounds to Mr Batterbee, 'who got me to sign to be an artist'. The Chairman of the

Central Land Council through the '80s, he is a leader of the Arrente community. One of his Western Desert style paintings hangs in the Catholic Church in Alice Springs, done for the Pope's special mass for Aboriginal Christians. He also designed the stained glass windows of the Araluen Arts Centre in Alice Springs. When his community responsibilities permit, Wenton paints both Hermannsburg landscapes and paintings using traditional designs. His dot paintings are distinctive for their medium — watercolour — and pointed, linear forms.

RUBY ROSE (YARDAYA) NAPANGARDI

Place of birth Janyinki c.1920 and language/tribe Warlpiri. She lives at Lajamanu, her country being Janyinki and her Dreamings are Kanakurlangu, Mardukuja-mardukuja, and Yunkaranyi (Pirrkanji). She began painting at Yuendumu in 1985 and has settled down in Lajamanu in the last few years after many journeys up and down the road to Yuendumu, despite her age, with linguist Mary Laughlen, whose main informant Ruby Rose has been for the Warlpiri language dictionary.

RUTH NAPALJARRI

A Warlpiri/Anmatyerre, she was born c.1940. Her country is Coniston and the Mt Allan area, which she shares with LUCY and Hilda MARTIN Napaljarri. One of the group of senior women at Yuendumu whose large vividly coloured and detailed collaborative paintings first drew attention to the painting enterprise and helped establish Warlukurlangu Artists.

S

SAM TJAMPITJIN

Born c.1930 'in the bush', on the north-west side of Lake Mackay, Sam Tjampitjin is a Kukatja speaker. His Dreamings are Tingari and Water, and his traditional country is the site of Lanta-lanta, the area north-west of Lake Mackay. The artist has only been painting for Warlayirti Artists since early 1990. His works impress with their strong, bold colours and design. The images speak from the deep well-springs of the artist's knowledge and experience as a senior person in Men's Law. All his works communicate something of the artist's sense of the power of the land. Many deal with Water Dreaming and associated rainmaking rituals.

SANDRA NAMPITJINPA

Born at Yuendumu on 2 November 1954, Sandra is the oldest daughter of Paddy Tjangala. A Walpiri speaker, her country is around Yuendumu, though she usually paints the Two Women Dancing story for Mt Leibig, where she lives with her father, her sister PETRA and her three children. Taught to paint on canvas in the early '80s by her father, she was one of the first women painters from Papunya Tula Artists to be purchased by the National Gallery of Australia. Collections: National Gallery of Australia, Canberra, Museums & Art Galleries of NT, Holmes à Court

SANDY, WILLIAM

Born 'in the bush' in 1944 in Pitjantjatjara country round Ernabella in SA. Winkilini, further to the south in SA, is William's country from his father and grandfather. Kunapi, far to the south of Papunya out towards Docker River, is his country from his grandmother and mother's side. He paints Dingo, Emu, Woman, Green Bean and other Dreaming stories for this country. He grew up walking around these places — and further north around Hermannsburg, Areyonga and Haasts Bluff. Eventually the family settled at Ernabella, where William attended the mission school. From here William came to Papunya in 1973 and married Violet Nakamarra, sister of Michael NELSON Jagamara. They have four children, a boy and three girls, one adopted. From the time of his arrival in Papunya settlement, William worked for the Papunya Council. From the late '80s, he and his wife have been health workers with the Papunya Medical Service. William has recently stopped other employment to concentrate on his painting. He did his first paintings in 1975, teaching himself after watching the other artists at work. However, it was not till the early '80s that he began painting regularly for Papunya Tula Artists, after Daphne Williams took over the running of the company. In 1985 he won the NT Art Award. His work was included in the 'Dreamings' show which toured the USA in 1988–9, and in the subsequent show of Papunya Tula Artists at the John Weber

Gallery in New York. He had a solo exhibition in 1990 at Gallery Gabrielle Pizzi. William's wife, Violet Nakamarra, has also painted occasionally since the early '80s. Collections: Holmes à Court, Broken Hill Art Gallery, Wollongong City Art Gallery

SCOBIE, JENNIE NAPURRURLA
Born at Lajamanu c.1955. A Warlpiri person, she is the sister of Mabel Tilawu JAMES. Miya-miya is her country and Ngurlu is her Dreaming. She started painting in 1987.

SCOBIE, JOHNNY TJAPANANGKA
Born in the Kintore Ranges c.1935, Johnny Scobie grew up 'in the bush'. A member of the Pintupi tribe, his father walked these regions with UTA UTA Tjangala. As a young man, Johnny went droving, north to Lajamanu and east as far as Broken Hill before returning to Alice Springs to marry his promised wife, Narpula SCOBIE, sister of Turkey TOLSON. The couple lived in Papunya, where Johnny began painting in the late '70s when John Kean was running the artists company. His work was included in the Peter Stuyvesant Collection of Papunya Tula paintings which began touring locally and then internationally in 1977. Johnny stopped painting for a time, starting up again after the move to Kintore at the beginning of the '80s. His country from his mother's side was Pinari — around the Kintore Ranges — out to Lake Mackay and the Balgo area. He also paints the Wedgetail Eagle Dreaming for the site of Tjanka, a hill to the west of Yuendumu. He is Chairman of the Walungurru (Kintore) Council, a position he has held for many years. Collections: Holmes à Court, Broken Hill Art Gallery, SA Museum, Supreme Court of the Northern Territory, Darwin

SCOBIE, (MIYANGULA) LILY NANGALA
Place of birth Jukakarinyi c.1930, her language and tribe are Warlpiri. She lives at Lajamanu, her country being Warlukurlangu (the one near Mongrel Downs — Warlukurlangu means 'belonging to the fire' and there are quite a few sites associated with it) and her Dreaming is Warlu (Bush Fire). She works with her sisters TOPSY, Yinarrki and Yurrurngali (all Nangalas), who started painting in 1986.

SCOBIE, NARPULA NAPURRULA
Also cited as: Narrpula Scobie Napurrula
Born in the Haasts Bluff region in late '50s, she is the younger sister of Turkey TOLSON. She grew up in the Haasts Bluff area and moved to Papunya when the settlement was established in the '60s. Married to Johnny SCOBIE, she started painting at Papunya in the early '80s, one of the first women to do so, and has continued painting in Kintore. She remains the only senior Pintupi woman painting for Papunya Tula Artists, though her young daughter-in-law, Fabrianne PETERSEN, has recently started painting. One of Narpula's paintings was included in the 'Art and Aboriginality' exhibition in Portsmouth in 1987 and in an exhibition of Australian Art which toured China in 1988. She paints Bush Tucker and other women's stories including the story of Two

Women who came up from Mitukutjarrayi in the south, stopping at the mountain outside Kintore before travelling on to the north-west. Collections: Holmes à Court, Art Gallery of SA, Australian Museum, Sydney

SCOBIE, NEIL JAPANANGKA

Place of birth Ngarrkakurlangu, his language/tribe is Warlpiri and he lives at Lajamanu. His country is Ngarrkakurlangu and his Dreamings are Mamingirri, Pakuru, Warlu, Tililturlpa and Ngarrka. He works with his wife, Janie Samuels Napurrurla and started painting in 1986.

SIMMS, AGNES (NGARNIYA) NAPANANGKA

Born at Yuendumu of the Warlpiri language/tribe. She lives at Lajamanu and her country is Ngarna, Janyinki and Mina-mina. Her Dreamings are Mardukuja-mardukuja (Kana), Warna and Ngalyipi and she started painting in 1986.

SIMMS, KITTY NAPANANGKA

A Warlpiri speaker, her place of birth is Yurntumu and she lives at Lajamanu. Her country is Mina-mina and her Dreamings are Mardukuja-mardukuja, Ngalyipi and Warna. She started painting in 1986.

SIMON, AGNES NAKAMARRA

Born in Darwin in 1964, her language/tribe is Warlpiri and she lives at Lajamanu. Her country is Yarturlu-yarturlu and her Dreamings are Ngurlu, Pirlarla and Laju. She works with her husband, Doug Tasman Japangardi, and started painting in 1987.

SIMON, PHYLLIS NAKAMARRA

Born at Lajamanu c.1970, she lives at Lajamanu and is the daughter — and student — of Victor SIMON Tjupurrurla, whose formidable influence is evident in her art. A Warlpiri speaker, her country is Yarturlu-yarturlu — the Granites — and her Dreamings are Ngurlu, Pirlarla and Laju. She started painting in 1987.

SIMON TJAKAMARRA (c.1947–1/1990)

Born in Pintupi country south-east of Kiwirrkura at Kulkuta in the Pollock Hills region in the late '40s, he walked in to Papunya from Muduk, west of Kintore when still a young man, not yet married. His older brother, ANATJARI Tjakamarra, was one of Geoffrey Bardon's group of 'painting men' at Papunya in 1971, and Simon did a few small paintings in the early days of the art movement before moving away to Tjukula, near Docker River. He returned to painting while living at Yai Yai outstation west of Papunya in the late '70s, becoming interested after watching the older men at work on their canvases. He joined his brothers, Anatjari and JACKIE Tjakamarra, in Kintore in the early '80s and began painting regularly for Papunya Tula Artists. He quickly emerged as a subtle and powerful exponent of the classic Pintupi style of circles and connecting lines. He usually painted Tingari stories from around the area of Kulkuta. Collections: Holmes à Court, Art Gallery of WA

SIMON, VICTOR JUPURRURLA

Born Yarturlu-yarturlu in 1945 of the Warlpiri tribe and language, he lives at Lajamanu and his country is Yarturlu-yarturlu — the Granites gold mine. His father, Pirlarla Jakamarra, whom Victor described as 'boss of his countrymen', organised Aboriginal people to work at Granites goldmine in the '30s. A few years after Victor was born, his father was killed when the army greatcoat he always wore became stuck in the wheels of the crusher. Victor was thirteen years old when he came to Lajamanu, where he is now a leading figure. He is one of the Lajamanu representatives for ATSIC. He paints Pirlarla, Ngurlu (bush seeds for grinding into damper) and Laju ('Witchetty in Gumtree') Dreamings. Simon works with his wives, Kitty, Pampirriya and Agnes Napanangka, and started painting in 1986. He won a prize at the Tennant Creek Art Award in 1988.

SIMS, BESSIE NAKAMARRA

Born c.1940, Bessie is Warlpiri and lives at Yuendumu. In the early '80s Bessie Sims joined the group of senior women at Yuendumu who were pioneers of the painting enterprise in the community. Her work has been included in many shows of Warlukurlangu Artists since the Editions Gallery exhibition in Perth in June 1986 and in Alice Springs, Adelaide, Sydney, Seattle, USA, Melbourne, Brisbane, and in Los Angeles, USA at the Caz Gallery. She is married to Paddy Japaljarri SIMS and is the older sister of Michael NELSON Jagamara, both well-known artists. She paints the Ngarlajiyi (Bush Carrot) Dreaming associated with Wapurtali near Mt Singleton, west of Yuendumu, also Janganpa (Possum), Pamapardu (Flying Ant) and Karntajarra (Two Women) Dreamings. Her work featured on the catalogue cover of a show of Yuendumu paintings held at the Sydney Opera House in 1987. In 1988 she was commissioned to paint a mural for the South Australian Museum in collaboration with five other artists. With Maggie and Peggy Poulson, she is featured in the video which accompanied the 'Dreamings: Art Of Aboriginal Australia' exhibition to the USA in 1988–9, painting an elaborately detailed Janganpa Dreaming. She is also depicted in the exhibition catalogue working with Paddy Sims on one of his paintings. Collections: South Australian Museum, Australian Museum, Sydney, Museums and Art Galleries of NT, Kohane Family collection, many other private collections. Reference: Diggins, L., *Myriad of Dreamings*; West, M., *The Inspired Dream*; Johnson, V., *The Painted Dream*; *Australian Aboriginal Art from the Collection of Donald Kahn*; all catalogues of major shows of Western Desert art which have included her work

SIMS, PADDY JAPALJARRI

Born c.1917 at Mt Nicker, NT, south-west of Yuendumu at the site of Kunajarrayi, which is associated with the Initiated Ngarrka (Men) and Warna (Snake) Dreamings.

He is Warlpiri and lives at Yuendumu, where he is one of the leading artists in the community. He was one of the main artists and motivators of the Yuendumu Doors project, and collaborated with Larry Jungarrayi SPENCER, JIMIJA Jungarrayi and Paddy Jupurrurla NELSON on the painting of *Munga Star Dreaming* which was purchased by the National Gallery of Australia from the first Yuendumu exhibition in Sydney in 1985. The artist paints Yiwarra (Milky Way), Ngarlkirdi/Warna (Witchetty Grub/Snake), Pirntirna (Woma Python), Liwirringki (Burrowing Skink), Wanakiji (Bush Plum) and Walpa (Wind) Dreamings. His work has been in numerous group exhibitions of Warlukurlangu Artists throughout Australia since the Yuendumu painters' first show at the Araluen Arts Centre in Alice Springs in October 1985. His paintings have also been shown in major overseas exhibitions including the 'Dreamings' exhibition which toured North America in 1988–9 and 'l'été Australien' at Musée Fabre, Montepellier, France, 1990. In 1988 Paddy Sims was selected by the Power Gallery, Sydney University, to travel to Paris with five other Warlpiri men from Yuendumu to create a ground painting installation at the exhibition 'Magiciens de la Terre' at the Centre Georges Pompidou in Paris. The trip took place in 1989 and the painting met with wide acclaim. Collections: National Gallery of Australia, Canberra; National Gallery of Victoria; SA Museum; WA Museum of Anthropology; Christensen Fund; major private collections in Australia and overseas etc. References: (ed) Caruana, W., *Windows on the Dreaming*; Ryan, J., *Mythscapes*; (ed) Sutton, P., *Dreamings*; Warlukurlangu Artists, *Kuruwarri: Yuendumu Doors*

SIMS, WENDY NUNGARRAYI (BROWN)

A Warpliri speaker, and daughter of Bessie and Paddy SIMS, Wendy Nungarrayi Sims lives in Yuendumu. She paints Ngalkirdi (Witchetty Grub), Wanakiji (Bush Plum) and Yanjylpiri (Star) Dreamings. Her work was included in 'Yuendumu: Paintings out of the Desert' at the South Australian Museum in 1988 and the 'Women's Exhibition' at the Women's Gallery in Melbourne in 1990 and in 1992 at Warlukurlangu Artists' exhibitions in Melbourne, Hobart and Sydney.

SKEEN, MILLIE NAMPITJIN

A Kukatja speaker, Millie Skeen was born in the Stansmore Ranges c.1932. Her country is Lirrwarti, and she paints Emu and Bush Carrot Dreamings. She lives in Balgo and has been painting since 1986. Like many of the older artists with Warlayirti Artists, her work has a strongly idiosyncratic look. Two common themes are showing tendrils of the bush carrot ('tjirilpatja') surrounding the canvas or, alternatively, 'narrative' works showing men's weapons and telling of the activities of her ancestors. The images are sometimes strikingly original. Collections: Art Gallery of WA, Gold Coast Art Gallery

SONDA NAMPITJINPA, see TURNER, Sonder Nampitjinpa

SPENCER, ANDREW JAPALJARRI

A Warlpiri speaker, originally from Yuendumu, he now lives in Alice Springs with his family, and works with HALT (Healthy Aboriginal Lifestyle Team). As part of this work, he produced a series of posters dealing with current issues and problems in Aboriginal communities such as family breakdowns, petrol-sniffing, alcohol abuse and AIDS, but using the traditional iconography of Western Desert painting to spell out his message. The success of this innovation in disseminating information to Aboriginal people has led to its adoption by others involved in health and community services — and more recently by other artists (e.g. the 'history paintings' of Malya TEAMAY of the Mutitjulu community at Uluru).

SPENCER, APRIL NAPALJARRI

Born at Yuendumu c.1965. A Warlpiri speaker, her country is Yarripilangu and she paints Goanna and Ngalyipi (Snake Vine) Dreamings. She lives in Alice Springs, but has connections with the community at Kiwirrkura. She began painting in 1989 after watching her brother, Andrew Japaljarri SPENCER, when she was living at Hidden Valley. Her brother taught her about their father's Dreamings. 'I dance and paint for the Dreaming.' She works with the Jukurrpa group based at the IAD in Alice Springs.

SPENCER, GARTH JAPALJARRI

Born in Yuendumu in 1946, Garth is a Warlpiri speaker. He lives on an outstation of New Haven, near his country Yarripirlangu. His father taught him about the Goanna Dreaming which he depicts in his paintings. He started painting in 1988/9, and was once associated with Warlukurlangu Artists in Yuendumu. His brother, Andrew Japaljarri SPENCER, also paints.

SPENCER, ISABEL NAPALJARRI

Born in Yuendumu c.1955. Isabel is Andrew and Garth Japaljarri and April Napaljarri SPENCER's sister. She has spent most of her life in Yuendumu, moving into Alice Springs only in 1991. In Alice Springs she was taught the techniques of acrylic painting by Rachel Napaljarri JURRA. Isabel paints Wardapi (Goanna) Dreaming, which she inherited from her father. She has strong connections to Willowra, Kiwirrkura and Yuendumu communities and is a Warlpiri speaker. In 1992/3 she attended the Literacy Course at IAD.

SPENCER, LARRY JUNGARRAYI (c.1919–1990)
Also cited as: Larry Spencer Tjungarrayi/Jungarai

Born c.1919 at Yarripirlangu, south-west of Yuendumu, a site associated with the Ngarrka (Initiated Men) or Ngalyipi (Snake Vine) Dreaming. He was one of the senior men whose painting of the doors of the Yuendumu school helped to start up the painting enterprise in the community. He collaborated with Paddy Japaljarri SIMS, JIMIJA Jungarrayi and Paddy Jupurrurla NELSON on *Munga Star Dreaming* 1985, purchased by the National Gallery of Australia from Warlukurlangu Artists's first Sydney show at the Hogarth Gallery in December of that year. In its fluid impulsive paintwork, his *Milky Way Dreaming* 1986, also purchased by the Gallery, typified the exuberance of the early Yuendumu style, which remained undiminished in Larry Spencer's work. Collections: National Gallery of Australia. Reference: Warlukurlangu Artists, *Kuruwarri: Yuendumu Doors*

SPENCER, WINKIE NAPALJARRI

Born in Yuendumu in 1960, Winkie is a Warlpiri speaker, and Andrew Japaljarri SPENCER's sister. She now lives in Hidden Valley town camp in Alice Springs. Apart from Goanna Dreamings, she paints Flying Ant (Pamapardu) Dreaming from her mother's country at Nyirrpi. She started painting in 1991 and has been selling most of her works through Jukurrpa artists' co-operative — she is a student of the IAD Bridging Course.

STAFFORD, BETTY (JAMINAKARI) NANGALA

A Warlpiri person whose country is Puyurru and Dreaming Ngapa (Water), she lives at Lajamanu. She works with three other older women, Topsy, Yinarki and Yurrurngali Miyangula — all Nangalas and all sisters. She started painting in 1987.

STAFFORD, DAVID JAKAMARRA

Born in 1960, he is an Anmatyerre speaker whose heritage country lies around Coniston. He paints Witchetty Grub Dreaming and is married to Kathy BAGGOT Napangardi. He lives at Mt Allan.

STAFFORD, LILLY PANANGKA
Also cited as: Lilly Stafford Napanangka (Amnatyerre and Warlpiri skin names respectively)

Born c.1950 at Coniston. An Anmatyerre speaker, she has been painting Witchetty, Yiparli (Bush Banana) and Sugarbag Dreamings for her country at Coniston since 1988 when the Yuelamu Museum and Art Gallery opened at Mt Allan. Collections: Australian Museum, Sydney

STEVENS, THOMAS TJAKAMARRA

Tommy Stevens is Pitjantjatjara — the skin name Tjakamarra was assigned after he married a woman from Papunya and resided there for a few years in the mid '80s. He was taught to use pen and brush by Ewald Namatjira, the son of Albert Namatjira, Thomas was an experienced and talented exponent of European representation (e.g. Thomas Stevens, *The Lost Boomerang* [Methuen, Australia, 1983]), illustrating books for the Papunya Literature Production Centre, when he turned his hand to Papunya painting in about 1985. He produced some strikingly original paintings incorporating elements of both traditions in what emerged in the late '80s as one of the dominant tendencies in 'town based' Western Desert art. Also wrote *Altyerre Ipenhe Anwernekenhe Akurneleke*

Kerte — Damaging Our Dreaming Land (Yipirinya School Council). More recently his paintings have returned to the Hermannsburg watercolour style of his earlier work. He lives in Alice Springs.

STEVENSON, (YIMIKILAYI) MOLLY NUPURRURLA

Born at Lajamanu in 1964, Molly is Warlpiri tribe/language and lives at Lajamanu. Her country is Yumurrpa and her Dreamings are Yarla and Wapurti. She started painting in 1986.

STEWART, PADDY JAPALJARRI
Also cited as: Cookie Japaljarri Stewart

Born c.1940 and a Warlpiri/Anmatyerre, Paddy lives at Yuendumu. His country is Mt Allan and Mt Denison area and his Dreamings are Kangaroo, Seed and Possum. He paints for Warlukurlangu Artists, with whom he has shown widely since the mid '80s. His work was included in the 'Dreamings' exhibition which toured the USA in 1988–9. Paddy Stewart and Roy Japaljarri Curtis assisted the old men of the Yuendumu community in the painting of the school doors in 1983 which helped to spark off the development of a painting enterprise at the settlement. At the time, all the men involved in this project were members of the School Council and the Yuendumu Tribal Council. Remarkably, Paddy Stewart also helped paint the original Papunya school murals, assisting his countryman Billy STOCKMAN Tjapaltjarri.

STEWART, PANSY NAKAMARRA

Born in 1946, Pansy Stewart is a Warlpiri speaker. Her Dreamings are Yarla (Yam) and Janganpa (Possum). She lives in Yuendumu and paints for Warlukurlangu Artists, with whom she began exhibiting in 1992. Her work has been shown in exhibitions in Hobart, Melbourne and Canberra. Collections: Art Gallery and Museum, Kelvingrove, Glasgow, Scotland

STEWART, QUEENIE NUNGARRAYI

A Warlpiri speaker, Queenie Stewart lives in Yuendumu and paints for Warlukurlangu Artists. Her dreamings are Marlu (Kangaroo), Wardapi (Goanna) and Janganpa (Possum). She exhibited with other Yuendumu painters in 1990 in Darwin and Melbourne, and in 1992 in Perth, Melbourne and Alice Springs.

STOCKMAN, ALBY JAPANANGKA

Born in 1946, Alby Stockman is an Anmatyerre speaker whose traditional country is Red Hill. He paints Water, Possum, Emu, Kangaroo, Caterpillar, Red Hill and Mt Wedge Dreamings. He is married to Beryl Nangala, who also paints. He is the Director of the Yuelamu Cattle Company at Mt Allan.

STOCKMAN, BILLY TJAPALTJARRI

Born at Ilpitirri near Mt Denison, north-west of Papunya, c.1927 of the Anmatyerre/ Western Arrente tribe. His first contact with whites was as an infant survivor of the Coniston massacre (1928): 'All the people were running. I was a little one — in a coolamon. My mother put me under a bush. My father had gone hunting — for rabbit and goanna. They killed my mother. I was grown up by her sister — Clifford POSSUM's mother.' Billy grew up at Napperby station and Aileron, was initiated at Napperby and then worked there as a stockman. Later he worked as a cook in the Papunya communal kitchen and with the Pintupi people brought in from the west, helping them to adjust to the settlement lifestyle. He was one of the Papunya Town Councillors in the '70s and an accomplished wood carver before he took up painting. Billy was one of the founders of the Papunya painting movement: watched over by Old MICK and Old Tom Onion, who gave permission for the use of their story, Billy, KAAPA, and Long Jack PHILLIPUS painted the Honey Ant Dreaming design on the school wall which set the painting movement in motion. An energetic campaigner in the outstation movement, he was one of first to shift to his own outstation west of Papunya. His country lies west of Napperby station around Mt Denison, Ilpitirri and Yuendumu. He paints Budgerigar, Spider, Yam and Wild Potato Dreamings for this region. Billy was a Central Australian delegate to the NAC during the '70s; Aboriginal Arts Board member 1975–79; and Chairman of Papunya Tula Artists during the '70s. Billy has visited the USA several times, most recently for the opening of the 'Dreamings: Art of Aboriginal Australia' exhibition in New York in 1988, also Papua New Guinea, New Zealand, and the 'All Black Festival' in South Africa. He occasionally paints in town for the Centre for Aboriginal Artists, but mostly lives with his family on his outstation at Ilili near Papunya. He and his wife Intinika have two sons and two daughters, of whom Gillian paints occasionally, having been taught by her father. Collections: National Gallery of Australia, Canberra, Art Gallery of SA, Art Gallery of NSW, Holmes à Court, Flinders University Art Museum, Peter Styvesant collection, South Australian Museum, Museums & Art Galleries of NT, University of WA Anthropology Museum, Art Gallery of WA, National Museum of Australia, Canberra, Victorian Arts Centre, Campbelltown City Council

STOCKMAN, TOPSY NAMPIJINPA

Born in 1920, Topsy is the mother of Alby STOCKMAN. An Anmatyerre, her country is Mt Allan and Ngarliyikurlangu. She paints Emu Dreaming. She lives at Mt Allan.

SUNFLY TJAMPITJIN

Born 'in the bush' in the Alec Ross Ranges, north-west of Lake Mackay, c.1920, Sunfly is a very senior man in the Balgo community, whose understanding of the Law is acknowledged by all. A Kukatja speaker, his country is Murrunpa (Alec Ross Ranges) and his principal Dreamings are Tingari and Luurnpa (Kingfisher). He began painting in 1984, several years before the establishment of Warlayirti Artists. His works show a great dramatic power and tell of things that cannot be described to outsiders. One of the artist's forceful designs has been used to form a mosaic in the Forrest Place redevelopment in the heart of Perth. Collections: National Gallery of Australia, Canberra, National Gallery of Victoria, Art Gallery of WA

SUSAN NAPALJARRI

Born at Wave Hill of the Warlpiri tribe, Susan Napaljarri lives at Lajamanu. Her country is Warlukurlangu, Yarrurmangu and Karlyardijaru (Ringers Soak) and her Dreaming Warlu. She works with husband Tingiyari (JACKO Jakamarra) and his co-wife LIZZIE Napaljarri, and started painting in 1986.

SYDDICK, LINDA JUNKATA NAPALJARRI
Also cited as: Linda Sims Napaljarri, Tjangkiya (Linda Syddick) Napaltjarri

Born in 1941 at Jigalong of a Pintupi mother and Pitjanjatjara father. In 1943 her mother went to Kintore after her father was killed in a spearing. At Kintore she was raised by her uncle (father's brother), Shorty LUNGKATA, who taught her to paint as an older girl — as did NOSEPEG Tjupurrula and UTA UTA Tjangala. She recalls her first experience of painting in the Papunya schoolroom. Her first husband was Musty Syddick, a Luritja man whose mother was a Pintupi/Aranda (Arrente) woman from the Jigalong/Kintore area, and whose father was an Afghan camel driver. Musty was a painter whose name appeared occasionally in Papunya Tula Artists' records from the '70s. He seems to have been the first artist to use the now popular stippled effect of flicked brushwork in his paintings during the '70s. Linda Syddick is also an innovator. A deeply religious woman, her paintings reflect both her extensive knowledge of the Dreaming and her Christian beliefs, one of the few artists working in the Western Desert style to have taken this direction. She uses the traditional symbols to denote her Dreaming and the Christian story she is trying to depict in the painting. She paints Tingari Dreamings — her father's Emu story from around Kintore, and her mother's Snake story. She has taught her daughter Ruby to paint. In 1990 she travelled to Sydney to see her painting *Ngkarte Dreaming* hung in the annual Blake Prize for Religious Art and included in a travelling exhibition of 37 paintings to tour the eastern states. Also in 1990 an exhibition in Santa Fe, New Mexico 'From the Australian Desert', featured her work. She works with the Jukurrpa group when in Alice Springs. More recently she has been living out at Kintore and painting for Papunya Tula Artists. She was included in 'Australian Perspecta 1993' at the Art Gallery of NSW and has three times been a finalist for the Blake Prize.

SYDDICK, Musty (d.), see SYDDICK, Linda

T

TAMERRE, GLORIA PETYARRE, see GLORIA Petyarre

TAPAYA, NYUWARA

Born on 5 August 1971, her language group is Pitjantjatjara. Nyuwara was born at Ernabella hospital. Her mother, who is an established artist, is Pitjantjatjara and comes from Antalya. Her father is from Tipany and his first language is Yangkunytjarjara. Nuywara attended Ernabella school and Woodville High School until 1988. The next year she began working in the screenprinting workshop at Ernabella Arts. She began experimenting with acrylic paints with immediate success. Later in 1989 she attended an information gathering tour of Darwin and Bathurst Island and began studying batik techniques. In November of that year she exhibited both paintings and batiks in Ernabella Arts's 'Wiritjuta' exhibition at Araluen Arts Centre in Alice Springs. In 1990 she continued her studies in design and fabric printing and attended the opening of Ernabella Arts's exhibition 'Ngura Kutjara' at the Tandanya Aboriginal Cultural Institute in Adelaide. In 1991, 1992 and 1993 her fabric prints have been exhibited in the Central Australian Aboriginal Art and Craft Exhibition at the Araluen Arts Centre. Her fabrics were also shown in 'Kutjupa-Kutjupa', Ernabella Arts's exhibition at the Aboriginal Artists Gallery in Sydney in 1991. In April 1992 Nyuwara attended the opening of 'Raiki Tjuta', Ernabella Arts's exhibition at the Women's Gallery in Melbourne. In June 1992 she spent two weeks in Jogjakata, Indonesia studying dye techniques and cap printing. In September 1992 one of Nyuwara's caps was exhibited in the National Aboriginal Art Award and purchased by the Art Gallery of SA. This exposure and an exhibition of her fabric designs in an Alice Springs gallery attracted several design commissions for T-shirts and a doona cover of the print *Waru* from the Community Arts Abroad catalogue. Nyuwara is continuing her studies of printmaking and lithography, while still producing her popular screenprint designs for fabrics. Collections: Art Gallery of SA

TARAWA, CHARLIE TJUNGARRAYI
Also cited as: Charlie Tjaruru Tjungurrayi, Jungarai

Born at a rocky hill called Tjitururrnga, west of the Kintore Ranges in Pintupi country, c.1921. His first contact with whites was with the Adelaide University expedition of 1932 at Mt Leibig. Before World War II his family lived around the missions at Haasts Bluff and Hermannsburg, meeting Dr Charles Duguid, who gave him the name Charlie. He has travelled extensively, working with the army around Adelaide River, south of Darwin, during World War II, then as a dogger out of Haasts Bluff, travelling by camel team in journeys westward to Pintupi homelands hunting dingoes whose scalps were exchanged for rations. He took rations out to his countrymen and women still living in the desert, some of whom rode back east on his camels to see for themselves. Because of his extensive experience with Europeans, he became the adopted spokesman for the younger Pintupi men in the early days of the painting movement. Later he became a friend of Papunya Tula Artists manager (1980–1) the late Andrew Crocker, with whom he travelled to England in the early '80s, and who organised a major retrospective of the artist's work, 'Charlie Tjaruru Tjungurrayi: A Retrospective 1970–1986' (Orange City Council, 1987), which toured four Australian states. A more detailed account of the artist's life written by Andrew Crocker is contained in the catalogue of this exhibition. Charlie Tarawa paints Emu, Wallaby, Water and Frog Dreamings and Tingari stories from the Tjitururrnga area. His sons, HILARY and BENNY Tjapaltjarri, also paint for Papunya Tula Artists. He lives in Kintore, where he is usually referred to as 'Wadama' or 'Watuma'. Collections: National Gallery of Australia, Canberra, Holmes à Court, Museums & Art Galleries of NT, Flinders University Art Museum, University of Queensland Art Museum, National Gallery of Victoria, Art Gallery of WA, Art Gallery of SA, National Museum of Australia, Canberra, SA Museum, University of WA Anthropology Museum, Burke Museum, University of Washington, Seattle

TASMAN, BARBARA NAPURRURLA

Born c.1955, she is a Warlpiri person who lives at Lajamanu and whose country is Yarturlu-yarturlu (the Granites) and Dreamings are Ngurlu (Seed), Janganpa (Possum) and Laju (Witchetty Grub). After working at Lajamanu School for several years as an assistant teacher, she went on to do two years teacher training.

TASMAN, DENISE NAPANGARDI
Also cited as: Denise Robertson Napangardi

Born at Yuendumu c.1960. A Warlpiri speaker, she lives at Lajamanu and her country is Yawul-lawulu and Dreamings are Yurrampi (Honey Ant), Wardapi (Goanna), Wintiki and Puurda. She works with her husband, Jimmy ROBERTSON, and started painting in 1986.

TASMAN, LYNETTE NAPANGARDI

Place of birth Yuendumu 1962, her language/tribe is Warlpiri and she lives at Lajamanu. Her country is Jirrparanpa, Kunajarrayi and Parralya and her Dreamings are Wardapi, Yarla, Ngurlu and Ngayaki. She paints her stepfather and mother's Dreamings. Lynette's father was a white man and to prevent the child being taken away, her mother, Molly TASMAN, had to stand up to Welfare authorities and argue that she could bring up the child equally well herself. Lynette works with Mary-Ann TASMAN, her sister-in-law, and with her mother and started painting in 1986.

TASMAN, MARY-ANN NAPALJARRI

Born at Lajamanu in 1956, Mary-Ann is a Warlpiri whose country is Kunajarrayi and Dreamings are Warna, Laju and Ngalyipi. Her Laju — Witchetty Grub — Dreaming painting was put onto a T-shirt. She sometimes works with her sister-in-law, Lynette TASMAN. Started painting in 1987 and is one of the most successful Lajamanu artists, especially amongst the younger women. She is very articulate, in Warlpiri and in English also — she negotiated the deal to have her painting on the T-shirt herself.

TASMAN, MELODY NAPURRURLA

Place of birth Kunalarrinyi c.1920 or earlier. Melody lives at Lajamanu and is the elder sister of Molly Naparrurla TASMAN. Her language/tribe is Warlpiri and her country is Minya-miya. Her Dreamings are Ngurlu, Jurlpu (Puntaru), Kulukuka and Pirdijirri. Started painting in 1986. Collections: National Gallery of Victoria

TASMAN, MOLLY NAPURRURLA

Born at Miya-miya c.1936 of the Warlpiri language/tribe. She lives at Lajamanu, her country is Miya-miya and Malungurru and her Dreamings are Ngurlu, Jungunypa and Kalajirri. She started painting in 1986. Was married to Johnny Scobie Tjapanangka, a Pintupi man who came from Papunya. Collections: National Gallery of Victoria

TAX, RICHARD TJUPURRULA

Born 'in the bush' in the area south of Southesk Tablelands c.1935. A Kukatja tribesman, his traditional country is south-west of Balgo at Kurtal. He began painting for Warlayirti Artists in 1989 and paints Rainbow Snake and Goanna Dreamings. The artist's works have a unique look and exhibit a strong sense of tradition and authority. Along with other Mulan painters, he uses brushwork along with dotting, and includes more figurative elements in his works. The designs are always interesting and every area of the canvas is filled with motifs and significance from Men's Law.

TEAMAY, MALYA

A Pitjantjatjara speaker, Malya was born at Curtin Springs, NT and grew up at Uluru /Ayers Rock, Ernabella and Areyonga. He now lives in the Mutitjulu community, Uluru. Self-taught, Malya began painting in about 1985, around the time of the Uluru handback. Unlike most of the small group of painters now at Uluru, he does not carve wood. His first painting, versions of which he is still doing, concerned petrol sniffing, and is sometimes described by him as a 'history' painting, as it shows the history of black/white relations in Australia from his perspective. Malya sells paintings both to Maruku Arts and Crafts and sometimes to individuals in the Uluru community. He says he paints the 'outside' story. His three common subjects in paintings are petrol sniffing, the Lasseter story, and the Kalgoorlie gold story. He has also done a painting for the community store which shows the food coming in, money changing hands, and all the workers in the store. Malya says he never paints little boards as there is not enough room on them to tell a story. Most other men in the Mutitjulu community, apart from Charlie Peipei, paint little paintings. KUNBRY and IMPANA also do big ones. For the tourists, Malya usually paints Tjala and Maku; if asked, he will do history painting, 'If they like history, I'll make history.' He also paints the Seven Sisters story and Liru (Snake) Dreamings. He sometimes paints his father's story (Kuniya), a Dreaming which comes across Uluru way. He says tourists are interested in the story; they want to learn: 'Every canvas, I tell story. Some Anangu paint it and sell it, and don't tell story; just painting for money.' Malya's wife assists in the painting process. Malya paints the Tjukurrpa and some colour; his wife does the colour background and the outlines of the design; then they both do the dots. It takes him about three days to do a large painting. His twelve-year-old daughter also paints occasionally. Malya is a particularly active member of the Mutitjulu community and has travelled widely throughout Australia to speak on Anangu issues. Collections: Museum of Victoria

TEDDY JUPURRURLA
Born at Coniston, Teddy is Warlpiri/Amnatyerre and lives at Willowra. Walpajurri (Bandicoot) is his Dreaming. 'When we got canvas that's when I started painting.' (From the CDEP coordinator at Willowra in 1989)

TEX, PETER JAPALJARRI
Born at Papunya in 1960, Peter has a Warlpiri mother and a Pintupi father. He now lives at Nyirrpi, but has relatives at Kintore, Papunya and Lajamanu. His country is Kunajarrayi. His first painting of Snake Dreaming was produced in 1986 (or '87), when his sister Nora Napaljarri (see ANDY, Nora Napaltjarri) gave him a canvas. Since then he has sold his paintings through the galleries in Alice Springs and participated in exhibitions in Adelaide and Canberra.

TILMOUTH, BOBBY JUPURRULA
Also cited as: Bobby Tilmouth Japarula
Born on Napperby station in 1942, Bobby Tilmouth is a cousin of artist Peter LEO. Teddy BRISCOE Tjampitjinpa from Mt Allan is his uncle. An Amnatyerre speaker, he now lives at Napperby. His traditional country is around Napperby Soakage and Coniston. He began painting in 1986, and usually paints Fish, Witchetty Grub and Corkwood Dreamings for this area. His work has been exhibited in several Australian capital cities.

TILMOUTH, DESMOND JAMPIJINPA
Born in 1963, Desmond's country is Ngarliyikurlangu and he paints Emu Dreaming. He is married to Carol FRANK and lives at Mt Allan.

TILMOUTH, DOREEN NAMPIJINPA

Born in 1970, Doreen's traditional country is Ngarliyikurlangu and Mt Wedge. She paints Emu and Bush Onion Dreamings and is an Anmatyerre speaker. She lives at Mt Allan.

TILMOUTH, JOSEPHINE NAKAMARRA

Born in 1965 at Napperby, where she still lives. Her grandfather's country is Yuendumu, and she is an Anmatyerre speaker. The Dreamings she paints are Honey Ant and Witchetty Grub. She occasionally sells her paintings through Jukurrpa artists' co-operative in Alice Springs, as well as the Napperby painting company.

TIMMS, SARAH NAPANANGKA

Born in the Yirningarra area in 1930, Sarah's language and tribe is Warlpiri and she lives at Lajamanu. Her country is Mina-mina and her Dreaming Mardukuja-mardukuja (Women Dreaming). She works with husband, Tiger TIMMS, and daughter Jennie and started painting in 1986.

TIMMS, TIGER JUPURRURLA

Born at Pirlipardu of the Warlpiri tribe and lives at Lajamanu. His country is Pirlipardu (Munjkurlurrpa — Tanami Downs) and Dreamings are Ngapa (Water) and Mukuparnta. Works with his wife, Sarah TIMMS, and daughter Jennie. He was one of the first to start painting in Lajamanu.

TINGIYARI, see JACKO Jakamarra

TJANGKIYA Napaljarri, see SYDDICK, Linda

TJIKATU, BARBARA NAPANANGKA

Born on 1 July 1935 at Waltjitjara, NT. A Pitjantjatjara speaker, her heritage country is Waltjitjara, Umutju, Katkurari and Kalyarintja, for which she paints Tjitji Tjukurrpa — Children Dreaming. She is married to Nipper Winmati and has been painting in acrylics since 1986. She lives in the Mutitjulu community at Uluru and sells her work through Maruku Arts and Crafts.

TJUMPO TJAPANANGKA

Born 'in the bush' c.1930, probably at Waterlander Breakaway, Tjumpo is a Kukatja speaker whose country lies around the site of Karnapilya and the area west of Lake Mackay, to the south of Balgo. His principal Dreamings are Tingari and Water Dreaming. He started painting in Balgo in 1986. His works are recognisable by their very tightly concentrated lines that swirl and squirm around the canvas. Usually done on a larger-sized frame, these works give the feeling of a big country alive with powerfully elemental forces. The area that the artist paints is where the 'First Contact' group of

1984 were living, and the artist is in fact a close relative of WALIMPIRRINGA Tjapaltjarri and others in that group. Collections: major public and private collections, including the Art Gallery of WA, the National Gallery of Victoria, Holmes à Court

TOBY JANGALA

Born at Yarturla-yarturla (the Granites mine) c.1945, his language/tribe is Warlpiri and he lives at Lajamanu. His country is Yumurrpa and his Dreamings are Janganpa (Possum) and Ngapa. He works with his wife, Pampirriya Nungarrayi BURNS, and started painting in 1986.

TOLSON, TURKEY TJUPURRULA

Born c.1938 about five miles (8 km) east of Haasts Bluff, Turkey's family had been moving between traditional country around Kintore and Hermannsburg mission, where they could collect rations of flour, tea and sugar, and after Turkey's birth they remained in the area around Haasts Bluff. Only when Papunya was being established and there was work to be had building the settlement did the family come in from the bush. This was in 1959, shortly after Turkey's initiation to manhood. Turkey was employed as a labourer on construction work around the new settlement and also in the Papunya communal kitchen. Later he married and moved to an outstation west of Papunya. His first wife died, and he remarried and later moved to Kintore in 1983. He now has an outstation on his traditional lands at Yuwalki, to the south-east of Kintore. Currently Chairman of Papunya Tula Artists and one of the best known of the company's artists, Turkey Tolson was one of the youngest of the original group of painters at Papunya. While some of his work is amongst the most innovative and figurative of that of all the Papunya Tula artists, he also paints in the classical, severely traditional Pintupi style of circles and connecting lines. He was artist-in-residence at Flinders University in 1979 with David CORBY, and paints Bush Fire, Emu, Snake, Woman and Mitukutjarrayi Dreamings from his traditional country south of Kintore around Yuwalki, Mitukutjarrayi and Putjya Rockhole. The artist and his work featured in 'East/West: Land in Papunya Paintings' at Tandanya Aboriginal Cultural Institute in Adelaide, 1990. The opening, including Turkey's speech and other interview material with the artist, is included in the documentary 'Market of Dreams'. Turkey's daughter-in-law, Brenda Rowe, has been painting since 1989. Collections: Holmes à Court, National Gallery of Victoria, Victorian Centre for the Performing Arts, Art Gallery of WA, Art Gallery of SA, National Museum of Australia, Canberra, University of WA Anthropology Museum, Flinders University Art Museum, SA Museum, Darwin Supreme Court etc.

TOMMY, MICHAEL TJAPANGATI
Also cited as: Michael Tommy Jabanardi

Born c.1960 in Alice Springs, Michael Tommy is the husband of artist Barbara CHARLES. Both are Amnatyerre speakers. Michael Tommy's country is around

Coniston, and he usually paints Snake Dreaming and another story of Hunting Emu from this area, though he also paints his father's Lizard (Perentie) Dreaming located around Mt Allan. Michael began painting in 1982 at Napperby. His work is strong with interesting effects of perspective and considerable tension between the design elements of the painting and the background dotting. His work has been associated with both the Napperby painters, and Yuelamu Artists, the painting enterprise at Mt Allan, where he and his wife now live.

TONY TJAKAMARRA

Born near Lake Mackay in Pintupi country, he is the younger brother of Freddy WEST. The family came in to Balgo in WA and Tony grew up at Balgo, moving to Kiwirrkura in the mid '80s when the settlement was established there in 1984. It was here that he began painting, in the late '80s, his work depicting Tingari stories from around the area of Lake Mackay in a manner influenced by the 'linked dotting' style of many Balgo artists. His painting of Nyuntjuri, a Storm Dreaming site associated with storms and lightning, was featured on the catalogue of 'Friendly Country, Friendly People' (Araluen Arts Centre, Alice Springs, 1990)

TOPSY NANGALA

Born at Mt Doreen in 1914, her tribe/language is Warlpiri. She lives at Lajamanu and her country is Puyurru and Dreaming Ngapa. She works with other Nangalas, including Yinarrki and Yurrurngali, and started painting in 1986. Collections: National Gallery of Victoria

TOPSY NAPANANGKA

Born c.1924 at Jarradajarrayi (Mt Theo), a site associated with Wardapi (Goanna) and Warna (Snake) Dreamings. She is Warlpiri and lives at Yuendumu. She collaborated with Liddy Napanangka WALKER and Judy Nampijinpa GRANITES on *Bean Dreaming* 1985, which was purchased by the National Gallery of Australia and shown in 'Windows on the Dreaming' at the gallery in 1989. Collections: National Gallery of Australia, Canberra. Reference: *Windows on the Dreaming*, (ed.) W. Caruana.

TOPSY NAPANGARDI

Born in 1931 of the Anmatyerre tribe, Topsy is the sister of Don MORTON. Her country is Yuelamu and she paints Honey Ant, and the Women Dreaming story for her father's country, which is the same as FRANK Japanangka's. She lives in Mt Allan and is one of the senior women of that community.

TURNER, MAUREEN NAMPIJINPA

Born at Mt Barkly in 1952, Maureen Turner paints the Warlpiri Fire Dreaming for her country Warlukurlangu. She also paints an Emu story for this country. She first appeared as a painter on the files of the Mt Allan company Yuelamu Artists, but now usually sells her work through the Centre for Aboriginal Artists and other galleries in Alice Springs. She has been painting since 1989 or earlier, and may have been influenced by her sisters, SANDRA and Sonder TURNER Nampitjinpa, from Mt Leibig, where Maureen was a teacher in the community school. More recently she moved to Alice Springs, and in 1990 travelled to Vanuatu for the Art Dock show, the first international art exhibition to be held in Vanuatu.

TURNER, SONDER NAMPITJINPA
Also cited as: Sonder Nampitjinpa, Sonda Nampitjinpa, Sonda Turner Nampitjimpa

Born outside of Yuendumu 1 March 1956, Sonder is the second daughter of Paddy Tjangala. She walked into Papunya with her parents as a young girl. Taught to paint in the early '80s by her father, Sonder was one of the first women painters in the Western Desert style to gain recognition for her work, winning the 1986 Canberra National Times Art Award. Her paintings usually depict the Two Women Dancing story for Mt Leibig. A Warlpiri speaker, she moved to Darwin in 1986 and thence to Katherine. She now has four children. Exhibitions: Gauguin Museum, February 1988, 'The Painted Dream', Auckland City Art Gallery, 1991. Collections: Flinders University Art Museum, Holmes à Court, Malcolm Forbes (USA), National Gallery of Australia, Canberra, Art Gallery of South Australia

TUTUMA TJAPANGATI (c.1915–1987)
Also cited as: Old Tutuma Japangardi

OF THE Pintupi/Pitjantjatjara tribe, Tutuma was one of the first Pintupi to own his own camels, which he used to go on extensive trips throughout his country west of Lake McDonald. An important ceremonial leader for the Pintupi/Pitjantjatjara, he was always eager to depict his Dreaming stories onto board with paint. One of the original artists whose vast output of work in the same loose, energetic 'action painting' style later practised by many of the older painters in communities where painting started up in the '80s. He travelled to Sydney in 1981 with Old Mick NAMARARI and NOSEPEG for an exhibition of paintings at Sid's Gallery. His country lay west of Lake McDonald across the WA border and around Lake Hopkins. He moved out to Kintore with the rest of the Pintupi at the beginning of the '80s and continued painting for Papunya Tula Artists until the mid '80s, although hampered by failing eyesight. Collections: National Gallery of Victoria, Museums & Art Galleries of NT, Flinders University Art Museum

TWO BOB TJUNGARRAYI

Born c.1938 at Haasts Bluff before the establishment of white settlement in the area. His family had fled to Warlpiri country round Mt Wedge after the 1928 massacre at Coniston. Later they moved to his mother's country at Haasts Bluff. Two Bob had no formal education. Like several of the other Papunya Tula artists, he was brought across from Haasts Bluff in the early '60s to the new settlement at Papunya, where he worked in the communal kitchen as a butcher. He was taught to paint by his older stepbrother, Paddy CARROLL, at the start of the '80s. One of a group of younger Warlpiri artists, which also includes DON Tjungarrayi, MAXIE Tjampitjinpa and Michael NELSON, who started painting at Papunya in this period and have since emerged as major artists for the painting company. Two Bob's country lies around Three Mile Bore and across to Kerrinyarra — Central Mt Wedge. The Dreaming stories he paints include Goanna, Man, Woman, Bush Tucker, Bush Grapes, Mukaki, Carpet Snake — and others he shares with Paddy Carroll. He and his wife, Nellie Nangala, a Luritja woman (who also paints occasionally), have three sons and two daughters. They live at Papunya. Two Bob has travelled to Canberra, Sydney and Adelaide with Papunya Tula Artists. Collections: National Gallery of Australia, Canberra, Art Gallery of SA, Holmes à Court, Parliament House, Canberra, Victorian Museum

U

UMBIDONG, EMANTURA

Born in Areyonga, NT, where she went to school, coming back to Uluru to spend the holidays there, since there was no school at the Rock in those days. She now lives at the Mutitjulu community, Uluru. She remembers making and selling carvings at Uluru when she was young, before the Maruku Arts and Crafts enterprise was established. Her mother and father used to make artefacts to sell to the tourists and taught her to carve and incise designs with hot wire. She enjoys wood carving, which her sister Barbara also teaches her. She only makes nulla nullas, having tried a lizard once and found it 'too hard'. She finds painting easier and likes to do both large and small paintings. She always paints her grandmother's country near Docker River, even her little paintings are about this place. The Dreaming track for this story comes through Uluru. Umbidong works in the community as a health worker, working at weekends on her painting and carving.

UTA UTA TJANGALA (c.1920–1990)
Also cited as: Uta Uta Jangala, Uta Uta Tjungala, Wuta Wuta Tjangala, Uata Uata Tjangala No 2

Born c.1920 in the Kintore Ranges, far to the west of Papunya. Part of the original group of painting men at Papunya in 1971; at the time it commenced, Uta Uta was a gardener in the Papunya school, where he worked with his friend Yarta. The friendship these two men had with Geoffrey Bardon, who supplied them with brushes, paint and board, sparked off the involvement of a dozen other Pintupi men at the very beginning of the painting enterprise at Papunya (Reference: G. Bardon, *Aboriginal Art of the Western Desert*). Despite his advancing years, Uta Uta emerged in the late '70s and early '80s as a master of the mature Pintupi style on a vast scale. He was assisted on his 1981 painting of the site of 'Yumari', which has been exhibited in the XVII Bienal de Sao Paulo, 1983 and the USA in the 'Dreamings' exhibition of 1988–9, by a team of eleven other artists, including ANATJARI Tjampitjinpa, Dinny CAMPBELL, JOHN Tjakamarra, KANYA Tjapangati, CHARLIE Tjapangati and YALA YALA Tjungarrayi. Another large canvas of the rocky outcrops near Yumari painted in 1983 was purchased by the Art Gallery of SA. In 1985 he won the National Aboriginal Art Award. Many of the stories he paints are based on the Tingari cycle — also sites associated with Yumari, a site which included some important waterholes across the WA border. He also paints Old Man, Emu and Carpet Snake Dreamings. Like most of the Pintupi living in Papunya, he returned to his homelands in the early '80s when Kintore was established and settled on his outstation at Muyinnga, west of Kintore. His son, Shorty Tjampitjinpa JACKSON, who lives in Kintore, has also begun painting in recent years, depicting the sites around Lake MacDonald in the Kutulu region where he walked around with his father as a boy.

Uta Uta died in Alice Springs Hospital on Friday 14 December 1990. Collections: National Museum of Australia, Canberra, National Gallery of Victoria, Art Gallery of SA, Queensland Art Gallery, Holmes à Court, Australian Museum, Sydney, National Gallery of Australia, Canberra, Parliament House, Museums & Art Galleries of NT, SA Museum

V

VIOLET PETYARRE

An Eastern Anmatyerre speaker, Violet Petyarre was born c.1925. Her country is Atnangkere Soakage, and she is associated with the Atneltyeye community. She has an Emu Dreaming in this area which she paints. Like most of the Utopia artists, she began to work with paint and canvas in the summer of 1988–9. Her sisters, Nancy Petyarre and Myrtle Petyarre, also paint occasionally.

W

WAKO, MORRIS JANGALA
Also cited as: Maurice Wako
Born in 1970, Maurice Wako is an Anmatyerre speaker who has country in the areas of both Napperby and Mt Allan. He paints Possum, Bush Tucker, Honey Ant and Witchetty Dreamings and lives at Mt Allan.

WAKURI, BARNEY TJAKAMARRA
Of the Pitjantjatjara language group, Barney resides at Mt Leibig. His paintings depict stories associated with the area around Wingkilina in WA, often Two Women Dreaming. He usually sells his work through Papunya Tula Artists.

WALKER JAPANGARDI
Born in 1945 of the Anmatyerre tribe, his country is Coniston and Mt Allan and he paints Corkwood and Dingo Dreamings. Married to painter Elsie MOORE, he lives at Mt Allan.

WALKER , JUDY NAPALJARRI (NYIRRPIYA)
Born at Mt Doreen, her language/tribe is Warlpiri and she lives at Lajamanu. Her country is Jila Well and her Dreamings are Warna and Mala and she started painting in 1986. A huge canvas of hers hangs in the Lajamanu school staff room, purchased with funds supplied to decorate the room.

WALKER, LIDDY NAPANANGKA
Also cited as: Liddy Napanangka
A long time resident of Yuendumu, Liddy Walker was born c.1930 at Jarradajarrayi (Mt Theo), which is associated with Wardapi (Goanna) and Warna (Snake) Dreamings. She is also responsible, through her father, for a Dogwood Dreaming. Liddy is part of the group of senior Warlpiri women who began painting ceremonial designs at Yuendumu in the early '80s. She has exhibited regularly with Warlukurlangu Artists since the community's first exhibition of paintings at Araluen Arts Centre in Alice Springs in October 1985. Her Dreamings are Warna (Snake), Kanta (Bloodwood Gall or Bush Coconut), Wardapi (Goanna) and Wakirlipirri (Acacia Seed). *Bean Dreaming* 1985, on which she collaborated with TOPSY Napanangka and Judy Nampitjinpa GRANITES, was purchased by the National Gallery of Australia's collection and was included in the 'Windows of the Dreaming' exhibition at the Gallery in 1989. Collections: National Gallery of Australia, South Australian Museum, Art Gallery of SA, private collections. Reference: *Windows on the Dreaming*, (ed.) W. Caruana.

WALKER, TOWSER JAKAMARRA

Born in 1925, Towser Walker is one of the senior men in the Warlpiri community at Yuendumu. He paints Yarla (Yam), Wapirti (Small Yam) and Ngarlalajiyi (Bush Carrot) Dreamings. His work was included in 'Yuendumu: Paintings out of the Desert' at the South Australian Museum in 1988 and in Warlukurlangu exhibitions in Darwin, Perth and Alice Springs in 1990–1. Collections: South Australian Museum

WALLABI, CHARLIE TJUNGARRAYI
Also cited as: Charlie Wallabi Tjungurrayi

Born near Jupiter Well, he walked in to Balgo with his family while still a young boy and grew up on the settlement. After he was married, he moved to Kintore in Pintupi country and lived there or back at Balgo till the mid '80s when he came to live in Kiwirrkura, closer to his traditional lands. He began painting for Papunya Tula Artists in the new community of Kiwirrkura in about 1987 and when interviewed in 1989, considered his work still a 'little bit rough: he taught himself and was 'still learning'. He paints Tingari stories around Jupiter Well, including a Snake story — Wanpurutinga. Collections: Holmes à Court

WALLABY, GEORGE TJANGALA

Born 'in the bush' around Lake Gregory c.1935, George Wallaby is a Walmatjari speaker. His traditional country is Lake Gregory, in the area where Sturt Creek and its many tributaries empty into the salt lake. The Dreamings which the artist paints are Wanayarra (Rainbow Snake) which now lives in the many waterholes and creekbeds created by its Dreamtime activities, and Water. He began painting for Warlayirti Artists in 1989 and lives at Mulan. He employs a large stick for his dotting and uses this sparsely on the canvas, then intermingles a variety of motifs in such a way that they are often hidden in a 'trompe d'oeil' effect. This creates intriguing effects that are suggestive of forces that lie beneath and 'behind' the land.

WALLACE, KATHLEEN KEMARRE

Born at Uyedye (Todd River) in 1948, she now lives in Santa Teresa, south-east of Alice Springs. Kathleen is an Arrente speaker whose country is Alyethenge. The Dreamings she paints are Kangaroo and Falcon. Kathleen has been working at the Keringke Arts Centre in Santa Teresa since it started in 1987, and in 1993 took over the position of arts supervisor.

WALLY PWERLE

An Alyawarre speaker, known primarily for his wood carvings, Wally Pwerle also paints occasionally. The Grass-Seed Dreaming in the area of Irrweltye outstation (a place called Aknumurrapa) is often the subject of his paintings. He is married to Janice Kngwarreye, who also paints occasionally.

WALTER, TJAMPITJINPA (c.1910–1981)
Also cited as: Talpulpa Tjampitjinpa

An elder stateman of the Pintupi community in Papunya, having been one of those who authorised the design work for the Papunya school mural at the very beginning of the painting movement. Described by Geoffrey Bardon in *Aboriginal Art of the Western Desert*, as 'a gentle and kind patron in my gradually improving understanding of the Aboriginal way of life', Old Walter was a senior custodian of the Water Dreaming that runs through Kalimpinpa west of Papunya. He had an extensive knowledge of ceremonial sites which were part of the Dreaming journeys mapping out the locations of water sources across a vast area of the Western Desert. Most of his paintings depict the classic Water Dreaming iconograph, though occasionally as his eyesight weakened towards the end of his life, he commissioned other artists to paint some of his other stories for him, including Billy STOCKMAN, who painted an Eagle Dreaming story for the site of Walkulpu near Yuendumu in Old Walter's name, Paddy CARROLL, who painted his Euro Dreaming for him, and possibly also his wife, GLADYS Napanangka, who married again, to artist Johnny WARANGKULA in the mid '80s. Collections: National Gallery of Victoria, University of WA Anthropology Museum, Museums & Art Galleries of NT, Flinders University Art Museum, SA Museum

WANTAMA, TREVOR

A Pintupi, Trevor began painting occasionally for Papunya Tula Artists in the late '80s. Formerly residing at Kintore, he now lives at Tjukula. His country is south-west of Kintore and he paints Nightbird Dreaming.

WARANGKULA, GLADYS NAPANANGKA, see GLADYS Napanangka

WARANGKULA, JOHNNY TJUPURRULA
Also cited as: Johnny Warangula Tjupurrula, Johnny Warrangula Tjupurrula, Johnny Warankula Tjupurrula, Johnny Warrangula Tjaparula, Johnny W. Tjupurrula, Jonny W.

Born at Minjilpirri, north-west of Illpili and south of Lake Mackay c.1925. This is Kangaroo Dreaming country dotted with limestone soaks. As a child, Johnny lived a traditional lifestyle in the desert, never attending European school. His mother was of mixed Luritja/Warlpiri/Pintupi descent and his father was Luritja/Warlpiri. He recalled his first frightened contact with whites when as a big boy he hid in the trees from a plane which his people took for a 'mamu' or devil. On another occasion, they saw camels from a hill they had climbed, and also took them for devils and again hid in fright. Later, the family moved in to Hermannsburg mission, where Johnny worked as a labourer constructing the airstrip. During the family's stay at Hermannsburg, Johnny passed through the ceremonies for manhood. From there he moved to Haasts Bluff for the construction of another airstrip, making roads, felling trees and shovelling dirt. For this work he received no money, just 'tucker', meaning flour, tea and tobacco, but also, according to Johnny, including fresh vegetables — cabbage and carrots. He followed the road making to Mt Leibig, Yuendumu and Mt Wedge and later worked on the construction programmes of various settlements, making bricks. In 1954 he was chosen, along with NOSEPEG Tjupurrula, as Aboriginal representative to meet the Queen. He was living in Haasts Bluff when the bulk of the population was moved to the new settlement of Papunya in 1960. Johnny was serving on the Papunya Council with Mick NAMARARI, LIMPI Tjapangati and Kingsley Tjungarrayi when Geoffrey Bardon arrived at the settlement, and they soon let their interest in obtaining art materials be known when painting started up. Johnny rapidly developed a distinctive personal style of overdotting, often several layers, creating effects of what Geoff Bardon called 'tremulous illusion'. He remained a major force in the painting movement for most of the '80s, though his output has been steadily reduced by failing eyesight. It was alongside his painting in the National Gallery of Australia that its Director James Mollison chose to be photographed in 1984, declaring the work of the Papunya artists to be the 'finest abstract art ever produced in this country'.(26 January 1984, *Sydney Morning Herald*). Johnny's work often depicts events around Tjikarri, Yipa, Kilyalnga and the Ehrenberg Ranges (Illpili and Kampurarrnga), where he established one of the first outstations in Central Australia. This is good water country and his work often depicts the Water Dreaming stories as well as Yam, Fire and Egret stories and stories from around Nyilppi and Nyalpilala — his father's Dreaming. Johnny is of the Luritja language group and lives in Papunya with his wife, GLADYS Napanangka. He has two daughters from a previous marriage and two sons and six daughters from his marriage to Gladys. Collections: Holmes à Court, Queensland Art Gallery, National Gallery of Victoria, Art Gallery of WA, Art Gallery of SA, National Museum of Australia, Canberra, National Gallery of Australia, Canberra, Orange Regional Gallery, Alice Springs Law Courts, Museums & Art Galleries of NT Darwin, Flinders University Art Museum, SA Museum. Reference: in press — Warangula, Johnny Tjupurrula, *Mala Tjukurrpa* (Papunya Literature Production Centre).

WARD, FRED TJUNGARRAYI
Also cited as: Fred Ward Tjungurrayi

Born 'in the bush' east of Kiwirrkura on the western side of Kintore and Yumari c.1955, Fred lived in Warburton, WA before returning to live in Pintupi territory at Kiwirrkura in August '87. He began to paint for Papunya Tula Artists soon after arriving in Kiwirrkura, exhibiting his work for the first time in the 1987 exhibition at Roar Studios. In 1989 he won the NT Art Award. He paints Tingari Cycle Dreamings in the classic Pintupi style of concentric circles linked by lines of travel, his work being distinctive for its powerful designs and austerely traditional palette. Collections: Holmes à Court

WARD, GEORGE TJUNGURRAYI

Born 'in the bush' south-east of Kiwirrkura on the Kuljuta side. Trucked in to Papunya in the '60s by Jeremy Long's Welfare Branch patrols, he lived in Warburton, Wiluna and Jigalong before returning to Pintupi country and the newly established settlement of Kintore across the NT border. Though he observed the work of the painting company in Kintore, it was not until the mid '80s when he moved deeper into Pintupi territory at Kiwirrkura that he began to paint for Papunya Tula Artists. He paints the stories of his country — Tingari stories including Snake and Kuningka (Native Cat) Dreamings in the Waralunga/Kulkuta area south-east of Kiwirrkura.

WARLIMPIRRNGA, TJAPALTJARRI

Born on a hillside east of Kiwirrkura in the late '50s, Warlimpirrnga was one of the small party of Pintupi whose arrival in Kiwirrkura in 1984 made national headlines. Until this point, at the age of about twenty-five, Warlimpirrnga had never encountered Europeans and their ways. The group had been following their traditional lifestyle in the country west of Lake Mackay. After three years at the settlement, Warlimpirrnga approached Daphne Willams of Papunya Tula Artists with the request that he be allowed to paint. The other artists instructed him in the use of paint and canvas, and he completed his first painting for the company in April 1987. His first 11 paintings were exhibited in Melbourne at the Gallery Gabrielle Pizzi in 1988, the entire group being purchased by the National Gallery of Victoria. Warlimpirrnga is married with a young son and paints Tingari stories for his country, around the sites of Marua and Kanapilya. Collections: National Gallery of Victoria, National Musée Des Arts Africains et Oceaniens, Paris

WATSON, BETTY NUNGARRAYI

Born at Yurntumu c.1955, her tribe/language is Warlpiri and she lives at Lajamanu. Her country is Kunajarrayi and her Dreamings are Warna and Ngarlkirdi. She is the step-daughter of Junti Japaljarri, with whom she worked before he died, and daughter of Liddy NELSON Nakamarra. She started painting in 1986.

WATSON, JUDY NAPANGARDI

A Warlpiri speaker, Judy Watson lives in Yuendumu and has been exhibiting paintings of her Ngalyipi (Snakevine) and Karnta (Women's) Dreamings with Warlukurlangu Artists since the beginning of the '90s.

WATSON, LAWRENCE JANGALA

Born Yuendumu c.1962 and a Warlpiri whose Dreamings are Ngapa (Water) and Yankirri (Emu). Lawrence Watson is one of the youngest male artists working with Warlukurlangu Artists. He began painting in 1988 and exhibiting in 1989. In 1990 the artist's work was included in 'Tigari Lia, Contemporary Aboriginal Art from Australia' at the Third Eye Centre in Glasgow, Scotland. His work combines elements of the older artists' approach e.g. asymmetrical layouts, with an exuberant exploration of the stylistic possibilities of Western Desert art. Reference: *Australian Aboriginal Art from the Collection of Donald Kahn*

WATSON, MAGGIE NAPANGARDI
(formerly Maggie Napangardi Ross)

A Warlpiri who lives at Yuendumu, she is another of the senior Warlpiri women at Yuendumu whose interest in rendering traditional women's designs in western materials was one of the driving forces behind early experiments with canvas at the settlement. Her work was included in the first exhibition of Yuendumu paintings at the Araluen Arts Centre in Alice Springs in October 1985. Since then she has shown in numerous exhibitions of Warlukurlangu Artists in cities around Australia, as well as in the 'Karnta' exhibition at Hogarth Galleries, Sydney, 1987 and 'Yuendumu: Paintings out of the Desert', SA Museum, 1988. She is pictured painting one of her canvases in both the *Dreamings* catalogue (p 106) and *The Inspired Dream*, (ed.) M. West. Collections: SA Museum, many private collections

WATSON, MARJORIE NUNGARRAYI

Born at Yuendumu c.1960, her language/tribe is Warlpiri and she lives at Lajamanu. Her country is Pirrpirrpakarnu and her Dreamings are Warla, Ngalyipi and Mala. She works with her sister, Beth PATRICK, and started painting in 1987. She has been described as a 'transitional' painter for the way she often does a very bold Aboriginal flag on the painting, sometimes other motifs, or divides the painting into Aboriginal colours, with the sun in the middle, and then puts the dots and design on top of that. According to those who know her, this is done in a quite conscious sense of pan-Aboriginal pride. She works in the pre-school at Lajamanu school.

WEST, FREDDY TJAKAMARRA

Born in the desert around present day Kiwirrkura in the early '40s, Freddy was still a young man when his family was brought in to Papunya by Jeremy Long's Welfare Branch patrols in the '60s. Freddy remembers meeting the patrols out near Jupiter Well in WA and arranging with them to be picked up the following year from the site of Kaluta, further to the east. He began painting in Geoffrey Bardon's time, and after a break of some years resumed work in the '80s. In 1981 he joined the move back to Kintore in the Pintupi homelands. His country lies around Muntardi and Jigalong to the north of Kiwirrkura along the western shores of the great salt lake Wilkinkarra, and Yunalla, a rockhole in the Great Sandy Desert where the snake who created Wilkinkarra now dwells. Freddy West was the moving force behind the establishment of Kiwirrkura in the mid '80s and now lives there with most of his 15 children, including his sons Bobby and Tony, who have also begun painting in the last few years. Collections: Holmes à Court, Australian Museum, Sydney, Art Gallery of WA, Art Gallery of SA, National Museum of Australia, Canberra, University of WA Anthropology Museum

WHITE, CONNIE NAKAMARRA

A Warlpiri speaker, Connie White lives in Yuendumu and has shown her paintings with Warlukurlangu Artists since the beginning of the '90s. Her main Dreaming is

Warnpa (Snake). She was one of 42 artists from Yuendumu who worked on a 7 x 3 m canvas which toured several European cities in 1993 as part of 'Aratjara — Australian Aboriginal Art'.

WHITE, MAGGIE NAPANANGKA

Born c.1935 and lives at Yuendumu. Now in her mid-fifties, Maggie White was one of the senior women whose work in the early '80s helped initiate the painting movement in the Yuendumu community. She has been showing with Warlukurlangu Artists since the Yuendumu painters' first exhibition at the Araluen Arts Centre in Alice Springs in October 1985. She has exhibited in Perth, Melbourne, Adelaide, the Gold Coast, at the Portsmouth Festival in England 1987, Sydney, Canberra, the Lewis-Warra Gallery in Seattle, USA, and Darwin. Her work was also included in the 'Windows on the Dreaming' exhibition at the National Gallery of Australia in Canberra in 1989. The Gallery has one of her paintings in its collection, as do the SA Museum and many private collections. Her work retains a looseness and boldness expressive of the importance which the artist attaches to the ritual act of invoking the Dreamings by representing them in European materials. References: Caruana, W., *Windows on the Dreaming*; *Australian Aboriginal Art from the Collection of Donald Kahn*

WILLIAM, KENNY TJAMPITJINPA

Born near present day Kiwirrkura after World War II, Kenny spent his boyhood travelling 'in the bush' with his family until Jeremy Long's Welfare Branch patrols brought them in to Papunya in the late '60s. From there Kenny moved to Balgo in WA, joining other tribesmen who had migrated north to the edges of Pintupi territory. He remained at Balgo during the '70s, moving back to Papunya and later to Kintore when the settlement was established at the start of the '80s. He now lives with his older brother, RONNIE Tjampitjinpa, at Redbank (Ininti) outstation west of Kintore and with his assistance has begun painting his Dreamings around Kiwirrkura for Papunya Tula Artists. He has been painting since 1988.

WILLIAMS, DULCIE NAPANGARDI

Born at Yuendumu in 1963, Dulcie now lives at Nyirrpi. She started to paint at the same time as her husband, Peter Japaljarri TEX, and they sometimes co-operate in paintings depicting Snake Dreaming. Dulcie also paints Possum and Goanna Dreamings.

WILLIAMS, EILEEN

A Pitjantjatjara/Arrente (Aranda) speaker, living in Hermannsburg. Eileen's father, Nahasson Unawanika, is an important elder of the Pitjantjatjara, whose country extends south to Uluru; she painted the mural at the Yulara Sheraton. The Dreamings she paints include Red Sandhill and Striped Fish in rockpools after rain.

WILLIAMS, PHYLLIS NAPURRURLA

A Warlpiri speaker from Yuendumu, Phyllis Napurrurla Williams first exhibited with Warlukurlangu Artists at the Sydney Opera House in 1987. She has since shown regularly in Warlukurlangu exhibitions in Seattle, USA, Adelaide, Melbourne, Brisbane, Perth, Sydney, Canberra, Darwin and Alice Springs. Her principal Dreamings are Janganpa (Possum) and Mukaki (Bush Plum).

WILLIAMS, VERA MBITJANA

Born in Alice Springs on 6 August 1966, her language group Pitjantjatjara. Her mother is a Warlpiri woman from Yuendumu. Her father is a Pitjantjatjara man who grew up at Hermannsburg. Vera grew up at Amoongana, Hermannsburg and Alice Springs, receiving her secondary schooling in Alice Springs. In 1984 she designed a stained glass window for the Araluen Arts Centre in Alice Springs as part of a college project. Today she speaks six Central Australian languages. Since 1987 she has been living at Ernabella with her husband. In 1988 she began working in the print workshop at Ernabella Arts. The following year she exhibited her screenprinted and handpainted designs in the Australian Conservation Foundation's 'Desert Impressions' exhibition in Melbourne and the Ernabella Arts exhibition 'Look at us Now' at Tandanya in Adelaide. Vera was awarded the 'Best Developing Artist in SA' in 1989. Her screenprints for fabrics have been exhibited in Adelaide, Alice Springs, Sydney and Melbourne. Vera also works on canvas, and has just begun to work with lithographs and etchings. Her screenprint *Cattle Dogs and Snakes* was included in an exhibition of Contemporary Australian Textiles in Krefeld, Germany. In July 1993 Vera attended a print workshop at the University of the NT in Darwin to further her studies in this medium.

WILLIE JAPANANGKA
Also cited as: Willie Reilly Japanangka

A Warlpiri speaker, Willie Japanangka's country is Mt Theo (Purturlu). He and all his relatives live in Willowra. He says he began painting on weapons e.g. boomerangs, and when painting materials were made available in Willowra in the late '80s through a community adviser, took up the enterprise along with many other men and women at Willowra. He is self-taught: 'I taught to do painting myself, because I remembered about my dreamings.' The artist did paintings for the children at Willowra school to learn about their Dreamings: 'I did one painting about my country which I put on the wall in the school. I also did a painting which I sold to the art gallery. But now I still paint and sell to people that are interested in buying my painting.' The artist's nephew, MALCOLM Jakamarra, remembers him painting on canvas in 1981, one of the first to do so in the Willowra community. However, Willie Reilly's involvement with the art movement can be dated back another decade to 1972 when a painting bearing the name William Reilly Jabanunga (Japanangka) was sold by Papunya Tula Artists. The painting is now in the Kelton Foundation collection. In 1980 paintings by William Reilly could be found in several Alice Springs art galleries. There seems little doubt that this

Dinny Nolan Tjampitjinpa and Paddy Carroll Tjungarrayi (Photo: Palani Mohan, courtesy **Sydney Morning Herald**)

Warlimpirrnga Tjapaltjarri (second from right) with his two brothers and Gerry Hand, then Minister for Aboriginal Affairs (Photo: John Corker)

Billy Stockman Tjapaltjarri (Photo: John Corker)

Maxie Tjampitjinpa (Photo: John Corker)

Clifford Possum Tjapaltjarri (Photo: Jon Falkenmire)

Lily Sandover Kngwarreye (Photo: Rodney Gooch)

Lyndsay Bird Mpetyane (Photo: Chris Hodges)

Louis Pwerle (Photo: Chris Hodges)

Gloria Petyarre and Emily Kame Kngwarreye (Photo: Dean Wilmot, courtesy **Sydney Morning Herald**)

Daisy Napanangka Nelson (Photo: John Corker)

Eubena Nampitjin (Photo: Neil McLeod)

Susie Bootja Bootja Napangati (Photo: Neil McLeod)

artist is one of those individuals who acted as a catalyst for the spread of the painting movement across the Western Desert, specifically to Willowra.

WILSON, NOLA NAPANGARDI

Born at Yuendumu in 1958, Nola is a Warlpiri speaker and the sister of EUNICE Napangardi. She started painting in 1987 while she was still living at Yuendumu and sold her work through Warlukurlangu Artists. She paints Bush Banana, Snake and Honey Ant Dreamings. Nola moved to Nyirrpi in 1989 and now sells her paintings mainly through the local community store.

WILLY TJUNGARRAYI
Also cited as: Willie Tjungurrayi

Born at Patjantja, south-west of Lake Mackay, c.1930. Willy was raised by Charlie TARAWA, who was Willy's father's brother. Willy was raised 'in the bush' — 'naked' with 'only nulla nulla and woomera'. It was Charlie's camels which eventually brought the family in to Haasts Bluff in the late '50s and from there to Papunya. Willy began painting for Papunya Tula Artists in 1976 during the '80s since emerged as one of the senior Pintupi painters. His country lies a short distance to the south west of Kintore — around Kulkuta, Tjukula, Warrabri, Malka, Yumari, Tjitikulpa and Patjanytja. In the early '80s he joined the move back to the Pintupi homelands and now lives with his family in Kintore. Collections: Holmes à Court, National Gallery of Australia, Canberra, Victorian Centre for the Performing Arts, Art Gallery of NSW

WIMMITJI TJAPANGATI

Born 'in the bush', probably near Percival Lakes, c.1925, Wimmitji is a Kukatja speaker who lives at Mulan and Balgo and has been painting since 1987. His country is Kuta Kuta, near Percival Lakes. He paints Tingari stories for this region, including the Native Cat ceremony for Tjatjati, north of Jupiter Well, Papa (Dingo) and Wati Kutjarra (Two Men) Dreamings for Tjawuwirpa, and Snake Dreaming at Nyinmingka. The artist spent all his early years in this area and knows all its sacred places. Wimmitji's works have a quite idiosyncratic look: they appear rough with much overlain dotting and many different shapes and forms. This gives them a look of great age which may add to perceptions of their 'authenticity' — though from the artist's perspective this comes from his great involvement in the Law. All speak volumes of the artist's country and its many associated stories. He sells his work through Warlayirti Artists. Collections: National Gallery of Australia, Canberra, National Gallery of Victoria

WINDEROO, ALAN TJAKAMARRA

Born 'in the bush' c.1920, probably near Hidden Basin, Alan Winderoo is a senior lawman of the Kukatja tribe within the Balgo community. His country on his father's side is Yinpirkuana (Impirrkarwanu) near Lappi Lappi and his principal stories are Tingari and Water Dreamings. He began painting in Balgo for Warlayirti Artists in 1987, but may have painted prior to this, through his links with the Yuendumu community. His works exhibit a stong sense of tradition. The often rough application of paint serves to confirm that what is important to the artist is the message, which in turn is concerned with powerful events and forces of the mythological past. A painting of the artist's was exhibited at the Madrid Art Fair in February 1990. Collections: National Gallery of Victoria, Holmes à Court

WIRRI, KEVIN TJAPALTJARRI
Also cited as: Kevin Wirri Tjabaltjarri

Born at Haasts Bluff on 1 April 1953, his language group is Luritja. His grandfather's country is Kintore and Kunajarrayi. His father's country is Lipa. The Dreaming Kevin paints is Witchetty Grub turning into Serpent. His community now is Docker River, but he has connections with Papunya. Kevin started painting in 1964. He first learnt to paint landscapes from Albert Namatjira's son. Other artists he has connections with are Barney DANIELS and Leslie BROGAS (Tjapangati). He paints the same Dreamings as Barney Daniels but they have different styles.

WOODS, DEMPSEY TJAMPITJINPA

Born in Pitjantjatjara country c.1930, Dempsey painted for Papunya Tula Artists in the late '70s. His former wife, Pauline WOODS, is one of the most successful women artists now operating out of Jukurrpa in Alice Springs.

WOODS, PAULINE NAKAMARRA

A Pintupi/Warlpiri speaker born at Vaughan Springs, west of Yuendumu in 1949 and raised in Yuendumu. Her traditional country, Mungkururrpa, lies west of Papunya. Her Dreamings include Bush Bean, Bush Potato, Spinifex, Seven Sisters, Bush Banana, Janganpa (Possum) and Paku-Paku (Birdmen). She lives in Alice Springs, but also has connections with the Granites. She is the sister of Long Jack PHILLIPUS Tjakamarra. In her early forties, and a mother of three, Pauline Woods was one of the leading figures in the formation and development of Jukurrpa as an Aboriginal-controlled concern. In the years since she began painting in 1986, she has developed an extremely fine and fluid style of painting. In February 1988 one of her works was included in an exhibition entitled 'The Australian Cultural Month' at the Australian Embassy in Manila. In September 1988 she became the first woman to win the National Aboriginal Art Award in Darwin with a painting that took her two months to complete. She is currently Vice President of Jukurrpa. In 1993 she became the first Aboriginal woman artist to have her work represented on an Australian stamp. Collections: many public and private collections.

Y

YALA YALA TJUNGARRAYI
Also cited as: Yala Yala Gibbs Tjungurai; Yala Yala Gibson Tjungarai; Yella Yella Gibbs Tjungurrayi

Born c.1925 at Iltuturunga, west of Lake McDonald, Yala Yala and his family were amongst those Pintupi who walked in to Papunya in the early years of the settlement. Yala Yala retraced the stages of their journey in his mind: Yininti, Wili, Illpili, Wirrinpili, Papunya. He has been painting since the beginning of the Papunya Tula movement and now lives at Kintore in the Pintupi homelands. He has an outstation at Muntardi, lying midway between Kintore and Kiwirrkura in desert oak country. His traditional lands encompass a wide area south-east of Kiwirrkura covering a vast network of sites, parts of which are depicted in his paintings. He is the senior custodian of Yawalyurru, a secret-sacred men's site in the Great Sandy Desert near his birthplace which is part of the Tingari cycle. Yala Yala is an authority amongst the senior Pintupi men on ceremonial matters in this region. He remains one of the classic exponents of the Pintupi style of Western Desert painting. Collections: Holmes à Court, Queensland Art Gallery, National Gallery of Victoria, Museums & Art Galleries of NT, Brooklyn Museum of Art, New York

YAPA, GEORGE TJANGALA
Also cited as: George Yapa Yapa Tjangala

Born at Witingu, close to Jupiter Well and present day Kiwirrkura, probably in the late '40s or early '50s, he is the son of ANATJARI Tjampitjinpa. He spent his early years 'in the bush', living the traditional nomadic lifestyle. His group was sighted by government patrols in 1963. Later they heard from relatives about the new settlement at Papunya. Yapa Yapa walked in with his family in the early years of the settlement. His first experience of painting was in the mid '70s, on UTA UTA and Charlie TARAWA's paintings, then in 1980 he began painting in his own right. His traditional country lies around Kirrpinga, a large well site north of Kiwirrkura. His paintings also depict an Eagle Hawk Dreaming, and Tingari stories from this area and Wala Wala, another large waterhole outside of Kiwirrkura. In recent years he has lived in Kintore and Kiwirrkura with his two wives and four small children. Collections: Victorian Museum

YIPATI (KUYATA) (1946–1992), see KUYATA, Yipati

YUKENBARRI, LUCY NAPANANGKA
Born near Kiwirrkura c.1932, Lucy Yukenbarri is a Kukatja speaker. Her country is Winpupulla and Puturr, north of Jupiter Well. She lives in Balgo and started painting

for Warlayirti Artists in 1989. A strong, senior woman who in recent times has been one of the hardest working artists in Balgo, she has developed a highly individual style where the paint is applied in heavy, coalesced dabs. A bold pattern of colours is created which serves to represent different areas of the artist's country. The works are usually totally abstract but all concern old campsites and their food and water sources.

YUMPULULU TJUNGARRAYI
Also cited as: Yumpalulu Tjungurrayi
Born c.1925 in Pintupi country across the WA border around Kiwirrkura, where he now resides. With his family he travelled across the country between Jupiter Well and Kiwirrkurra, living in the traditional way. Yumpululu was in Papunya in the early years of the painting movement and may have tried his hand at a few boards, but it was not until 1980, two years before the move back to Kintore, that he emerged as a distinctive figure in the painting movement. One of his paintings from this period was purchased by the Chase Manhattan Bank in New York. His son, Noel Thomson Tjapaltjarri, has also recently begun to paint for Papunya Tula Artists. Collections: Museums & Art Galleries of NT

YUPUPU, DAVID TJAMPITJINPA (d. 1992)
A Pintupi whose country is Yawurrungu, south-west of Mt Webb, he came from Balgo to live in Papunya. There is a heavy influence of early Balgo style in his rough, fused dotting technique. He first painted for Papunya Tula Artists in early 1990, producing paintings sporadically until his death in June 1992. Collections: Holmes à Court

Z

ZIMMARON, SMITHY TJAMPITJINPA

The younger brother of RONNIE Tjampitjinpa, Smithy came in to Yuendumu settlement as a baby and later joined other relatives at Papunya. One of the most literate people in European terms in Kintore, Smithy has been Administrator of the Community Health Service and has painted occasionally in the past few years. His country lies south-west of Kintore around Lampintja.

Appendix A
Guide to Artists included in this Dictionary
By Community

Note: This is not an index. The technical limitations of the wordprocessing package on which most of the entries were originally entered prevented my generation of an exhaustive listing of the artists in this dictionary. The following lists were manually prepared and updated for publication in 1993, but some omissions are to be expected because of the piecemeal way in which the data has come in over the last few years. That an artist is not listed here does not necessarily mean they are not included in the dictionary itself, where their biography will provide information about the community (or communities) with which they are associated.

PAPUNYA TULA ARTISTS

Papunya
1. ANDERSON, Alison Nampitjinpa
2. BROGAS Tjapangati
3. BROWN, Jeannie Nakamarra
4. BROWN, Theo Tjapaltjarri
5. BUSH, George Tjangala
6. CAMPBELL, Gordon Tjapanangka
7. CARROLL, Paddy Tjungarrayi
8. CORBY, Natalie Nungarrayi
9. DON Tjungarrayi
10. EGALIE, Charlie Tjapaltjarri
11. ENTALURA Nangala
12. GLADYS Napanangka
13. GOODWIN Tjapaltjarri
14. KAAPA Tjampitjinpa (d.)
15. LEURA, Daisy Nakamarra
16. LEURA, Tim Tjapaltjarri (d.)
17. MAXIE Tjampitjinpa
18. Old MICK Tjakamarra
19. NELSON, Michael Tjakamarra (Jagamara)
20. NOLAN, Dinny Tjampitjinpa
21. NORMAN, Lily Napaltjarri
22. PANTIMAS, Dick Tjupurrula (d.)
24. PHILLIPUS, Long Jack Tjakamarra
25. REGGIE Tjupurrula (d.)
26. SANDY, William
27. STOCKMAN, Billy Tjapaltjarri
28. TWO BOB Tjungarrayi
29. Old WALTER Tjampitjinpa (d.)
30. WARANGKULA, Johnny Tjupurrula
31. YUPUPU, David Tjampitjinpa (d.)

Mt Leibig
32. BULLEN, Andrew Tjapangati
33. DIXON, Colin Tjapanangka
34. DIXON, Mary Nungarrayi
35. JACK Tjupurrula
36. JOE Tjakamarra
37. KELLY, Lily Napangati
38. MARINGKA Nangala
39. MARSHALL, Charlie Tjungarrayi
40. PETERSEN, Maudie Nungarrayi
41. PETRA Nampitjinpa
42. SANDRA Nampitjinpa
43. TURNER, Sonder Nampitjinpa
44. WAKURI, Barney Tjakamarra

Haasts Bluff
45. GIDEON (Jack) Tjupurrula
46. JUGADAI, Timmy Tjungurrayi (d.)
47. LIMPI Tjapangati (d.)
48. LIONEL Kantawarra (d.)
49. Old MICKINNINIE (d.)
(See also Postscript: Ikuntji Women's Centre)

New Bore
50. GINGER Tjakamarra

Kintore
51. ADRIAN Tjupurrula
52. BENNETT, John John Tjapangati
53. BENNY Tjapaltjarri
54. CAMERON Tjapaltjarri
55. CHARLIE Tjapangati
56. CAMPBELL, Dini Tjampitjinpa
57. GEORGE Tjangala (d.)
58. GEORGE Tjapaltjarri ('Dr George')
59. GEORGE Tjapanangka
60. GEORGE Tjungarrayi
61. HILARY Tjapaltjarri
62. INKAMALA, Ray (d.)
63. JACKSON, Shorty Tjampitjinpa
64. JOHN Tjapaltjarri
65. JURRA, Joseph Tjapaltjarri
66. KUNTI KUNTI, Jack Tjampitjinpa (d.)
67. MAJOR, Riley Tjangala
68. MINOR, Richard Tjangala
69. NAMARARI, Mick Tjapaltjarri
70. NOLAN, Billy Tjapangati
71. PETERSEN, Fabrianne Nampitjinpa
72. PINTA PINTA Tjapanangka
73. RONNIE Tjampitjinpa

74. ROWE, Brenda Napaltjarri
75. SCOBIE, Johnny Tjapanangka
76. SCOBIE, Narpula Napurrula
77. TARAWA, Charlie Tjungarrayi
78. TOLSON, Turkey Tjupurrula
79. Old TUTUMA Tjapangati (d.)
80. UTA UTA Tjangala (d.)
81. WANTAMA, Trevor
82. WILLIAM, Kenny Tjampitjinpa
83. WILLY Tjungarrayi
84. YAPA YAPA, George Tjangala
85. ZIMMARON, Smithy Tjampitjinpa

Kiwirrkura
86. ANATJARI Tjakamarra (d.)
87. ANATJARI Tjampitjinpa
88. BROWN, Jimmy Tjampitjinpa
89. GEORGE Tjapaltjarri ('Jampu')
90. JACKIE Tjakamarra
91. JOHN Tjakamarra
92. KANYA Tjapangati
93. PAYUNGKA, Timmy Tjapangati
94. SIMON Tjakamarra (d.)
95. THOMPSON, Noel Tjapaltjarri
96. TONY Tjakamarra
97. WALLABY, Charlie Tjungarrayi
98. WARD, Fred Tjungarrayi
99. WARD, George Tjungarrayi
100. WARLIMPIRRINGA Tjapaltjarri
101. WEST, Freddy Tjakamarra
102. WEST, Tony Tjupurrula
103. YALA YALA Tjungarrayi
104. YUMPULULU Tjungarrayi

Also
105. LOWRY, Tommy Tjapaltjarri (d.)
106. LYNCH, Johnny Tjapangati (d.)
107. STEVENS, Thomas Tjakamarra
108. POSSUM, Clifford Tjapaltjarri
109. EDIMINJA, Eddie Tjapangati

WARLUKURLANGU ARTISTS: YUENDUMU
1. BROWN, Lena Nungarrayi
2. BROWN, Sheila Napaljarri
3. COLLINS, Ruby Nakamarra
4. DANIELS, Dolly Nampijinpa
5. EGAN, Jeannie Nungarrayi
6. EGAN, Matthew Jampijimpa
7. EGAN, Ted Jangala
8. GALLAGHER, Carol Napangardi
9. GALLAGHER, Jack Jampijinpa
10. GOREY, Dadu Nungarrayi
11. GRANITES, Judy Nampijinpa
12. GRANITES, Kurt Japanangka (see also Lajamanu)
13. GRANITES, Loraine Nungarrayi
14. JIMIJA Jungarrayi (d.)
15. JONES, Florrie Napangardi

16. JURRA, Peggy Nangala (d.)
17. JURRA, Tilo Nangala
18. KENNEDY, Lucy Napaljarri
19. LANGDON, Molly Nampijinpa
20. LEWIS, Margaret Napangardi
21. MARTIN, Andrea Nungarrayi
22. MARTIN, Hilda Napaljarri
23. MARTIN, Una Nampijinpa
24. NELSON, Daisy Napanangka
25. NELSON, Frank 'Bronson' Jakamarra
26. NELSON, Helen Napaljarri
27. NELSON, Jorna Napurrurla
28. NELSON, Norah Napaljarri
29. NELSON, Paddy Jupurrurla
30. OLDFIELD, Dave Jupurrurla
31. OLDFIELD, Eva Nungarrayi
32. OLDFIELD, Ruth Napaljarri
33. POULSON, Clarise Nampijinpa
34. POULSON, Ivy Napangardi
35. POULSON, Maggie Napurrurla
36. POULSON, Michael Japangardi
37. POULSON, Mona Napurrurla
38. POULSON, Peggy Napurrurla (see also Alice Springs)
39. RICE, Thomas Jangala
40. ROBERTSON, Beryl Napangardi
41. ROBERTSON, Lady Nungarrayi
42. ROSS, Darby Jampijinpa
43. ROSS, Jack Jakamarra
44. ROSS, Theresa Napurrurla
45. SIMS, Bessie Nakamarra
46. SIMS, Paddy Japaljarri
47. SIMS, Wendy Nungarrayi (Brown)
48. SPENCER, Andrew Japaljarri
49. SPENCER, Larry Jungarrayi (d.)
50. STEWART, Paddy Japaljarri
51. STEWART, Pansy Nakamarra
52. STEWART, Queenie Nungarrayi
53. TOPSY, Napanangka
54. WALKER, Liddy Napangardi
55. WALKER, Towser Jakamarra
56. WATSON, Judy Napangardi
57. WATSON, Lawrence Jangala
58. WATSON, Maggie Napangardi
59. WHITE, Connie Nakamarra
60. WHITE, Maggie Napanangka
61. WILLIAMS, Phyllis Napurrurla

YUELAMU ARTISTS: MT ALLAN
1. ALLAN, Mary Nangala
2. ANDY, Ada Napaljarri
3. ANDY, Emily Napaljarri
4. BAGGOT, Kathy Napangardi
5. BRISCOE, Teddy Mjbba Jampijinpa
6. BROWN, Frank Jangala
7. BROWN, Peggy Napangardi
8. CHISOLM, Charlie Jangala (d.)
9. COLLINS, Andrew Jangala

10. COOK, Anne Nungarrayi
11. COOK, Jack Jangala
12. COOK, Lisa Nampijinpa
13. COLLINS, Beryl Nangala
14. DAISY Napangardi
15. DANIELS, Leslie Jampijinpa
16. DENNY Jampijinpa
17. DIXON, Harry Japanangka
18. DIXON, Karen Nungarrayi
19. DIXON, Lucy Napurrurla
20. DIXON, Tiger Japanungka
21. ELMA Napanungka
22. FRANK, Carol Napangardi
23. FRANK Japanangka
24. GOREY, Veronica Napurrurla
25. HAGAN, Isobel Nungarrayi
26. HUDSON, Jean Nampijinpa
27. JOHN Japangardi
28. LINNY Nampijinpa
29. LORRAINE Nampijinpa (d.)
30. McCORMACK, Lola Nampijinpa
31. McCORMACK, Tim Japangardi
32. MAVIS Nakamarra
33. MELODY Napaljarri
34. MOORE, Elsie Nampijinpa
35. MORTON, Don Japangardi
36. MORTON, Sarah Napanangka
37. NORMAN, Allan Jampijinpa
38. PATTERSON, Banjo Jampijinpa
39. PATTERSON, Glenda Nungarrayi
40. PATTERSON, Rosie Napangardi
41. ROSS, Michael Jangala
42. ROWENA Nungarrayi
43. STAFFORD, David Jakamarra
44. STAFFORD, Lilly Pananka
    (Napanangka)
45. STOCKMAN, Alby Japanangka
46. STOCKMAN, Topsy Nambijinpa
47. TILMOUTH, Desmond Jampijinpa
48. TILMOUTH, Doreen Nampijinpa
49. TOPSY Napangardi
50. TURNER, Maureen Nampijinpa
51. WALKER Japangardi
52. WAKO, Morris Jangala

NAPPERBY

1. CAMPBELL, Nancy Napanangka
2. CASSIDY Tjapaltjarri
3. CHARLES, Barbara Napaltjarri
4. COCKATOO, Kitty Pultara
5. DIXON, Beatrix Nangala
6. EILEEN Napanangka
7. JESSIE Napaltjarri
8. KENNY Tjakamarra
9. KITTY Pultara Napaltjarri
10. LEO, Peter Tjakamarra
11. LEO, Susan Dixon Napaltjarri
12. LISA, Pultara

13. LYNCH, Brenda Nungurrayi
14. McNAMARA, Ronnie Tjapanangka
15. MORRIS Tjapanangka
16. TILMOUTH, Josephine Nakamarra
17. TILMOUTH, Bobby Jupurrula
18. TOMMY, Michael Tjapangati

ALICE SPRINGS (and Beyond) ARTISTS

1. ABBOTT, Mary
2. ANDY, Nora Napaltjarri
3. ANGELINA Na(nga)la Pwerle
3. BERGER, May
4. BOKO, Eileen
5. BOKO, Patricia
6. BROWN, Meggerie Napanangka
7. BROWN, Peggy Nakamarra
8. BROWN, Priscilla Napanangka
9. BUTLER, Sally Napurrula
10. COLLINS, Connie Nungarrayi
11. DANIELS, Barney Tjungurrayi
12. DANIELS, Carol Nampijinpa
13. DEMPSEY, Young Timothy
    Tjungurrayi
14. DICKSON, Bertha Nakamarra
15. DOOLAN, Monica Nakamarra
16. EGAN, Betty
17. EGAN, Rebecca Nampijinpa
18. EVANS, Kitty Nakamarra
19. EUNICE Napangardi
20. FLEMING, Rosie Nangala
21. FORRESTER, Janet Na(nga)la
22. GORDON, Julie Napurrurla
23. GOREY, Daisy Napanangka
24. GRANITES, Rex Daniel Japanangka
25. JURRA, Rachel Napaljarri
26. KELLY, Norman Tjampitjinpa
27. LANGDON, Charlotte Nabanangka
28. LEO, Barbara Leo Nakamarra
29. LIDDLE, Bessie
30. LYNCH, Norbett Kngwarreye
31. MARTIN, Peggy Napangati
32. MILLER, Kitty
33. MOTNA, Erna Nakamarra
34. NELSON, Geraldine Nakamarra
35. NELSON, Maudie Napanangka
36. NEIL, Dorothy Petyarre
37. OLDFIELD, David Jupurrurla (see also
    Warlukurlangu Artists)
38. PANSY Napangati
39. POLLY Napangati
40. POSSUM, Clifford Tjapaltjarri (see
    also Papunya Tula Artists)
41. POSSUM, Gabrielle Nungurrayi
42. POSSUM, Michelle Nungurrayi
43. POULSON, Peggy Napurrurla (see
    also Warlukurlangu Artists)
44. ROBERTSON, Yvonne Nampijinpa
45. ROBINSON, Rene Nampijinpa

46. ROBINSON, Dorothy Napangardi
47. RUBUNTJA, Wenton
48. SPENCER, April Napaljarri
49. SPENCER, Garth Japaljarri
50. SPENCER, Isabel Napaljarri
51. SPENCER, Winkie Napaljarri
52. SYDDICK, Linda Junkata Napaljarri
53. TURNER, Maureen Nampijinpa
54. WALLACE, Kathleen (Santa Teresa)
55. WOODS, Pauline Nakamarra

Note: These artists are listed here as Alice Springs based artists because they sell their paintings primarily through outlets in Alice Springs. In most cases they also currently live in Alice Springs, though some are based on communities (Mt Leibig, Yuendumu, Santa Teresa etc.) close to Alice Springs. In some cases an artist has been listed both here and under one of the community-based painting companies through which they also sell their work.

WARLAYIRTI ARTISTS: BALGO HILLS

1. BOOTJA BOOTJA, Susie Napangati
2. BRANDY Tjungurrayai
3. BROWN, Dinny Tjapanangka
4. BYE BYE Napangati
5. DOONDAY, Bill Tjampitjin
6. EUBENA Nampitjin
7. FRED Tjakamarra
8. GIBSON, Kenny Tjakamarra
9. GILL, Matthew Tjupurrula
10. GILL, Mick Tjakamarra
11. GIMME Ena Nungurrayai (d.)
12. GORDON, Palmer Tjapanangka
13. GORDON DOWNS, Johnny Tjangala
14. GREEN, Albert Tjampitjin
15. HALL, David Tjangala
16. KUNINTJI, Rita Nampitjinpa
17. LEE, Donkeyman Tjupurrula
18. LEE, Patricia Napangati
19. LEWIS, John Tjapangati
20. LOOMOO, Lucy Nungurrayai
21. MARTIN, Dominic Tjupurrula
22. MILLIGA Napaltjarri
23. MILNER, Boxer Tjampitjin
24. MOSQUITO, John Tjapangati
25. MUDJIDELL, Bridget Napanangka
26. MUNTJA Nungurrayai
27. MUTJI, Michael Tjangala
28. NAGOMARA, Albert Tjakamarra
29. NANYUMA, Rosie Napurrula
30. NJAMME Napangati
31. NYUMI, Elizabeth Nungurrayai
32. OLODOODI, Patrick Tjungurrayai
33. POSSUM Tjapangati
34. SAM Tjampitjin
35. SKEEN, Millie Nampitjin

36. SUNFLY Tjampitjin
37. TAX, Richard Tjupurrula
38. TJUMPO Tjapanangka
39. WIMMITJI Tjapangati
40. WALLABY, George Tjangala
41. WINDEROO, Alan Tjakamarra
42. YUKENBARRI, Lucy Napanangka

LAJAMANU ARTISTS

1. ABIE Jangala
2. BAKER, Belinda Nakamarra
3. BARNES, Beryl Puyurrpa Nakamarra
4. BARNES, Lady Nakamarra
5. BIRRELL, Jeannie Napurrurla
6. BLACKSMITH, Peter Japanangka (d.)
7. BURNS, Pampirriya Nungarrayi
8. COOKE, Henry Parti-Parti Jakamarra
9. DAISY Purlpurlngali Napurrurla
10. DANIELS, Robin Napaljarri
11. DIXON, Fabian Japanangka
12. DIXON, Iris Napanangka
13. DIXON, Valda Napurrurla-Nangala
14. FENCER, Andy Japanangka
15. GIBSON, Barbara Nakamarra
16. GIBSON, Beryl Nakamarra
17. GIBSON, Paddy Japaljarri
18. GIBSON, Sister Nakamarra
19. GRANITES, Kurt Japanangka
20. GREEN, Joe Japanangka/Jungarrayi
21. GREEN, Robyn Napurrurla
22. HARGRAVES, Jennie Nampijinpa
23. HARGRAVES, Joy Nangala
24. HARGRAVES, Lila Nungarrayi
25. HARGRAVES, Lily Nungarrayi
26. HECTOR, Linda Yinarrki Nangala
27. HECTOR, Lucy Yurrurngali Nangala
28. HECTOR, Menzies Japaljarri
29. HERBERT, Lindy Nakamarra
30. HERBERT, Patsy Nangala
31. JACKO Tingiyari Jakamarra
32. JAMES, Irene Napurrurla
33. JAMES, Joe Japanangka
34. JAMES, Mabel Napurrurla
35. JIGILI, Fred Jampijinpa
36. JIGILI, Judy Napangardi
37. JIGILI, Margaret Napangardi
38. JIGILI, Yulanti Nangala
39. JOHNSON, Cecil Japangardi
40. JOHNSON, Marlene Nampijinpa
41. JOHNSON, Martin Japanangka
42. KELLY, Alice Napaljarri
43. KELLY, Gladys Napangardi
44. KELLY, Jimmy Jampijinpa
45. KENNEDY, Tim Jupurrurla
46. KINALUJA Nungarrayi
47. LAWSON, Louisa Pupiya Napaljarri
48. LAWSON, Ronnie Jakamarra
49. LIKIRRIYA Napaljarri

50. LIZZIE Napaljarri
51. LONG, Joe Tjangara Jangala
52. LORNA Napurrurla
53. McDONALD, Kay Nungarrayi
54. MAISIE Napangardi (Kajingarra)
55. MARSHALL, Joe Japangardi
56. MILLER, Liddy Nampijinpa
57. MORRISON, Teddy Jupurrurla
58. NELSON, Irma Napanangka
59. NELSON, Liddy Nakamarra
60. PATRICK, Beth Nungarrayi
61. PATRICK, Freddy Jangala
62. PATRICK, Myra Nungarrayi
63. PATRICK, Paddy Jangala
64. PATTERSON, Sergeant Jupurrurla
65. PATTERSON, Valerie Napanangka
66. PATTERSON, Rex Jupurrurla
67. PETERS, Janie Nakamarra
68. RAYMOND, Dick Japaljarri
69. ROBERTSON, Jimmy Jampijinpa
70. ROCKMAN, Biddy Napaljarri
71. ROCKMAN, Mona Napaljarri
72. ROCKMAN, Peggy Napurrurla
73. ROCKMAN, Peggy Yalurrngali
     Napaljarri
74. ROSIE Napurrula
75. ROSS, Elizabeth Nungarrayi
76. ROSS, Peter Jangala
77. RUBY ROSE Yardaya Napangardi
78. SCOBIE, Miyangula Lily Nangala
79. SCOBIE, Jennie Napurrurla
80. SCOBIE, Neil Japanangka
81. SIMMS, Agnes Ngarniya Napanangka
82. SIMMS, Kitty Napanangka
83. SIMON, Phyllis Nakamarra
84. SIMON, Victor Jupurrurla
85. SIMONS, Agnes Nakamarra
86. STAFFORD, Betty Jamanakari
     Nangala
87. STEVENSON, Yimikalayi Molly
     Napurrurla
88. SUSAN Napaljarri
89. TASMAN, Barbara Napurrurla
90. TASMAN, Denise Napangardi
91. TASMAN, Lynette Napangardi
92. TASMAN, Mary-Ann Napaljarri
93. TASMAN, Melody Napurrurla
94. TASMAN, Molly Napurrurla
95. TIMMS, Sarah Napanangka
96. TIMMS, Tiger Jupurrurla
97. TOBY Jangala
98. TOPSY Nangala
99. WALKER, Judy Napaljarri Nyirrpiya
100. WATSON, Betty Nungarrayi
101. WATSON, Marjorie Nungarrayi

WILLOWRA — WIRLIYAJARRAYI ARTISTS
1.   ANNE Napangardi
2.   BANDY Jupurrurla
3.   BETTY Napanangka
4.   DORA Napaljarri
5.   GEORGINA Napangardi
6.   HILDA Napaljarri
7.   KATHY Nangala
8.   JOHNNY Japaljarri
9.   LADY Napaljarri
10. LILLIAN Nakamarra
11. LONG, Janet Nakamarra
12. LUCY Nampijinpa
13. MALCOLM (Maloney) Jakamarra
14. MAY Napurrurla
15. MINNIE Napanangka
16. MOLLY Napurrurla
17. NORA Napanangka
18. NORAH Napanangka
19. PEGGY Nampijinpa
20. REILLY, Willie Japanangka
21. TEDDY Tjupurrurla

ERNABELLA SA: ERNABELLA ARTS INC.
1.   ATIRA-ATIRA, Michael
2.   ATIRA-ATIRA, Tjulkiwa
3.   BAKER, Nyukana
4.   DAVEY, Jillian
5.   KUYATA, Yipati (d)

UTOPIA
1.   BILLY Petyarre
2.   BIRD, Ada Petyarre
3.   BIRD, June Ngale
4.   BIRD, Lyndsay Mpetyane
5.   COWBOY Louie Pwerle
6.   EDIE Kemarre
7.   EMILY Kame Kngwarreye
8.   GLORIA Tamerre Petyarre
9.   HOLMES, Michelle Pwerle
10. HOLMES, Sandra Kemarre
11. JANICE Kngwarreye
12. JONES, Freddie Kngwarreye
13. KATHLEEN Petyarre
14. LENA Pwerle
15. LILY (Sandover) Kngwarreye
16. LOUIE Pwerle
17. LUCKY Kgnwarreye
18. MORRIS, Harper Tjungarrayi
19. PURVIS, Julie Mpetyane
20. QUEENIE Kemarre
21. ROSEMARY Petyarre
22. ROSS, David Pwerle
23. VIOLET Petyarre
24. WALLY Pwerle

NYIRRPI

1. BENNY Jangala
2. BROWN, Mary Napangardi
3. GALLAGHER, Charles Jampijinpa
4. GALLAGHER, Pauline Napangardi
5. GIBSON, Nancy Napanangka
6. MARSHALL, Susan Nakamarra
7. MORRIS, Tiger Japaljarri
8. TEX, Peter Japaljarri
9. WILLIAMS, Dulcie Napangardi
10. WILSON, Nola Napangardi

Other painters based at Nyirrpi for whom biographies have not been collected include: Margaret Napangardi Brown; Esther Nungarrayi Fry; Ormay Nangala Gallagher; Jeannie Napurrurla Lewis; Paddy Japanangka Lewis; Dora Napurrurla Long; Molly Napurrurla Martin; Mary-Anne Nampijinpa; Mosquito Jungarrayi Morris; Valerie Napurrurla Morris; Banjo Jungarrayi Tex; Biddy Nangala Tex

MARUKU ARTS & CRAFTS: MUTITJULU COMMUNITY, ULURU; AMATA, FREGON, INDULKANA

1. COLLINS, Impana
2. DIXON, Matala
3. EDIMINJA, Eddie (See also Papunya Tula Artists)
4. KITSON, Jimmy Jungarrayi
5. LEWIS, Wanatjura
6. MUNTI, Yipati (Riley)
7. PATTERSON, Nellie Nungarrayi
8. PEIPEI, Kunbry
9. TEAMAY, Malay
10. UMBIDONG, Emantura

Other painters, who have sold their work through Maruku Arts and Crafts but for whom biographies have not been collected, include: Barbara Nipper, Elyawarri Teamay, Ross Dixon, Bill Edemintja (Ediminja) and Hazel Peipei

IKUNTJI WOMEN'S CENTRE, HAASTS BLUFF

1. JACK, Eunice Napanangka
2. JUGADAI, Narputta Nangala
3. JUGADAI, Daisy
4. JUNABEE Napaltjarri

Appendix B
Artist's Dreamings — Yuendumu

In some cases, no English translations of the Jukurrpa were provided. These Dreamings usually name sites in the artist's heritage country. In Western Desert society, each Dreaming (Jukurrpa) is the shared responsibility of individuals from different skin groups in the complementary roles of kurdu (owner) and kurdungurlu (manager). Most artists paint the Dreamings over which they personally have ownership, and these are the ones listed below for the Yuendumu artists. However, they may also paint their parents' and other close relatives' Dreamings or, with the kurdu's permission, those for which they are kurdungurlu.

KURDU	KURDUNGURLU
Napurrurla/Jupurrurla	Napaljarri/Japaljarri
Napaljarri/Japaljarri	Napurrurla/Jupurrurla
Nungurrayi/Jungurrayi	Nakamarra/Jakamarra
Nakamarra/Jakamarra	Nungurrayi/Jungurrayi
Napanangka/Japanangka	Nampijinpa/Jampijinpa
Nampijinpa/Jampijinpa	Napanangka/Japanangka
Napangardi/Japangardi	Nangala/Jangala
Nangala/Jangala	Napangardi/Japangardi

NAPURRURLA

Artist	Jukurrpa	Dreaming
Agnes Napurrurla Dixon	Ngalajiyi	Bush Yam
Connie Napurrurla Walker	Janangpa Ngalajiyi	Possum Bush Yam
Dora Napurrurla Long	Ngapa Yarla	Rain Bush Yam
Erica Napurrurla Ross	Ngalajiyi	Bush Yam
Irene Napurrurla Williams	Janangpa	Possum
Jorna Napurrurla Nelson	Ngalajiyi	Bush Yam
Lorna Napurrurla Williams	Janangpa Wapirti	Possum
Monica Napurrurla White	Warna	Snake
Morna Napurrurla Poulson	Yankirri Janangpa Warna Ngalyipi	Emu Possum Snake Snake Vine
Molly Napurrurla Martin	Janangpa Ngapa Yarla	Possum Water Bush Yam
Marlette Napurrurla Ross	Warlukurlangu	Fire
Maggie Napurrurla Poulson	Ngalyipi Janangpa Wapirti	Snake Vine Possum
Nancy Napurrurla Oldfield	Yarla Miinypa Kirdalangu	Bush Yam Native Fuschia Father and Son
Nancy Napurrurla Dixon	Warna	Snake
Peggy Napurrurla Poulson	Janangpa Patanjarnngi Ngalajiyi Mantala	Possum Bush Yam
Phillis Napurrurla Williams	Janganpa Mukaki	Possum Black Berries

Artist	Jukurrpa	Dreaming
Polly Napurrurla Wheeler	Janganpa	Possum
Peggy Napurrurla Granites	Wakirlpirri Yarla	 Bush Yam
Ruby Napurrurla	Yarla	Bush Yam
Topsy Napurrurla Butcher	Warlpajirri	
Theresa Napurrurla Ross	Miyikirlangu Ngalajiyi Wardilyka Pamapardu Yirriwara	Bush Fruits Bush Yam Turkey Flying Ant Headband

NAPALJARRI

Artist	Jukurrpa	Dreaming
Biddy Napaljarri White	Wurrkarli	Bloodwood
	Wurrpardi	Acacia
	Lingka	Snake
	Yarla	Bush Potato
	Ngatijirri	Budgerigar
Doris Napaljarri Jurra	Ngalyipi	Snake Vine
Hilda Napaljarri Martin	Ngatijirri	Budgerigar
	Marlu	Kangaroo
	Jurrpa	Owl
	Ngalajiyi	Bush Yam
	Yanyilingi	Native Fuschia
Helen Napaljarri Nelson	Warlpajirri	
	Wardapi	Goanna
	Yurnkaranyi	Honey Ant
	Janmarda	Bush Onion
	Ngarlkirdi	Witchetty Grub
	Ngalyipi	Snake Vine
Kitty Napaljarri Oldfield	Karnta	Women
Kaye Napaljarri Ross	Ngalyipi	Snake Vine
	Ngarlkirdi	Witchetty Grub
Lucy Napaljarri Kennedy	Miinypa	Native Fuschia
	Yanyilingi	Sugar Leaf
	Ngarlajiyi	Bush Carrot
	Warlawurru	Eagle
	Janmarda	Bush Onion
	Wurlpayi	River
	Ngarlkirdi	Witchetty Grub
	Miyikirli	Bush Fruits
	Marlu	Kangaroo
	Wardapi	Goanna
Maggie Napaljarri Ross	Janmarda	Bush Onions
	Miinypa	Native Fuschia
Norah Napaljarri Nelson	Ngarlkirdi	Witchetty Grub
	Karnta	Women
	Ngaru	Bush Plum
	Yiwarra	Milky Way
	Witi	Ceremonial Pole
	Mala	Hare Wallaby
	Kinki	Giant Women

Artist	Jukurrpa	Dreaming
Ruth Napaljarri Oldfield	Miinypa	Native Fuschia
	Janmarda	Bush Onion
	Yanyilingi	Sugar Leaf
	Janangpa	Possum
	Marlu	Kangaroo
	Yurrampi	Honey Ant
	Ngarlu	Rockhole
	Ngatijirri	Budgerigar
Sheila Napaljarri Brown	Ngarlkirdi	Witchetty Grub
	Ngalyipi	Snake Vine
	Yiwarra	Milky Way
	Karntajarra	Two Women
	Witi	Ceremonial Pole
	Liwirringki	Burrowing Skink
	Wati	Man
Selina Napaljarri Sampson	Ngapa	Water
Tess Napaljarri Ross	Ngalajiyi	Bush Yam
	Ngarlkirdi	Witchetty Grub
	Yarla	Bush Yam
Valerie Napaljarri Martin	Karnta	Women
	Yarrungkanyi	

JUPURRURLA

Artist	Jukurrpa	Dreaming
David Jupurrurla Oldfield	Warna	Snake
	Puurda	Bush Potato
	Purla-Purla	Black Kite
	Yankirri	Emu
	Maliki	Dog
	Ngama	
	Yarla	Bush Yam
	Wiji	
	Kurlarda	Spear
	Janangpa	Possum
	Ngarlkirdi	Witchetty Grub
Johnny Jupurrurla Walker	Janganpa	Possum
	Warna	Snake
	Wardilyka	Bush Turkey
Paddy Jupurrurla Nelson	Janangpa	Possum
	Watijarra	Two Men
	Yarla	Bush Yam
	Marrkirdi	
	Warna	Snake
	Karnta	Women
	Ngapa	Rain
	Karrku	
	Mukaki	Black Berries
	Pamapardu	Flying Ant
	Marnikiji	Bush Berries
	Ngalajiyi	Bush Yam
	Marlu	Kangaroo
	Ngalyipi	Snake Vine
Roy Jupurrurla Curtis	Puurda	Bush Potato
	Jajirdi	
	Yarla	Bush Yam
	Ngalajiyi	Bush Yam
	Ngapa	Rain
Victor Jupurrurla Ross	Kinki	Giant Women
	Warlpa	Wind
	Yarla	Bush Yam

JAPALJARRI

Artist	Jukurrpa	Dreaming
Dudley Japaljarri Brown	Mala	Hare Wallaby
	Luwajirri	Goanna
	Ngarlkirdi	Witchetty Grub
	Ngapa	Rain
	Warna	Snake
Garth Japaljarri Spencer	Yarripilangu	New Haven
John Japaljarri Brown	Janganpa	Possum
Paddy Japaljarri Stewart	Janganpa	Possum
	Puurda	Bush Potato
	Jarlji	Frog
	Wakulyarri	
Paddy Japaljarri Sims	Karnta	Women
	Ngaru	Bush Plum
	Yanyjirlpiri	Star
	Liwirrinki	Burrowing Skink
	Warna	Snake
	Kurlarda	Spear
	Warlpa	Wind
	Ngarlkirdi	Witchetty Grub
	Ngalyipi	Snake Vine
	Wati	Man
	Wanakiji	Bush Tomato
	Ngatijirri	Budgerigar
	Witi	Ceremonial Pole
	Pirntina	
	Lingka	Snake
	Warlu	Fire

NUNGARRAYI

Artist	Jukurrpa	Dreaming
Alma Nungarrayi Granites	Wanakiji	Bush Plum
	Ngarlkirdi	Witchetty Grub
	Ngalajiyi	Bush Carrot
	Witi	Ceremonial Pole
Andrea Nungarrayi Martin	Yanyilingi	Sugar Leaf
	Janangpa	Possum
	Wardapi	Goanna
	Marlu	Kangaroo
	Puurda	Sweet Potato
	Kirdalangu	Father/Son
	Kirdiji	Shield
Biddy Nungarrayi Robertson	Liwirringki	Burrowing Skink
	Ngalyipi	Snake Vine
Dadu Nungarrayi Gorey	Janmarda	Bush Onions
	Yanyilingi	Native Fuschia
	Ngarlajiyi	Bush Carrot
	Jintirr-Jintirrpa	Willie Wagtail
	Purla Purla	Black Kite
	Wardapi	Goanna
Eva Nungarrayi Oldfield	Yanyjirlpiri	Star
	Yanyilingi	Snake Vine
	Warlawurru	Eagle
	Witi	Ceremonial Pole
	Ngarlkirdi	Witchetty Grub
Esther Nungarrayi Fry	Kunajarrayi	Country
	Ngarlkirdi	Witchetty Grub
Jeannie Nungarrayi Egan	Puurda	Bush Potato
	Pangkalangu	Giant Women
	Janangpa	Possum
	Wanakiji	Bush Tomato
	Miinypa	Native Fuschia
	Wardapi	Goanna
	Yiwarra	Milky Way
Loraine Nungarrayi	Karnta	Women
	Warna	Snake
Lyn Nungarrayi Sims	Ngarlkirdi	Witchetty Grub
	Ngalyipi	Snake Vine
	Yakajirri	Bush Raisin
	Kurlarda	Spear
	Witi	Ceremonial Pole
	Ngarlajiyi	Bush Carrot
	Ngaru	Bush Plum

Artist	Jukurrpa	Dreaming
Lena Nungarrayi Brown	Yarrungkanyi	Mt Doreen
	Janmarda	Bush Onion
	Liwirringki	Burrowing Skink
	Mamapurunpa	Barking Spider
	Ngapa	Water
	Ngarlkirdi	Witchetty Grub
Lady Nungarrayi Robertson	Liwirringki	Burrowing Skink
	Wakulyarri	Striped Rock Wallaby
	Witi	Ceremonial Pole
	Yartulu-Yartulu	Tanami Desert
	Yarrungkanyi	Mt Doreen
Mary Nungarrayi Robertson	Liwirringki	Burrowing Skink
	Pirrpipakarnu	Country
	Witi	Ceremonial Pole
	Warna	Snake
Queenie Nungarrayi Stewart	Janangpa	Possum
Ruth Nungarrayi Spencer	Ngalyipi	Snake Vine
Rosalie Nungarrayi Wayne	Wakulyarri	
Teresa Nungarrayi Martin	Wardapi	Goanna
Wendy Nungarrayi Sims	Ngarlkirdi	Witchetty Grub
	Mala	Hare Wallaby
	Watijama	Two Men
	Janangpa	Possum

NAKAMARRA

Artist	Jukurrpa	Dreaming
Bessie Nakamarra Sims	Janganpa	Possum
	Ngalajiyi	Bush Yam
	Karntajarra	Two Women
	Wapiti	
	Yarla	Bush Potato
	Pamapardu	Flying Ant
	Mukaki	Bush Berries
Connie Nakamarra White	Warna	Snake
	Yawakiyi	Black Berries
Clara Nakamarra France	Ngalajiyi	Bush Yam
Joanne Nakamarra White	Ngurlu	Grinding Seed
Janie Nakamarra Brown	Lukarrara	
Mona Nakamarra Collins	Punujutu	
Pansy Nakamarra Stewart	Ngalyipi	Snake Vine
	Janganpa	Possum
Ruby Nakamarra Stewart	Lukarrara	
	Yawakiyi	Bush Berries
	Jaralypari	
	Ngurlu	Grinding Seed

JUNGARRAYI

Artist	Jukurrpa	Dreaming
Mosquito Jungarrayi Morris	Mamupurunpa	
Otto Jungarrayi Simms	Wati	Man

JAKAMARRA

Artist	Jukurrpa	Dreaming
Frank Jakamarra Nelson	Janganpa	Possum
	Jilimi	Single Women's Camp
	Ngapa	Rain
	Wapiti	
	Ngalajiyi	Bush Yam
	Pamapardu	Flying Ant
	Yampirri	
	Japantarra	
	Warlpa	Wind
	Karlanjirri	
	Warna	Snake
	Marlu	Kangaroo
	Mukaki	Black Berries
	Yarrirdi-Yarrirdi	
Jack Jakamarra Ross	Luwarrinki	
	Yarla	Bush Yam
	Ngalajiyi	Bush Potato
	Marlu	Kangaroo
	Pamapardu	Flying Ant
	Warlpajirri	
	Yurduwaruwaru	
	Karlanjirri	
	Patanjarnngi	
	Warlu	Fire
Towzer Jakamarra Walker	Wapiti	
	Puurda	Bush Potato
	Yarla	Bush Yam
	Ngalajiyi	Bush Yam
	Watijarra	Two Men
Freddy Jakamarra	Ngapa	Water

NAPANANGKA

Artist	Jukurrpa	Dreaming
Alice Napanangka Granites	Janyinki Walya-Walya Ngalyipi Karnta	Country Death Adder Snake Vine Women
Aileen Napanangka Nelson	Karnta Ngalyipi	Women Snake Vine
Biddy Napanangka Hutchins	Purluntari Karnta Kanakurlangu	Fungus Women
Cecily Napanangka Granites	Janyinki Kanta Warnajarra Ngalyipi	Country Bloodwood Gall Two Snakes Snake Vine
Charlotte Napanangka Langdon	Kanta Wanakiji	Bloodwood Gall Bush Tomato
Daisy Napanangka Nelson	Yuparli Pikilyi	Bush Banana Vaughan Springs
	Yurrampi Warnayarra Purrpalangi	Honey Ant Rainbow Serpent Bush Vine
Elsie Napanangka Granites	Kanakurlangu Yurrampi Ngalyipi Karnta	Honey Ant Snake Vine Women
June Napanangka Granites	Yurnkaranyi Purluntari Warna Ngalyipi Karntajarra	Honey Ant Snake Snake Vine Two Women
Jean Napanangka Brown	Wardapi	Goanna
Maudie Napanangka Nelson	Warnayarra	Rainbow Serpent
Kelly Napanangka	Puurda Ngalajiyi	Big Bush Yam Small Bush Yam
Liddy Napanangka Walker	Warna Wakirlpirri Karnta Wardapi Ngapa	Snake Women Goanna Rain

NAPANANGKA (continued)

Artist	Jukurrpa	Dreaming
Maggie Napanangka White	Ngalyipi	Snake Vine
	Yarla	Bush Yam
	Wakirlpirri	
	Karnta	Women
	Ngayaki	
	Walya-Walya	Death Adder
	Warna	Snake
	Jarrardajarrayi	Country
	Wardapi	Goanna
Priscilla Napanangka Brown	Yuparli	Bush Banana
Topsy Napanangka Collins	Ngayaki	
	Wanakiji	Bush Tomato
	Wardapi	Goanna
	Janardajarrayi	
	Ngalyipi	Snake Vine

NAMPIJINPA

Artist	Jukurrpa	Dreaming
Alice Nampijinpa Michaels	Karnta	Women
Clarise Nampijinpa Poulson	Yankirri	Emu
	Pamapardu	Flying Ant
	Ngapa	Rain
Dolly Nampijinpa Daniels	Warlukurlangu	Bush Fire
	Watiya Wanu	Bush Grain
	Yilinkarri	Burrowing Skink
	Yankirri	Emu
	Ngapa	Rain
	Pamapardu	Flying Ants

JAPANANGKA

Artist	Jukurrpa	Dreaming
Douglas Japanangka Marshall	Kumpu Jungunypa Yankirri Mala	 Mouse Emu Hare Wallaby
Harry Japanangka Dixon	Yurrampi	Honey Ant
Jack Japanangka Butcher	Yuparli	Bush Banana
Kurt Japanangka Granites	Kanakurlangu Janyinki Purluntari	 Country
Peter Japanangka Dixon	Karnta	Women
Robin Japanangka Granites	Karnta Kanakurlangu	Women

JAMPIJINPA

Artist	Jukurrpa	Dreaming
Archie Jampijinpa Marshall	Kurdiji Warna-jarra	Initiation Two Snakes
Darby Jampijinpa Ross	Ngarlikirlangu Watijarra Yankirri Pamapardu Warlpa Warna Ngapa Liwirrinki Watiya-Wanu	Country Two Men's Emu Flying Ant Wind Snake Rain
Charlie Jampijinpa Williams	Marlu-Jarra Pamapardu Yankirri	Two Kangaroos Flying Ant Emu
Dinny Jampijinpa Nolan	Ngapa	Rain
Jack Jampijinpa Gallagher	Yankirri	Emu
Matthew Jampijinpa Egan	Ngapa Yipilanyji	Rain

NAPANGARDI

Artist	Jukurrpa	Dreaming
Beryl Napangardi Robertson	Warrarna Janyinki Yurrampi Pulurntari Karlangu	Country Honey Ant Fungus Digging Stick
Coral Napangardi Gallagher	Wardapi Ngayaki Karnta Yarla Wakirlpirri	Goanna Women Bush Yam
Dianne Napangardi Wilson	Ngalyipi Karlangu	Snake Vine Digging Stick
Florrie Napangardi Jones	Pikilyi	Vaughan Springs
Ivy Napangardi Poulson	Mulyukuna	
Judy Napangardi Watson	Janyinki Karnta Warrarna Wardapi Karlangu Ngalyipi	Country Women Goanna Digging Stick Snake Vine
Judith Napangardi	Yurrampi Kanakurlangu Yarla Janyinki	Honey Ant Bush Yam Country
Lottie Napangardi Robertson	Kanakurlangu Wanakiji Ngayakiyi Kanta	Bush Tomato Bloodwood Gall
Mary Napangardi Butcher	Yuparli	Bush Banana
Margaret Napangardi Lewis	Janyinki Karnta	Country Women
Maggie Napangardi Watson	Ngalyipi Yarla Wanakiji Karnta Janyinki Kanakurlangu Wati Karlangu	Snake Vine Bush Yam Bush Tomato Women Country Man Digging Stick

NAPANGARDI (continued)

Artist	Jukurrpa	Dreaming
Maggie Napangardi Ross	Janyinki	Country
Runa Napangardi Williams	Janganpa Yarla	Possum Bush Yam
Ruby Napangardi Ross	Janyinki	Country
Rosie Napangardi Watson	Yarla Wardapi	Bush Yam Goanna
Vera Napangardi Marshall	Pikilyi	Country

NANGALA

Artist	Jukurrpa	Dreaming
Enid Nangala Gallagher	Warlukurlangu Kanta Watiyawamu	Fire Bush Coconut Bush Grain
Holly Nangala Gallagher	Pamapardu manu Yankirri	Flying Termite and Emu
Elizabeth Nangala Gallagher	Pamapardu manu Yankirri	Flying Termite and Emu
Joy Nangala Brown	Watiyawarnu	Bush Seed
Peggy Nangala Jurra (d)	Ngapa Parardi	Water Rainbow
Rosie Nangala Fleming	Warlu manu Warna Jangala Kurlangu Ngapa Pamapardu Pamapardu manu Yankirri	Fire and Snake belongs to Jangala Water Flying Ant Flying Ant and Emu
Ruby Nangala Robertson	Ngapa	Water
Tilo Nangala Jurra	Ngapa Yankirri Warna	Water Emu Snake
Winnie Nangala Brown	Lingka	Snake

JAPANGARDI

Artist	Jukurrpa	Dreaming
Eric Japangardi Fisher	Warnayarra Mala Yurrampi	Rainbow Serpent Hare Wallaby Honey Ant
George Japangardi Ellis	Janganpa	Possum
Johnny Japangardi Miller	Wanakiji Yarla	Bush Tomato Bush Yam
Murray Japangardi Woods	Wardapi	Goanna
Michael Japangardi Poulson	Pikilyi Yurrampi Wataki	Country Honey Ant
Neville Japangardi Poulson	Yurrampi Witi	Honey Ant Ceremonial Pole

JANGALA

Artist	Jukurrpa	Dreaming
Jack Jangala Cook	Ngarlkirdi	Witchetty Grub
Lawrence Jangala Watson	Ngapa Pirntina	Rain
Tommy Jangala Watson	Ngapa	Water
Ted Jangala Egan	Warlukurlangu Ngapa Wakulyarri	Water
Thomas Jangala Rice	Ngapa Jarlji Munga Lungka	Water Frog Night

Appendix C
Guide to using this Dictionary

So long as they are included in the dictionary, and not every Western Desert artist is, it should be easy to find the entry for a particular artist you want to look up, but if you are having difficulty, the following rules of thumb may be helpful.

For convenience of reference, the biographies have been arranged alphabetically, in order of the names by which the artists are known to the world outside Western Desert society, particularly the Art world. Given the European practice of referring to artists by their surnames as 'Picasso' or 'Namatjira', this will usually mean listing the artist under their European-style surname if they have one, e.g. Alison ANDERSON Nampitjinpa or Paddy Jupurrurla NELSON (the order of skin name and surname varies from community to community).

Don't try looking up artists under their skin names. It actually misrepresents the role skin names play in Western Desert society to treat them as European surnames, as some curators and writers do. There are, in any case, just too many different spellings of skin names coming in and out of circulation and too many local variations (see *Notes on the Biographies* 'Spelling'), for this to be a workable way of ordering the entries. Should all Jakamarras be listed under 'J', or only those who use this Warlpiri spelling for their skin name, with Tjakamarras listed under 'T'? — and Djagamaras, if there are any, under 'D'? What about next year, when local usages or linguistic orthodoxies change again? What about Pitjantjatjara artists like William SANDY, who don't have skin names, or are part of another system of skin names than the familiar Western Desert one, like Kitty COCKATOO Pultara?

If the artist is only known by only one name other than their skin name, e.g. ABIE Tjangala, then their biography will be listed uner this name, even if it is a 'Christian' name like JOHN Tjakamarra. Also, when an artist is best known by their first name, even though they have something corresponding to a 'surname', e.g. EMILY Kame Kngwarreye, the entry will appear under the better known first name. In most cases, the reader will be cross-referenced to the entry if they look under the 'surname', e.g. KAME, Emily Kngwarreye, see EMILY Kame Kngwarreye. When artists have supplied an additional Aboriginal name used by their countrymen and women, this is also cited, but has not been used to determine the placing of their entry in the book.

If you are unsure of the details of an artist's name, but know their community of residence or the painting company through which their work is usually sold, *Appendix A: Guide to Artists by Community* may be a useful place to start looking. The capitalised form of a name within the entries, e.g. 'He is the older brother of Clifford POSSUM Tjapaltjarri', indicates there is an entry in the dictionary for that artist, which can be looked up under the name in capitals.

Alternatively, the reader may just browse ...